Galloping Through Life

MAJOR HUGH DAWNAY

SOMERVILLE PRESS

Somerville Press Ltd,
Dromore, Bantry,
Co. Cork, Ireland

First published in 2014 by Somerville Press Ltd

Designed by Jane Stark
seamistgraphics@gmail.com
Typeset in Adobe Garamond

ISBN: 978 0 9573461 9 2

Printed and bound in Spain
by GraphyCems, Villa Tuerta, Navarra

Contents

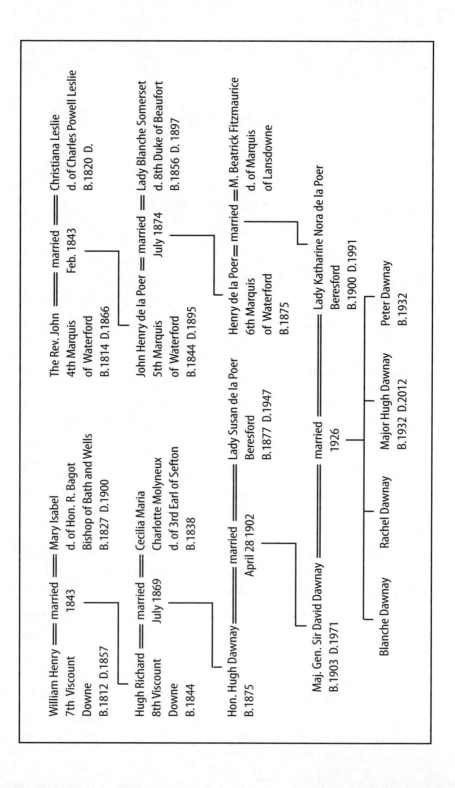

William Henry == married == Mary Isabel
7th Viscount   1843   d. of Hon. R. Bagot
Downe   Bishop of Bath and Wells
B.1812 D.1857   B.1827 D.1900

The Rev. John == married == Christiana Leslie
4th Marquis   Feb. 1843   d. of Charles Powell Leslie
of Waterford   B.1820 D.
B.1814 D.1866

Hugh Richard == married == Cecilia Maria
8th Viscount   July 1869   Charlotte Molyneux
Downe   d. of 3rd Earl of Sefton
B.1844   B.1838

John Henry de la Poer == married == Lady Blanche Somerset
5th Marquis   July 1874   d. 8th Duke of Beaufort
of Waterford   B.1856 D. 1897
B.1844 D.1895

Hon. Hugh Dawnay == married == Lady Susan de la Poer
B.1875   April 28 1902   Beresford
                                    B.1877 D.1947

Henry de la Poer == married == M. Beatrick Fitzmaurice
6th Marquis   d. of Marquis
of Waterford   of Lansdowne
B.1875

Maj. Gen. Sir David Dawnay == married == Lady Katharine Nora de la Poer
B.1903 D.1971   1926   Beresford
                                           B.1900 D.1991

Blanche Dawnay   Rachel Dawnay   Major Hugh Dawnay   Peter Dawnay
                                    B.1932 D.2012   B.1932

Foreword

I FEEL DIFFIDENT ABOUT WRITING a foreword to Hugh's memoirs. Our tastes, careers, skills and characters were as different as could be. All we seemed to have in common was our blood relationship (cousins twice over) and, all too soon, our bald heads, the downside of our Beresford genes.

Yet I knew him for well over seventy years, always liked him, and grew to regard him with increasing affection and respect. I admired him because he did not hide or neglect his talents but discovered them by trial and error and then developed them to the full. Of course it all started with horses. At Whitfield Court, the home of the Dawnays in County Waterford, the horse was King, as I learnt from experience as a boy, yet I will always be grateful for their hospitality and tolerance of a non-riding townee cousin.

Horses filled Hugh's life, first in hunting, then in racing, finally in polo. And through polo he came to the knowledge that he, who had always been bottom of the class at school, had a gift for teaching. A key moment came when he seized the salt cellars and pepper pots at dinner in an army mess in Düsseldorf, and showed to a group of German officers what was wrong with their polo tactics. In his memoirs Hugh vividly describes how the simple demonstration caught their attention and led to the invitation to come and coach them in polo. It was an important moment for several reasons. From it led to his subsequent career as a renowned polo coach, writer on polo, and doyen of the Whitfield Court Polo School, remembered with affection and gratitude by polo players of many nations. Moreover it showed him the usefulness of simple vivid methods to ram home teaching points, which was to be a feature of his coaching.

Not least Hugh's work at Düsseldorf used polo to bring about friendship between German and English and help heal old wounds. This was typical of Hugh, for one of his most attractive characteristics was his readiness to be friendly with people of all types, nations, religions and backgrounds. He was interested in people and concerned about their problems; although he got a lot of fun out of life he was a serious, simple and thinking man who gave up time to help others. This was recognised and appreciated in Waterford city and county, where 'the Major' became a much liked and respected figure.

Another attractive quality of Hugh's was his enthusiasm. He went full tilt at everything, and got completely absorbed in the activity of the moment. It is a characteristic that comes out in his memoirs. Even I, with my lack of sporting instincts, find myself caught up by his enthusiasm and excitement, traversing a racecourse or a polo field with him, and savouring every moment up to the final success or failure. I remember with amusement and affection the absorption with which he set about teaching himself to play the piano. He approached this like a military operation: one learnt the notes and then struck them in the right order. He forgot that a sense of time is also important, and the results were curious.

For many years I used to do a tour of friends and relatives in Ireland. Whitfield, and later Clashes were always part of the tour, first with Hugh's mother and then with Hugh and Maria-Ines, and sometimes their sons, David and Sebastian. It was a delightful part, because one could be sure of a warm welcome, and could relax there, sit round the kitchen table, gossip and laugh; and casting a glow over everything was Hugh's love for Maria-Ines and hers for him. Their meeting and marriage had been the best of the LCMs (Life Changing Moments), clocked off by Hugh with military precision in these memoirs which so vividly reflect his personality.

Mark Girouard

Author's Preface

MORE TIMES THAN I CAN REMEMBER I have listened to people talking about winning the lottery. I have heard many say 'If I could just win the lottery, all my problems would be solved'. Others have said 'All I need now is a lottery win'. Then I heard that the statistics about lottery winners clearly shows and demonstrates the horrific problems and unhappiness experienced by the majority of those, who have received big lottery payouts. I suddenly realised that many of these hopeful idiots, quoted above, had failed to appreciate that they had already won one or more lotteries, which were far more important than enormous sums of money. These wins concerned moments that had changed their lives, sometimes without them being aware of the significance of what had taken place. This made me consider many of the different experiences, that could be classified as 'life changing moments' (LCMs).

After deep reflection I concluded that there were too many LCMs to list, but that they could be placed under a few headings. These appeared to be personal relations, career opportunities, educational openings and sporting recognition. Next I looked for the order, in which the above should normally happen, and came up with the following four occasions that the majority are likely to experience in similar order. First Birth, second a Significant Teacher, third a Significant Boss and fourth the Suitable Spouse. In all four categories, a person can win or lose a lottery, but the initial loser, in any of them, may have a change of luck, later on, when a new significant person or happening becomes a life changing moment. Separately to the four, a Sports opportunity or a distinct different interest, which has been acquired at a crucial later time in life, could also produce a LCM. Finally I adjusted the above in to 6 stages, which I have examined individually below.

Birth is naturally the one lottery, that is completely out of our control. The enormous luck of being born with useful talents, has given many people a head start. Who our parents are, how they bring us up and the location of our first proper home, enormously influences our lives. There are surprising statistics, showing that children, of extremely wealthy parents, can have similar disadvantages to those from very poor families. Conclusions drawn suggest that it might be better to suffer than to be spoilt, because those born super rich may never understand reality and the meaning of incentive.

Any disadvantages of birth are difficult to rectify, but those who do battle to overcome them, especially if helped by a lucky encounter at the right moment, surely find glorious fulfilment, which is superior to anything felt by anyone born with a silver spoon in their mouth. A significant teacher is almost certain to appear during our educational years. A bad one can destroy children's confidence, sending them in to adult life, unprepared to fight for survival. A good teacher can make them proud of themselves and able to impress all the important people, whom they will meet in interviews and during their operational working days.

A significant boss could hugely affect anyone's professional life. An unfair superior can taint a reputation and the ability to inspire others, while a caring thoughtful head of a department will prepare employees to meet and handle the decisions and problems of the future. Only exceptionally lucky people will survive the former and then encounter and benefit from the latter, having learnt key lessons from both bad and good experiences.

Where and when you come face to face with your future spouse, is full of countless ramifications, that are mostly totally unpredictable. There are a few exceptions, seen in arranged marriages and examples of methodical people, who carefully plan whom they wish to meet. The percentage chance that any two people, who marry and turn out to be the perfect soul mates and ideal partners, for the rest of their lives, is quite low. Those who have an immediate passionate relationship and tie the knot quickly, seldom survive more than a few years. Any couple who thrive together for many years and are mutually helpful to each other, in multi dimensions, have won an amazing brilliant lottery that will bring them concrete happiness and unbelievable security. Following the birth of children the after effects are variable. Some husbands may stray in search of alternative female company and mothers can transfer their deep affection and love from their spouse to their children. The parents who avoid both of the above, to maintain their solidarity as a pair, are truly blessed and more likely than others to give their offspring the best possible upbringing, which in turn wins them that first lottery.

Sports people, besides being involved with winning or losing the above four lotteries, can add or lose golden chances, through several different dimensions of the game or event, in which they compete. Actual brilliant athletic talent goes back to your birth, but the luck of being in the right place at a good time, in order to be available to fill a vacancy in an outstanding team, is separately priceless. Being exposed to a coach, who is perfect for you and/or your team, probably only happens to a highly fortunate minority. The profound saying 'You can only play as well as you are allowed to' has endless ramifications. One clear example is that the day you are at peak performance, may or might not be the occasion, when an opponent is equally good or better than you. The equestrian fraternity cannot succeed without good horses. The rider, who just once in his life owns or rides a horse, which performs magnificently and consistently, has really won a lottery. If the horse has the flexibility to win in more than just one dimension of competition, it will be the equivalent of a multimillion lottery.

Lastly in my list, are the extremely lucky people, who when well established in one profession, through pure coincidence or an completely unexpected event, encounter a new or different interest, in which they quickly acquire sufficient proficiency, to lead them in to a second career, that provides them with success and fulfilment late in their life.

They may have won the second to none lottery, because in their old age they will have meaning, involvement and constructive use of the brain, that all combine in the avoidance of several dangerous pitfalls, which can make their last days inspiring instead of miserable. I dare to claim that compared to many others, whom I know and have known, I have had more than my fair share of the luck that goes around, and I realise, in hindsight, that I just may have won six lotteries. In the ensuing chapters I will try to explain how such amazing fortune crossed my path, although as a child, the frightening era of the Second World War threatened my home security. Also I had little apparent academic talent at school, only barely passing my exams. However I inherited my father's love of sport and horse riding. Then while at school was given an extremely useful background in sport, from having sufficient experience in several different dimensions, such as football, rugby, cricket, tennis, squash and swimming. Best of all my father gave me exceptionally wonderful opportunities, with ponies and horses, that installed a confidence within me, that stood to me more times than I can remember. Frequent examples of how the horse protected me are given in my description of this life, including the purchase by my father of a multidimensional winning horse, which has blessed me with so much luck.

Hugh Dawnay

CHAPTER 1

My First Lottery – Birth

THE VERY FIRST MEMORY OF MY LIFE was a frightening event in 1937, when I watched an out of control fire burn our home to the ground. College Farm House, in Upavon, Wiltshire, England, had been rented by my parents, as our temporary residence, while my father worked a few miles away as a major at Tidworth. He was commanding a Squadron of the 10th Royal Hussars (PWO), which would also be my future regiment. He was a member of their polo team, which had just won the much coveted 1937 inter-regimental polo tournament. They had an incredible polo team, with a handicap total of 25 goals, three more than the present day teams are allowed, in the annual British Open Tournament. My mother had gone away to County Waterford in Ireland, our real home then and now, and we, the four children, had been left under the care of a governess and a nanny. My father had been up most of the night at a stag party celebrating the feat of being the first ever regiment to win, back to back, the inter-regimentals in India and England.

I had two elder sisters and a twin brother. Blanche was five years older and Rachel had been born three years before us. Peter and I are unidentical twins, born five hours apart and, although we do look like brothers, have nothing else in common. I am three inches taller and Peter stole the brains, to be always a year ahead of me at school. He went on to become a well read intellectual. We four had been rushed into the garden, at about 7 a.m., and watched flames licking the thatched roof, while a local hero climbed a ladder, carrying a bucket of water. Suddenly a face, covered in shaving cream, looked out of an upstairs window, to enquire what was going on. Nobody had thought about waking my father, as he slept in, after the stag party. He then jumped into action to bring, most of our valuable belongings, out into the garden. We raised a special cheer when he arrived with the rocking horse. A fire engine eventually arrived, but failed to contain the fire. My father telephoned Tidworth to say he would be late but, not surprisingly, nobody believed him about the fire. We were driven to Badminton, the home of a distant relative, the Duke of Beaufort, where later in life I would have some enjoyable days. The 8th Duke's only daughter, Lady Blanche Somerset, married the 5th Marquis of Waterford, whose eldest daughter, Lady Susan Beresford, was my grandmother. After a short stay, we travelled to Whitfield Court, our real home in Ireland, to wait for a family quarter in Tidworth to become available for my parents and their four children.

Sadly I have no memory of the first four years of my life, which preceded that fire. Born in December 1932 at Lucknow, India, the station of the 10th Hussars, I would like to claim that as my first lottery win. Only as my story reached adulthood, did I start to appreciate some of the enormous luck of my birth. Much later, when I replayed my life, I suddenly fully realised that my parents had provided me with a fabulously privileged background and wonderful opportunities, many of which I had happily been able to take advantage of. Of course I would love to remember something of those colourful days in India, with so much sport, pomp and ceremony. I understand that I showed enthusiasm about the brilliant standard of polo, in which my father played, and that I loved to hit a ball with a tiny mini stick, while running along the side of a polo field.

My father, David, was the eldest of four brothers, who grew up without their father, Hugh, because he had been killed in France during the First World War. Second son of the Viscount Downe, my grandfather is described as a brilliant officer by Field Marshal French in his memoirs, where he also wrote about his death as 'the loss of one of the finest and most valuable Staff Officers I have ever come across'. His four sons all appeared to inherit much of his ability and together were wonderful friends, with a marvellous and simple sense of humour. My father was a loving fair parent, who cared deeply about every detail of my life. He was a brilliant all round games player, who loved horses and became an outstanding rider and polo player. In the height of his sporting achievements, with a 7 goal handicap, he won a silver medal in the 1936 Berlin Olympics, when he captained the British team (this episode will be fully written about in his obituary tributes page 163). Outside equestrian sports he had success at tennis, cricket and football, but he could have been good at almost any other game. Because of his enthusiasm for me to succeed, he seemed to presume that I would be equally good as him and he planned my sporting career with this misguided belief. Perhaps a subconscious knowledge that my father was over hopeful, gave me an early interest in how coaching could improve athletic performances. As a result, rather later than most, I probably did become an above average all round sportsman, and added to it the valuable bonus of having learnt some useful points about the art of coaching. Added to this, from my childhood right up till his sad death at only 68 years old, he provided me with so many wonderful ponies and horses, for hunting, racing, cross-country, show jumping and polo, giving me unbelievable opportunities.

My mother was Katherine Beresford, one of six children, born to the sixth Marquis of Waterford, who lived in the enormous Curraghmore Estate, nine miles from our home. She was prevented from being a demonstrative loving mother, by a combination of her genes and the old fashioned system of nannies, governesses and house staff. Yet she overcame the gigantic difficulties of the Second World War, to give her four children caring supervision and security, while our heroic Dad was away fighting in France, Africa and Italy. She also was a talented horsewoman, who had been one of the first of her generation to change from riding side-saddle to astride, and had ridden in and won point-to-point races. With her sister Lady Blanche Beresford, she was joint MFH with the Waterford Hunt for 10 years. Without doubt to be their son, born with their genes to appreciate their healthy outlook on life, while sharing the love of horse sports with them, started my life with a winning lottery ticket. Sadly for my twin Peter, he was not able to share much of my luck, as described, because of health problems and clearly having genes very different to mine, even though he was my twin brother.

My mother kept a diary all her life, which has helped me to write these memoirs. We returned with her from Ireland, to live in a military quarter at Tidworth, No. 1 Hampshire Cross in 1938. My main memories of this period are the many traffic accidents, which happened outside our front door, at the crossroads, and our two small ponies which we regularly rode. Named Pickles and Freckles they used to be full of mischief, finding many ways to deposit us on the ground. The most frightening of these would be a sudden dive under a tree, with low branches, which brushed us from the saddle. However we had a compensation, in that we had each been promised one pound sterling, when our own total of falls reached twenty. A tiny fortune at that time, this pledged reward enormously helped my courage, although it was sometime later, when in Ireland, that I finally earned my pound. Here at home I quickly reached the total when a pony, which had been sold to us as the 'perfect animal', immediately set about bucking all of us off, besides kicking and biting anything that went near her.

The polo at Tidworth in the late 1930s must have been sensational. In 1938 the mighty 10th Hussars team was beaten in the inter-regimental tournament by the 12th Lancers, who went on to lose the final in London. Then in 1939 the 10th Hussars had their revenge over the 12th Lancers, before winning a thrilling last pre-war inter-regimental final, despite one of their team scoring a goal in the wrong direction! Besides the inter-regimental battles, Tidworth and elsewhere staged many other tournaments, for which several officers, including my father, were in keen demand. Sadly after the war the standard in British Army polo has never reached the same heights, although there have been many exciting matches and finals in England and Germany, and I was very fortunate to play in some of them.

Just before the Second World War began we four children had gone to stay in Ireland with my grandmother, Susan Dawnay, daughter of the 5th Marquis of Waterford. As a war widow she had bought Whitfield Court, in County Waterford, and to me this has always been the most beautiful house in the world, my glorious home and part of my first incredible lottery win. Granny Sue always gave us a wonderful welcome and was a very generous hostess. Apparently she also showed incredibly kindness and friendliness to everyone, in the local area, and as a result we all enormously benefitted from her good will, in our neighbourhood, for many years and even up to this present time.

My father went to France in command of a 10th Hussars tank squadron and as history shows at that time the Allies were no match for the might of Hitler's army. Lucky to survive and not suffer a similar fate as his father, nearly thirty years before, he must have distinguished himself, because, soon after his return to England, the army promoted him to Colonel and posted him to Northern Ireland, to command and train the North Irish Horse, another tank regiment. We children had temporarily lived in another beautiful house, Kilcooley Abbey, in Tipperary, where we pooled our governess with others, belonging to five first cousins, and the kind Ponsonby family, the owners. One of those cousins was Mark Girouard, son of Major Richard Girouard and Lady Blanche Beresford, who has become a renowned writer about famous old houses. There we experienced many small adventures, including learning to fish in the lake with our congenial host, Tommy Ponsonby. Also we contracted mumps, measles and even scarlet fever, as far as I can remember. Our hosts must have been very patient and kind because they succeeded in giving us some memorable happy weeks and days.

Then we went to be reunited with our parents in Northern Ireland, where we stayed two years. The first was spent at Portrush, a seaside town on the north coast of Ireland, where the sea is often extremely rough and always very cold. The reward of a delicious hot chocolate drink from my parents, often enticed me to swim and nearly die of the cold, but this experience gave me a confidence in the water, and has made me appreciate any chance to swim in warmer water ever since. The second year we went to County Down, where we rented Ardelaigh House, a lovely old home, situated between the towns of Dundrum and Clough. This was close to Ballykinler barracks, where the North Irish Horse had moved to continue their training for war. Here they did their final exercises in Ireland, with the Churchill tanks, before going to England, en route to Africa. This did not prevent the regimental rugby team, which included the famous international player, Sammy Walker, from playing and winning many matches and at the age of eight I had the thrill, sometimes, to be a passenger in the team truck.

My uncle, Hugh Beresford, in the Royal Navy, who soon afterwards was killed near the island of Crete when the Kelly sunk, came from his ship to visit us. He could have been interned, when by mistake we drove together over the border into Southern Ireland and what appeared to be an amusing adventure might have prevented the tragedy of his death. He was my mother's youngest brother, who had been much loved and respected for his charity work with organisations like Toc H.

In England my father took the North Irish Horse to a training area in the county of Norfolk on the east coast. My parents rented a flat in a large mansion, owned by the Walsingham family in a beautiful estate, called Merton Hall. My brother and I sailed across the Irish Sea to a boarding school for the first time. Stonehouse School had been evacuated from the danger of bombing at Broadstairs in Kent to the West Riding of Yorkshire, where a handsome mansion had been rented. Close to Ingleborough mountain, with woods and a scenic lake, just above the house, it made a lovely country setting for a school. My memories of three and a half years at this school are mostly happy although academically I struggled, while my brother excelled. The teaching standard was inevitably affected by the demands of war. Hence no significant teacher was there to give me the inspiration I needed to elevate my academic level. However I did greatly enjoy all the school sport, which was well organised and involved many inter-school matches. My best sport was rugby and I remember being thrilled, when I first played for the school team and then overjoyed, when I was presented with my colours. I played wing forward and from good coaching, I much enjoyed tackling opponents, especially the big ones. I also somehow made the school cricket team, despite the disadvantage of unnaturally batting left-handed, because my dear father had taught me to play this way. Presuming I would be brilliant, he believed this would help me to upset all bowlers, but instead it made me be a boring batsman rather than a big hitter. Occasionally I made runs and took wickets and annoyed everyone with my conceit. Swimming and athletics were also well organised, but the former took place in the cold lake, where the temperature is normally in the low sixties. The compulsory cold shower, for which we queued every morning, must have helped us accept the cold water and my experience in the sea at Portrush certainly gave me extra courage to swim in it, and I became quite a strong swimmer. But although there was a spring board, from which I practised an amount of diving, I never learnt how to do it skilfully. For a long time I flunked plunging from the rock, which was at least fifteen feet above the lake surface, and was generally used by the good divers, until my very last week at school, when I entered the senior diving competition. For this the rock was obligatory and I still remember that moment, when I stood on it, knowing that I had to dive and the relief I felt when I found myself safe in the cold water, although I had gone deeper than ever before.

Twice a year we ran the U-boat gauntlet across the Irish sea to return home for the summer and Christmas holidays. Today most people, even without the U-boat threat would regard that journey as horrendous, as now the flight from London to Australia would take much less time, but I remember it as an adventure with the wonderful reward, at the end, of being at home again. It took the best part of three days, beginning in a train from Leeds to the port at Heysham, where we boarded the boat to Belfast. This crossing took most of the night and the fear of being sunk by the enemy, which did happen to at least one ship on that route, could normally be forgotten, while we tried to counter the effects of a rough sea. On the second day we went by train from Belfast to Dublin, where we stayed the next night in a hotel. Then came the worst part of all, the third day by train, from Dublin to Waterford, over one hundred miles, which took for ever, with frequent stops to clean the clinkers or to collect peat and wood for the engine.

A pony and trap conveyed us the last six miles to Whitfield Court. What joy we felt when we finally arrived to be greeted by Granny Sue, with a meal superior to anything that could be obtained in England. Throughout the war somehow food appeared to be plentiful in Ireland and this included sweets, which I smuggled in my luggage during the return journey to school in England by the same tortuous route.

During the Christmas holidays we enjoyed riding, which included our first experiences of foxhunting, that in hindsight must have provided an excellent preparation for my adult equestrian career.

The third school holiday was spent at Merton Hall, in Norfolk, at the rented flat, where my mother was based after Dad went to Africa. We made some good friends there, yet my limited memory only recalls four beautiful girls, who shared experiences with my two sisters, while I admired them from a distance. Two were the Walsingham daughters, known as M and K and the others were Elizabeth and Catherine Hind, whose father had been in the Olympic polo team, captained by my Dad.

I am very proud that my father had such a successful war. In Tunisia he led the North Irish Horse to achieve many victories using the Churchill tanks. Perhaps the most well known of these was the Battle of Long Stop Hill where they completely surprised the Germans, by appearing behind their positions, after climbing a very steep hill. For this he received the DSO medal, but he also counted himself extremely lucky not to be killed on at least three occasions. The first he recounted to me as a humorous story, but it must have been terrifying, because a German fighter plane literally hunted him with its machine gun blazing. Each time it swooped at him he ran to the opposite side of a tank and lay underneath only to see the plane turn round and attack again. The second occasion, after one victory, an upset tummy prevented him from walking on a battlefield tour with other commanders, during which a mine exploded killing the man deputising for him. The third time happened when driving a jeep, whose brakes failed going down a steep hill, with hairpin bends and he never understood how he survived.

Promoted to full colonel, my father became second in command of a brigade which did not take part in the invasion and capture of Sicily. He then thought his career had been ruined, because he had disagreements with the Brigade commander, but luckily he found it had not hindered him, when suddenly he was further promoted to command an armoured brigade in Italy. To his delight he found his original regiment, the 10th Hussars, under his leadership and received a second DSO medal, after a long successful campaign in Italy, where he finished the war safe and sound, besides being established as a very distinguished soldier. Also his three brothers all survived this terrible conflict with honour. Peter, a sailor, took part in various sea battles in different capacities, but signalling was his speciality and soon after the war he became an Admiral, to command the Royal Naval Signals School, before becoming the Captain of the Royal Yacht. Ronald, in the Coldstream Guards, had been taken prisoner at Tobruk, in North Africa, and after some years as a prisoner in Italy, he escaped to Switzerland and later retired as a Colonel. Michael, in the Air Force, was a brilliant pilot who flew many combat missions and finished the war with the rank of Group Captain, deeply involved in strategic planning for all three services. Tragically he lost his life, soon after the war, in an unfortunate accident.

My mother, who had been a nurse in the First World War, played her part in the Second World War by belonging to a Voluntary Force which took care of salvage and many other important works. She drove a tiny left-hand drive baby Austin, which I think had been in the Spanish Civil War, for miles, full of paper and tins. She must have been thrilled when my father temporarily returned from his triumphs in Italy and as a complete family of six we went to the VJ celebrations in London, an occasion which is implanted in my memory. Together with the Hind family of five, we all crossed the city on the underground, carrying a ladder. We changed trains at least twice and every time we entered or exited a carriage, fellow passengers were swept aside, or had to duck quickly and we nearly died laughing, at the hilarity of the situation, on such a joyful day of celebration. Then when we reached the bank of the Thames, we built a grandstand around the ladder and thereby enjoyed a marvellous view of the incredible fireworks. In the middle of the show sister Blanche cried out 'I am being pushed off' and we had to eject a gatecrasher, who bitterly objected in a voice, with an accent, that could have been German.

CHAPTER 2

My Second Lottery –
Significant Teacher in Eton

In September 1945 after only a few weeks of world peace, my brother and I went to Eton College to be in Mr R.C. Martineau's house. Peter had distinguished himself by passing into the highest possible grade for non scholars, otherwise known as oppidans. Although a whole year behind him, I was thrilled to be a student at this famous school. At only twelve and a half years old, probably the youngest in the whole school, for the first half (Eton language for term) we must have been the only boys sent to bed before evening prayers. My first impressions of Eton were that the opportunities for sport could be exciting, the threat of fagging frightening and the food disgusting. For the latter we had a compensation in that we ate tea in small groups in one of our own rooms, which we called 'messing together'. Supplementing the bread and tea, provided for us, with food bought and received from home, we ate the most incredible mixture of a meal. On a set of gas rings we could cook eggs, bread could be toasted in front of a fire, in the grate, and we often finished with cornflakes, to which ice cream and tinned fruit used to be added on special days.

Peter and I discovered that we had been selected for the Lower Chapel Choir without taking a proper test, because of the great reputation of my two Dawnay uncles, Ronny and Michael. They were still remembered for their solo singing, but we failed to live up to their name, although I enjoyed rehearsing and singing the Sunday anthems. I enormously appreciated the privacy and privilege of having my own room, although it was very small. Eton may be the only school in the world that gives all the boys their own room and all extra studies, like home work, had to be done there by oneself. This tested my self-discipline to the extreme and too often I returned from the classroom with my test paper torn across the top. That was called a 'rip' which signified failure and it had to be signed by your house master, who naturally showed much displeasure.

I found fagging to be not as bad as expected. Literally all the lower boys had to be the servants of the very senior ones. This consisted of preparing their tea, tidying rooms in the evening and at any time, during non lesson hours, answering 'boy calls'. From somewhere in the house a senior would yell 'boyyyyyyy' long and loud and we all scampered up or down stairs to where he stood. The last to arrive had to do a task. The excitement of trying not to be last, including sometimes jumping over banisters, could be enjoyable. Also preparing tea for the big boys enhanced our comradeship, as we worked in groups to do the shopping, cooking and toasting. The latter revives memories of enormous toasting forks in front of a big fire, which often felt too hot for comfort. I used to encourage myself with the thought that one day I should be the recipient of this service.

My mother and sister Rachel had gone to Italy to join my father. He then enjoyed the fruits of victory, while undertaking various interesting tasks. One of these placed him in charge of hundreds of thousands of prisoners of war. He duly ordered an orchestra to be formed, from the best German musicians, and on many nights my parents listened to the symphony of their choice, while eating dinner. Together with an American and a Russian General he also served on a special board in relation to Trieste and the complications with borders and boundaries. To every suggestion the Russian replied 'Niet' and hoping to soften him up the American often drove the jeep, which had been allotted to them, along the edge of steep cliffs at speed. The Russian sat in the front seat next to the sea and his nervous reactions provided some amusement to the other two, which compensated for his awkward behaviour.

I believe that my time at Eton gave me a wonderful education in almost everything except academic subjects, because I took the easy course of just doing enough to survive and lost the opportunity offered by the excellent educational facilities there. However during one half (term) a master, Mr Milligan, found a way to inspire me to be top of his class, for the only time ever at school. Although never repeated, this experience lifted my confidence, for the rest of my time at Eton, sufficiently to allow me to pass vital exams, for the school certificate and the Army entrance. The combination of studying under such a significant teacher, while being at this great school provided me with my lucky second lottery win. Without passing those exams, my life would have been dramatically altered, denying me many golden opportunities in the future. Also the general system of life in the school, beneficially taught me much about independence, because it compared to living in a small town, with school rooms, sports fields and other places scattered over a wide area. I had to find my own way around, arrange my room, select my clothes and purchase books required for classes.

In sport I achieved little that could be shown, but I gained a background from multi participation and the knowledge that I had come close to success at Eton football, otherwise known as the Field Game. This I enjoyed playing more than rugby and soccer although it is a mix of the two, with some special skills of its own. Possibly it is the only game in which a foul is only blown, when verbally appealed for, and only if the correct name of that foul is shouted. Between the houses the game is played with great competitiveness, at three levels, lower boy, intermediate and senior with raucous support from the sidelines. In my day house colours were only awarded for Eton football, although the houses played each other in many other sports. The number of boys to receive colours depended on how the house had advanced in the annual tournament. In 1948 my house, Martineau's, won the Cup with great rejoicing, especially as the whole team, including the 12th man, were given their colours. In an unusual situation only one boy had left by 1949, my last year, and I became 12th man only to see the team, hot favourites for a repeat win, lose in the quarter finals to the eventual winners. The team captain made it worse by telling me, that I would have replaced an injured player, if we had reached the semi-finals and I deserved my colours, which added to my grief. I took a long time to recover from the disappointment, as I had dreamt of playing in the prestigious finals and being awarded the colours.

My winter games playing also included Eton fives, singles and doubles, which was a fascinating experience, because there were hundreds of courts, in two long lines, full of people making an incredible noise, as the hard balls ricocheted around to shouts of both joy and dismay. There were only a few squash courts, which had to be booked in a Sunday morning queue, but I played enough to become quite useful especially at drop shots. Then a good compensation for my football, in my last year, I had the opportunity to try rackets, played in a court five times the size of a squash court, with a hard ball. I had lessons from a brilliant coach, called Cooper, an ex-international, and occasionally felt the thrill of hitting the half volley correctly, which made the ball fly at high velocity. Also I made one attempt at boxing by entering the annual school competition in my weight, but my main reason was to obtain a ticket to the final, besides having an experience to remember. I lost in the first round of my weight, in a close contest, and then enjoyed the rest of the week, in safety, on a chair watching.

The holidays provided the best training for my future in sport, because of the opportunity to ride. During the five weeks for Christmas I had the extra special thrill of foxhunting across the exciting Waterford countryside. During the war my first hunt, off the leading rain, had ended when my little pony had sunk in a bog with only his nostrils showing. Robin Hunt, later to become a renowned huntsman, had arrived in the nick of time to hold the pony's nose above ground before extracting him from the bog. Now as a teenager on a bigger pony I loved the challenge of jumping the wide variety of obstacles, which fenced the farmlands, while trying to stay in the leading group of followers. Twice a week, on a hunting day, I spent 8 to 9 hours in the saddle, leaving home at about 9 a.m. to ride and lead another horse to the 'meet', which often was more than 12 miles away, and then after hunting returning the same way. This experience must have helped me develop a strong seat and powerful legs, which later in life was so helpful to my career as a jockey, cross-country rider and polo player. The adventure and thrill from many of those hunts gave me much satisfaction and a feeling of achievement, when afterwards

I lay in a glorious hot bath, back at home. This would be followed by a delicious tea, including egg and toast, during which we reminisced about our day, the countryside crossed and obstacles jumped. The experience which remains clearest to me happened on a very cold day after a sharp frost. While crossing a river my pony tried to jump out of the water at the wrong place and, failing to reach the top of the bank, fell back in to the freezing water with me beneath him. Shivering with cold I was instructed to go to a nearby house, belonging to an aunt, but en route saw a fox cross the road in front of me closely followed by the hounds. I duly joined in and had an incredibly fast twenty minute hunt, at the end of which I was dry, warm and thrilled.

Back at Eton I tried to limit the amount I would boast about my hunting exploits only to be surprised how few of my contemporaries had had a similar opportunity, probably prevented by the recent war. In my house we had our own sport called 'Passage Football', a mini version of the 'Wall Game' only played by the elite sportsmen of the school. Two opposing scrums fought their way along a passage wall without any clear rules. We also indulged in another sport at the expense of the unfortunate Mr Martineau, our house master, who read to the lower boys from a literary masterpiece, for an hour every Sunday morning, in his private sitting room. Called 'Sunday Private' we wickedly conspired to disrupt the proceedings in various ways. Prior to one session we had all been outside to fill a matchbox with insects and, at a given signal, we released them, filling the room with dragon flies, butterflies, spiders and many flies. The sudden cloud across the ceiling and the buzzing noise emitted made our poor Tutor jump from his armchair in shock and fury. The following week we were banished to the house pupil room to sit on the hard desk seats. A smouldering piece of string was strategically placed in a slightly opened draw of Mr Martineau's desk. The ensuing smoke, from the imperceptible opening, slowly but surely emerged into the face of our Tutor. He took a long time to realise what was happening and before that he coughed and spluttered, at a gradually increasing rate, while reading with difficulty, as we giggled. Suddenly he put down the book, opened the offensive drawer and screamed 'Who did it, who did it?'. Much to my relief one boy immediately owned up and received the punishment of having to write out 500 lines of Virgil.

During summer holidays competing at show jumping, a few times, was a useful experience and often enjoyable. I believe that this requires more courage than all the other equestrian sports, because you are completely on your own all the time and the actual minutes of enjoyment are far less than the others, while everything you do can be seen by a discerning public. My memory is rather vague but I know that my confidence was boosted by the lucky purchase of a grey jumper, thought to be ten years old, for a cheap price. At several gymkhanas I think the grey and I always finished in the first three and I clearly remember winning a bareback competition, in which I became airborne over every jump and felt lucky to stay on. A year later the grey dropped dead under me with a heart attack and nearly all the neighbourhood cheerfully said 'If you had asked me I could have told you the grey was 25 years old'. After the shock and disappointment and a badly swollen ankle I spent two weeks at the famous riding school of Colonel Hume Dudgeon in Dublin. Although I felt humiliated to find how many skills I lacked, I had a wonderful time and learnt some important lessons for the future. The daughter of the Colonel, called 'K', gave some of the instruction and a few years later she married Robin Hunt, our famous Huntsman in Waterford, who had saved my little pony from sinking many years earlier.

Another year an elderly great character, Mrs Bright, asked me to jump her big wild bay gelding at the Waterford Show. This experience provided extra excitement, because the bay liked to fly jump, during the approach to every fence, and sometimes did two or three leaps in the air. If he arrived at the correct distance for take off, he would give a magnificent jump well above the fence, but if he was wrong, the whole jump would be totally demolished.

In sport for my last two summers at Eton I enjoyed the combination of cricket, tennis and swimming. I became the opening batsman for a rather indifferent house team and as a left-hander tried to take the shine off the new ball. I often did this but never scored a big total and once took a ball on the point of my chin. For a few days I looked a rare sight with a swollen jaw and found both eating and talking painful. At tennis with so many grass courts spread around the famous Eton playing fields, I took advantage to play doubles, often with a group of good players, which gave me some valuable experience. To swim entailed a mile walk to a lock in the river Thames. We found this less boring than expected, because of the fun of spotting courting couples in the long grass. Plunging into the dirty cold water could be unpleasant, but the incredible atmosphere generated by many boys, swimming at the same time, countered this.

I remember June being an exciting month, with the rowing event, the house bumping fours, giving us scope to scream and shout on the banks of the River Thames, in competition against the coaches, with megaphones, on bicycles. Then the incredible holiday, the Fourth of June, when parents tried to outshine each other, in appearance and in the provision of food for picnics, around the playing fields. The day culminated with the pageantry procession of boats and the fireworks. As the rowers in each boat stood up, we all hoped that one would fall in and sometimes it happened, with a suspicion of saboteurs being in the water. The fireworks with Windsor Castle, as a background, were magnificent and induced loud cheers and applause. Later in June, during Ascot race week, my brother, myself and two cousins had a unique bit of excitement for four successive years. This was provided by our distant relation, the Duke of Beaufort, who was Master of Horse to the King, and always stayed that week with the Royal Family, at Windsor Castle. He arrived in a mini bus to take us to the Castle, to eat strawberries and cream with the Royal Family and their house guests and each time we shook hands with King George, Queen Elizabeth and Princesses Elizabeth and Margaret. The first year I caused consternation with the state of my Eton clothes and Mary Beaufort desperately tried to remove stains from my jacket, before the introductions took place.

Badminton, the ancestral home of the Beauforts, which had been our refuge after the house fire, became a place, where I enjoyed many wonderful experiences, to be recounted later, but also one of shame, when we stayed there for a summer long leave (Eton language for half term). We were made to play for the local village junior cricket team against a Bristol school team, with much expectation on our performance.

Our opponents had an opening bowler, whose deliveries were faster than anything we had ever previously faced and my two cousins, the Beresfords from Curraghmore, my brother and I had our stumps quickly flattened, without scoring any runs. Then the Bristol boys hit all our bowling to the boundary as they made an enormous score.

Despite my laziness at academic subjects, which I have always regretted, as previously recorded, with the confidence giving to me by the kind Mr Milligan, I squeaked through the school certificate exams in 1949. A year later I passed the Army entrance exam, by only a few marks, giving me the first step, required to become an army officer. (A vital result of my second lottery win). This led to an invitation to attend the RCB, the Regular Commissions Board, which lasted three days and consisted of all kinds of tests. For one I had to give a short talk on any subject and I chose the story of the escape, by my Uncle Ronny, from an Italian prison of war camp to Switzerland. Another challenge put me in a group, without an appointed leader, which had to cross a complicated obstacle. For us to succeed someone had to take charge and we all shouted out suggestions, before, with much relief, we arrived on the other side. The Brigadier in charge of the RCB, knew my father, and I suspect that this piece of corrupt luck, helped me to pass and qualify to enter the Royal Military Academy Sandhurst, if I first successfully completed four months recruit training at Catterick Camp, in Yorkshire. This choice of career came about, because I simply could not think of another that might suit me, and I had obediently obeyed my father's directions to join the Army, in order to be a 10th Hussars, the regiment in which he had had such a wonderful pre-war life.

I returned from RCB to spend my last few weeks at Eton. As a member of the House Library, the equivalent of being a prefect in other schools, I felt very privileged and enjoyed a position of authority, with all the advantages that went with it, including having fags! I enjoyed having little boys attending to my comforts and it did improve the standard of life. I look back with amazement that I felt so happy about leaving school, because it meant exchanging a top position in life for one at the bottom, but I suppose that the appeal of becoming an adult excited me.

Sometime prior to the end of my Eton career my father had come home, from Italy, to attend the Staff College. Before the war he had been too occupied with polo and equestrian sports to take the entrance exams, but now he qualified through his war record. He found it difficult to be instructed by men, considerably younger than himself, but in his typically determined way, he pushed himself to qualify with honours. Then to his delight he heard that he had been appointed to command his beloved regiment, the 10th Hussars, although this meant demotion to colonel. He made all the arrangements to move to Germany and changed some internal appointments, to suit his requirements, only to find the War Office had altered their plans and had posted him to command a brigade, in the midlands of England. So the 10th Hussars had to wait for my arrival, before a Dawnay would again wear their uniform, but destiny would anyway place me under my father's command, before I reached the regiment. In an incredible twist of fate, he became the Commandant of Sandhurst, just before I arrived there, early in 1951, as an officer cadet.

CHAPTER 3

Joining the Army

AFTER THE LONGEST HOLIDAY OF my life, I left home in Waterford, Ireland, to join the British Army. On the way I visited my old prep school, Stonehouse, then safely returned from Yorkshire to the town Broadstairs in Kent. Before submitting to the humiliating rigours of the army ranks, I spent two days feeling very important, especially when I taught a class for one period and, while on the football field, I found that I could run with the ball so much faster than the small boys. From there I set out via London for Catterick Camp, in Yorkshire, to join the army on a day in November 1950, which I will never forget. Three fellow Etonians travelled with me on the train, which took us to Darlington and they helped to bolster my courage, when from the station an army lorry conveyed us to Catterick Camp. All four of us joined the same training regiment, organised by the famous cavalry regiment, the 17/21 Lancers, also known as the 'death and glory boys'.

At the camp the shock of the total military atmosphere and the Spartan barrack rooms increased, when I found myself separated from my school friends. As I put on my pyjamas that first night, a big ugly looking thug asked me what they were, but to my relief another man told him not to be so ignorant. The second day consisted of being marched all over the barracks, to be issued with uniform, clothes and equipment. Then we had to wait in a long queue to face the ordeal of receiving five injections, but a broad cockney, temporarily strengthened our morale, by telling us a string of wonderful jokes. When he stepped forward to receive his first jab, still laughing at his last joke, we watched in horror as he fainted when the first needle entered his arm. That night we all suffered from a fever, caused by one injection, and sore arms from the others.

The cold at Catterick was unbelievable and with perpetually numb hands, I found it extra difficult to do much of the work. To stay out of trouble proved to be difficult for me, especially during inspections, because something would always be found to be either dirty or insufficiently polished. I felt that the many drill periods were overexacting and I experienced great relief as each one finished. I did not like the food and one day in the cookhouse, a voice I knew said 'Any complaints', and there in officers' uniform I saw Harry Ponsonby from Kilcooley, Tipperary. Embarrassment and surprise struck both of us, but I felt comforted by his friendliness and indeed he turned out to be an ally on various occasions. To add to the unexpected, to my horror, I received a summons to the office of the colonel of the 17/21 Lancers. Expecting trouble I had difficulty with cold hands making myself smart before reporting to be marched in front of him. To my relief a big smile covered the face of Colonel Dick Hamilton-Russell, who told me that he had been a pre-war polo-playing friend of my father. Then to my delight he said that I would be welcome to bring a friend to ride his two horses, on days that he was not out fox-hunting. I duly invited Richard Coxwell-Rogers, a fellow Etonian, son of a general and new recruit, who much later became a great friend, to ride with me. We discovered, to our joy, that the Colonel's two big elegant hunters outclassed all the other horses in the regimental stables, and immensely enjoyed riding them. I do not recall what time of day we did this, but I do remember that being dressed in army denims, we knew that we looked strange on such fine horses, but when we passed well-dressed officers, on inferior-looking beasts, we suddenly felt superior. Any increase in our self-esteem helped, when the basic recruit training finished, to counter the move we then made to the potential officers' block. We then had to put little white tabs on our shoulder epaulettes, which immediately transformed us into the lowest form of life in the barracks. We were known as the f---ing POs. A very fierce Sergeant whose surname was also Sergeant, became responsible for our discipline and general military training. Luckily we escaped his clutches for much of the time, when visiting other squadrons, to be instructed in how to drive lorries and the procedure for operating radios. But Richard and I received an extra shock one day, when we were both summoned to the colonel's office, thinking that we might receive another good offer. Snow covered the ground and my numb fingers could not do up the buttons on my uniform, making us arrive late, outside the regimental headquarters, with some of my buttons still undone. The regimental sergeant-major shouted orders at us and tried to smarten me up, before marching us into the Colonel's office. To our dismay, in place of the friendly colonel, we saw a nasty little major, with a big moustache, glaring at us. 'You are both sons of generals and it is disgraceful that you are not doing better,' he said, before going on to threaten us with a ghastly fate, if we failed to produce an instant improvement during the coming week.

A few days later, while in a radio class, I saw another fierce-looking major, standing at the back of the room. When the period finished he announced, in a loud voice, that he wished to speak to me and thinking 'I am in further trouble', I approached nervously. Then he said almost angrily, 'Why the hell have you not been hunting?' His name was George Brooke, a great character, later as Sir George, who was to marry Lady Melissa Wyndham-Quin, daughter of the Earl of Dunraven, sister of Caroline Waterford, wife of my cousin, the Marquis of Waterford. I had presumed that it was impossible to get away, although I knew about an offer to go with the Middleton hunt, by none other than Lord Middleton himself, who had seen my grandfather die at the battle of Ypres in the First World War. By coincidence Christopher Willoughby, son of the Lord, had recently joined our squad and I rushed to ask him if we could call his father to make arrangements. The next weekend we were both driven to Birdsall Manor, the Middleton home, and the sudden change from army life with cookhouse food, to the comfort of a lovely mansion, with pheasant and red wine, felt like an unbelievable and magical dream. This became further enhanced when I found myself on probably the best hunter that I have ever ridden, jumping enormous fences effortlessly, as the Middleton hunt flew across the countryside.

The shock of returning to Catterick was softened by knowing that Christmas was close and we would soon have a few days leave at home.

To reach Ireland I went by train to Paddington, London, where I intended changing on to another for Fishguard. From the back of a very long queue an official ushered me, amongst others, through a different gate directly to the designated platform, where I duly boarded a carriage. Almost immediately, before the departure time, the train moved out and I discovered, from another passenger, that our destination would be Newbury, not Fishguard, and that only one other person, a young Kerry man, had made the same mistake. He kept saying 'I followed you' as together we looked for an official. We found the guard, who showed great sympathy and promised to try and have the train stopped at Reading, where we could change for Fishguard. As we passed through Slough station we watched him throw out his written request, after which we went through a dramatic period of waiting for the result. During the approach to Reading, the guard kept saying that we should already have started slowing down and how sorry for us he was. Then suddenly the brakes went on violently and in a short time the train had stopped at a densely crowded platform with a loudspeaker blaring 'Stand back nobody is to board this train'. The Kerry man and I, for a few seconds, felt important as we proudly stepped on to the platform. The rest of the journey went smoothly and I arrived safely in Ireland to join the rest of my family for a wonderful Irish Christmas.

My last month at Catterick gave us many extremely tough moments, including frequent threats that I would not qualify for Sandhurst. As my father had just taken over as Commandant there, it would have been a dramatic start for him if I had failed to arrive. On the other hand it might have saved him an amount of pain during the eighteen months I did spend there. Before leaving Yorkshire there was one more weekend pass in January '51. I went to stay with my cousins at Howick Hall, in Northumberland. This beautiful house and estate, which I had visited once during school holidays, belonged to Earl Grey, whose daughter Nisset had married my Uncle Ronny and had given him four children, before tragically dying from a brain tumour. His other daughter Molly, a very charming person, had married Evelyn Baring, later to be created Lord Howick, in recognition of his work as Governor of Kenya, throughout the Mau Mau troubles. Molly and the Greys made me gloriously welcome and once again I much appreciated the comparison to life at Catterick and I rejoiced that I only had two weeks left in that cold godforsaken place. Yet in hindsight I must admit that, when I became an officer, I often had cause to be grateful for that experience as an ordinary soldier, because it gave me an understanding in situations, where either soldiers needed my sympathy or when they were trying to be clever by pulling the wool over my eyes to fool and deceive me.

We only had a few days leave between Catterick and starting life, as an officer cadet, at Sandhurst and these I spent at Government House, the official residence of the Commandant. This imposing white house had a lovely large garden and at the end of this in a stable block I met the horse, who would give me more pleasure than I could ever have dreamed of. Rendez-Vous II, a handsome red bay with a lovely white blaze on his face, had been bought by my father to give me the opportunity to launch my career as a jockey. I soon found out just how big Rendez-Vous could jump when I rode him in the Sandhurst drag hunt and, at the first fence, he gave such an enormous leap, that we landed on top of other horses and fell. My pride had been a little dented, but luckily I had no bruises and I then knew that I had a wonderful horse for an exciting introduction to point-to-point racing.

The day for enrolment as a cadet arrived and I walked a few hundred yards to join Burma Company in Victory College. Sandhurst then had three Colleges, called Old, New and Victory and each College had four companies. Cadets had to do three terms, each of five months, before being commissioned. In the ensuing weeks I experienced the most incredible mixture of enjoyment with unpleasant times, happiness with depression, and fame together with shame. Six people as they interviewed me all said 'Look here Dawnay, in your special situation, don't expect any favours, because you will be treated just the same as all the other cadets'. My platoon corporal, our junior under officer, the company senior under officer, my platoon commander – a captain, Burma company commander – a major, and lastly the colonel who ruled Victory College, all followed this up, within two weeks, with the words 'Look here Dawnay, in your position, your results are not good enough'. Equally astonished by the apparent necessity to mention it and the obvious contradiction given, I struggled to survive that first month as a cadet. Then came the Junior Steeplechase, in which the new cadets in each company had to run, as a team, against the clock, an experience not easily forgotten. After five hundred yards we went through the mud splash and emerged covered in slime, an awkward condition, in which to continue running. Near the finish, completely exhausted, we passed through the deep ice cold wishstream, helped each other to scale a high wall before sprinting to the line.

All my life my likeness in looks to my father has been commented on, but at Sandhurst it plagued me, as I found myself recognised by all cadets and instructors and waved to by many from long distances. On the parade ground the sergeant-major often screamed my name either, for example, saying 'Mr Dawnay keep your hand still by your side' or 'The man five to the right and three behind Mr Dawnay stand still'. Many minor acquaintances greeted me as a long lost friend and although I despised this false friendship, it became difficult not to enjoy such popularity even though I knew it to be so insincere.

Being very immature for my age and a year younger than most of my contemporaries, during the second month at Sandhurst, the pace of life seemed to be impossible to contend with. To add to the pressure, because I was a good rider, without my consent, my dear father, the Commandant, had registered me to train for the army pentathlon competition. This meant training for swimming, running, fencing and pistol shooting besides the riding and on top of all this I had to be prepared for my first point-to-point race on Rendez-Vous. I had the privilege of being coached in the skills of jockeyship by the famous Monkey Blacker, who had achieved dizzy heights as a jockey and a show jumper and later became a senior general in the army. I remember that instead of listening in class, my mind went round and round the racecourse. Suddenly every kind of trouble overtook me and I had to go on punishment parades and do extra work for bad academic results.

The big day arrived for my first race in a point-to-point. The excitement must have clouded my thought process because, despite the training,

I used the wrong tactics and finished unplaced in the knowledge that Rendez-Vous could have won. Even so the experience thrilled me as my horse, jumping brilliantly, galloped into fence after fence at what felt like an incredible speed. Of course in racing fear has to be a factor, but I believe the principal cause is making a fool of oneself and this further increased for my second race, which took place, in front of all the cadets, at the local Tweseldown racecourse. Those in Burma Company had all backed Rendez-Vous and everything went well for the first circuit, but then without warning another horse ran out through the wings of a fence, taking me with him. My intense disappointment further increased the next day, when the vet announced that Rendez-Vous had broken down, with a strained tendon, and could not race again that year. I felt that life had betrayed me and when I continued to be in trouble, as a cadet, I started to smoke, despite all the warnings from my parents.

Somehow, miraculously, I went from that stage of feeling that I could not survive, to one of sensing that I had assimilated the fast pace of cadet life and could cope. This further improved when the training for pentathlon finished and we had time off for the competition itself. On the first day the riding took place at Tweseldown and I came third out of seventy but more memorable to me is an incident with my father during that day. 'The Commandant wants you urgently' I heard somebody shout and I ran to find him, to see a wide smile across his face. 'Look over there and you will see a Brigadier,' said my father. 'He has just saluted me as a General and he is the bastard, who nearly stopped my promotion in North Africa. Now he is still a Brigadier and has to salute me.' I had never seen him so elated, almost dancing on the spot.

The rest of that pentathlon competition provided a nightmare experience that I will never forget. The fencing, épée style, placed novices like me against experts, including the army champion. There were seventy-two competitors and we had to fight one hit only, against each one. I began badly losing every fight, but in another group I spotted the army champion winning all his bouts, the same way, with a quick prod at the hand, which held the sword. When I faced him I tried his tactic to win, before he had moved, and even though I finished almost last, I consoled myself with this victory and the memory of the expression on his face, when the buzzer announced my hit.

In the pistol shooting I had been quite good in practice, but on the day my right hand shook with nerves, as I aimed, and I recorded a low score. Then the swimming, my second best event, but ten lengths of a thirty yard pool took its toll, as I tried too hard and swallowed gallons of water. Lastly day five, we had to run 3,000 metres, against the clock, individually at minute intervals. I thought, as my team was out of contention for any prize, I would be able to take it a bit easy, but to my horror there were Sandhurst officer instructors, positioned all around the course, yelling at each of us to run faster, and I finished more exhausted than any other time in my life.

In June in the middle of the Sandhurst grounds I came face to face with my father, who proceeded to tell me everything I had done during the past two weeks, while I recounted to him all the events which he had attended. This was the result of people always feeling obliged to say to us 'saw your dad/son doing etc', whenever they met either of us. He also told me about his new plan to have an extra work period on Tuesdays and Thursdays, in order to start weekends from mid-morning Saturdays, to help those who lived far away from Sandhurst. Hence we all started to make great plans for the following weekend, until a notice appeared on the company blackboard, ' Victory College Juniors Blues fitting 12 noon Saturday'. Of course the cadets all told me to sort out the Commandant! I felt that I already had enough problems with authority, and refused to call him. On the Friday evening, in need of some clothes from my room, in Government House, I went there intending to slip in and out unseen. By coincidence on my way out I met the General, on the stairs, and then could not resist from saying to him, 'WHY did you give us something with one hand and take it away with the other?' With delight I saw that he did not know about the situation and then I watched his initial fury, turned into humour, as he rushed to the telephone to hatch a cunning plan. That evening at an official cocktail party a civilian instructor, obeying his brief, waited for the Commandant to be surrounded by all the colonels and then said in a loud voice 'General have you heard that

Victory College have a blues fitting at noon tomorrow?' My father only said one word 'WHAT?' and then had great difficulty, keeping a straight face, to act as if highly annoyed. Meanwhile an hilarious scene unfolded, with the staff officers conferring urgently to arrange the cancellation.

My intermediate term at Sandhurst passed by relatively smoothly, except for one incident with a car. Only seniors were allowed to have cars and they could not drive within the Academy grounds. A fellow cadet, who illegally kept a car in nearby Camberley town, lent it to me for a Saturday night dance, but forgot to tell me that it had a faulty petrol gauge. At the end of the dance, in the early hours of Sunday morning, I happily gave a lift home to a lovely young lady and, with the gauge reading a quarter full, the car suddenly spluttered to a stop on an isolated road. Accused of deliberately setting up the situation, I had to walk for miles to find a garage and buy petrol. By the time I had delivered the young lady, still complaining, to her home and had reached the Camberley garage, there was only half an hour left, before I had to be on a church parade, in the Sandhurst chapel. So I drove on to the back gate of Government House, abandoned the car outside the stables and ran for my life to change into uniform. I arrived at the chapel with one minute to spare. After the service we went straight on a two-day exercise and I completely forgot about the car. Four days later by chance I bumped in to my father, who said to me, 'You won't believe it, some unscrupulous bounder, last Sunday, dumped his car outside my stables.' With horror I remembered my drama on Sunday morning and asked him what had happened to the car. 'I called the police and told them to handle it,' he replied. I managed to keep a straight face and agreed that it was the work of a bounder and then took twenty-four hours to decide what to do about this predicament. In trepidation I went to the house of the Colonel Quartermaster of Sandhurst and explained the awkward situation, deliberately in front of his wife, seeking her sympathy. To my relief he understood the problem of implicating the car owner and embarrassing the Commandant and arranged for the car to be returned to the Camberley garage, without telling my father. Many years later I confessed to my Dad and we had a long laugh together.

The Commandant by tradition had to be escorted by two 'Stick Orderlies, selected by himself from the cadets in the intermediate term', as he marched from Government House to the Chapel, for the Sunday service. From my intake dear Dad could not resist choosing two cadets, who were both six foot seven inches tall and who dwarfed him at six foot one inch. This caused considerable amusement and a report came back to him that someone had asked 'Who is the little fellow in the middle?' Near the end of the intermediate term obligatory boxing provided a frightening part of the Sandhurst curriculum. We each had to fight against someone of equal stature and weight. I remember standing toe to toe with my opponent, in the knowledge that the authorities had devised this as a test of courage, throwing punches as fast as I could. I woke up in my bed to be told that I had been knocked out at the beginning of the second round.

1952 is a year which I will always remember. Rendez-Vous reappeared after a long rest with his legs scarred by that cruel treatment called 'firing'. But it had worked and he showed high spirits on exercise terrifying my father's groom and dictating to him where they should go. One day I rode Rendez-Vous around the hills and woods and he tried the same with me, by rearing up to refuse to pass a piece of paper. Several times I tried to coax him forward, but the rearing went higher and became more dangerous. With my heart in my mouth I lifted the whip and the longest fight I ever had with a horse ensued, as he jumped and stood on his hind legs many times, before suddenly giving in and going past the paper. After that, whenever he tried being obstinate, I only had to raise the whip and he immediately obeyed me. The preparation for our first point-to-point of the year went well with several gallops and schools over fences. I woke up in bed to discover that I had fallen off at Tweseldown in that first race and had been knocked unconscious. Apparently one of the Sandhurst instructors, who had seen me being lifted into an ambulance, later met my Dad and enquired 'How is he?' and received the reply 'Safe and uninjured, thank you, because he was caught quickly!'

Being my final term the pace of work became tough again and I struggled to survive, although I knew I had a place waiting for me in the 10th Hussars. Indirectly corruption protected me, as many other senior cadets still had to find a regiment to accept them and, with limited vacancies, the order of merit from the passing out results could have been crucial. Luckily it appeared that nobody dared to ask for the 10th Hussars, because they knew that the regimental representative, at Sandhurst, was the Commandant!

For the next race we took Rendez-Vous all the way to Dorset. The opposition turned out to be very weak and not only did we quickly go into the lead, but on arrival at the last fence, there seemed to be no other horse in sight. In this situation the thought of falling at the last is extra alarming, but Rendez-Vous jumped it perfectly and we had our first winner. I felt a wonderful exhilaration and the drive back to Sandhurst, with my parents, became a happy experience. Then a week later we went to the Vine Hunt point-to-point at Hackwood Park, near Basingstoke, and I remember the race vividly. The fences were small and upright and Rendez-Vous appeared to have no respect for them, so much so, that I thought something must be wrong with him and that I should pull up. He jumped every fence badly, nearly falling two or three times, until we reached the third last and the leaders looked to be a fence ahead. On a sudden impulse and as a last resort, I thrashed him with the whip several times, to find his stride majestically lengthening, before he stood off the jump in brilliant fashion. Then we literally ate up the ground and with another enormous leap, at the second last fence, we landed a hundred yards adrift of the leaders. I thought 'what a pity we could have won if I had beaten him earlier', but to my astonishment the gap seemed to diminish faster than before and as Rendez-Vous took off at the last fence I hoped we would make third place. Then in the finishing straight, we went by horse after horse, hitting the lead as we passed the winning post.

By pure luck I had found out the best way to ride Rendez-Vous in a race, just in time for the 1952 Cadets' Race, which followed two weeks later at Tweseldown. My old friend from Catterick, Richard Coxwell-Rogers, had a horse, which some people said could be good enough to beat us, but we were the hot favourite. Unluckily for Richard he ran into some trouble as a cadet, which prevented him from fully completing the final preparations for the race. I heard a libellous murmur that suggested that the Commandant might have arranged this. Anyway I enjoyed an armchair ride on Rendez-Vous and the new tactics worked perfectly. I sat quietly on him until half a mile from home. Then I drew the whip approaching the third last and felt him lengthen his stride to give fabulous jumps over the three final fences and win. Poor Richard came second, closer than I realised, and afterwards moaned about missing this vital last week of training. At the prize ceremony I received the cup from the Commandant and as I walked towards him I heard a loud whisper 'Take your hat off', an order I quickly obeyed.

All the senior cadets went to camp for the final outdoor training. I understood that my prospects of being commissioned depended on my performance in some initiative tests. The last of these required me to bring a group of re-supply vehicles to a designated location, in the middle of a wood at midnight. En route I thought I had lost the way several times, but luckily we arrived in the right place on time and I had passed all the tests. For the next race we went to Larkhill, the gunnery range in Wiltshire. Once again the tactics, learnt at Hackwood Park, worked perfectly and Rendez-Vous lengthened his stride over the last three fences to win comfortably. Two weeks later I returned to Larkhill, accompanied by a beautiful titled lady admirer, but Rendez-Vous had to carry a ten-pound penalty and he could not produce the normal acceleration when asked, leaving me shocked and sad that we had finished unplaced. I had failed to impress my first female fan and the 1952 season was over. As the end of our time at Sandhurst came in sight, I witnessed some unbelievable behaviour by future officers. I suppose they had to release pressure somehow, but it felt like a riot when they picked up all the bicycles they could find, and threw them in the lake.

The Sovereign's Parade provided the grand finale for a cadet at Sandhurst. It ended with the senior cadets marching up the Old College steps and in to the building. As they passed through the door they became a second lieutenant. The practice parades seemed to be endless, but gradually we were drilled into shape and the big day arrived. Immaculately dressed in Blues, white buff belts and shining boots, while carrying a rifle polished like a mirror, we marched from Victory to the Old College parade ground.

The inspection took place and the music made me feel a little emotional, before the parade began, besides my fear of miscounting the number of steps for 'the advance in revue order'. Then twice round the parade ground, first time slow marching followed by quick time and I wondered if I would catch the eye of my father, as we gave the eyes right. Lastly the thrill of climbing the steps and suddenly realising that the journey through Sandhurst had ended. As I emerged from Old College a sergeant-major saluted me and for the first time I returned the compliment instead of giving one. That night the Sovereign's Ball took place in the gymnasium and I much enjoyed it, despite having my face slapped by my girl friend and being reprimanded by my mother for dancing cheek to cheek.

There followed the best holiday of my life. It started with an incredible week at the Dublin Horse Show. Every day I attended the show to see the international jumping and other horse classes, followed by all night dancing at fabulous hunt balls. I will never forget the wonderful atmosphere of enjoyment at the dances and, although I had little sleep, pure adrenaline seemed to keep me in fantastic form. At the end of the week I moved to stay with a cadet friend, Peter Harvey, who had won the medal of honour at Sandhurst, for being first in the order of merit. His father, a retired British General, held the position as director of personnel, at the famous Guinness brewery. Peter and I played in a tennis tournament at Bray and, when on court, I felt the effects of the previous week's high living. When I threw the ball up to serve, I could hardly see it and to be quick about the court was difficult. Needless to say I did not win many games in the singles, but Peter and I had success in one doubles match. In the Harvey household the kind hospitality included a daily ceremony, when a barrel of draught Guinness was delivered and gleefully received. The General was a great character, who had spent much of his life in India. He played in a cricket match, between the office staff and the brewery workers and when he came in to bat, everybody helped him to score runs. The bowlers sent down easy balls, the fielders ran in the wrong direction and threw the ball in badly, while the General scored a number of runs, apparently oblivious of all the assistance. The look of pleasure on his face was wonderful.

CHAPTER 4

Becoming an Officer - Racing Career as a Jockey

THE REST OF THE HOLIDAYS I SPENT at Whitfield Court going to many good parties, including dances, besides enjoying, once again, the peace and beauty of the Irish countryside. Then the big day arrived for me to put on officers' uniform for the first time. I went to Bovington Camp, Dorset, in England, to learn some of the skills for handling tanks, with all the other new young armoured corps officers. Inevitably there had to be shocks and the first came when I found my bedroom to be in a nasty cold wooden hut and secondly that I spent most of the time in denims, instead of my smart new uniform. But we became excited when the tank driving phase began, out on the local moors. Initially I remember feeling a little desperate when trying to double de-clutch with the enormous pedals, while pulling the steering levers and hearing the inevitable grating of gears. Also I went through the experience of stalling the engine and allowing the tank to run backwards downhill, with an angry voice in my earphone berating me from the commander's turret. Then I gained confidence to get up to ten miles an hour, which in a tank felt like sixty, but my instructor had a wicked sense of humour and he directed me towards two little hillocks beyond which, unknown to me, lay a water hole. The tank rose majestically over the first hillock so I accelerated towards the second and too late saw the water on the far side. A wave of water came over me, soaking me from head to foot, and the laughter in my headset went on and on as I struggled to regain control of the enormous metal beast.

We went to the radio wing for the next phase of training. I tried to learn how to operate the temperamental 19 set, which had a long range and provided a very effective means of communication in the hands of an excellent operator. I will always remember the piercing whistle, which had to be tuned out to achieve good reception. My podgy fingers normally moved the button too far creating a louder whistle to the annoyance of those standing nearby. On some day exercises we drove long distances and attempted to talk to each other through horrendous noisy interference, because we lacked the experience to be, what is called, perfectly on net. We then moved to Lulworth, a few miles further south, on the coast of Dorset, to be trained on tank gunnery. There I enjoyed the comfort of living in a modern comfortable officers' mess, but heartily disliked our small and officious staff sergeant gunnery instructor. The combination of his loud boring voice and the roar of the guns nearly deafened me, while I struggled with the sequence of stripping and reassembling the machine gun. However I learnt all the range procedures and fire orders, how to load and the way to aim with the tank sighting gear. Somehow I avoided having an accident on the range, but always felt close to causing one.

With my young officer training completed, I spent a short leave at Government House, Sandhurst and prepared to go to Germany to join my regiment, the 10th Hussars. In one month I would be twenty years old yet, when I set out for Germany in November 1952, I felt like a small boy, going to school for the first time. I boarded the boat at Harwich, in England, to find that Colonel Michael Morley, the commanding officer of the 10th Hussars (PWO), also happened to be travelling. My introduction to him increased my nervousness throughout the journey. We disembarked at the Hook of Holland and from there went by train to Iserlohn in Germany. I had a peculiar feeling as I took my first look at the German people and their countryside, knowing that only seven years ago they had been our deadly enemies and in two world wars had been responsible for the death of my grandfather, Hugh Dawnay, and my uncle, Hugh Beresford. I immediately formed an opinion that both the German language and their architecture are ugly but soon discovered that, like other countries, they had some very charming people.

The Officers' Mess of the 10th Hussars owned much impressive furniture, pictures, silver and gold plate. This had been laid out in an imposing building, to provide a comfortable place for officers to sit, eat and drink. In the same street, in various houses, our bedrooms could be found and mine had to be the furthest away from the Mess. The walk of 300 yards felt like a mile on a cold morning and I could not afford to be late for breakfast or I would miss my lift to the barracks, which had been built three kilometres away. Following regimental custom, initially my fellow officers treated me coolly, until I had done a month or two at duty, except for one, who appeared to be a walking *Debrett*, by recounting my family tree to me. He knew more about my relations than I did, making me aware and surprised that there were far more titles connected to us than I had realised.

I joined C Squadron and became 3rd Troop leader, to be responsible for eleven men and four Valentine tanks. The Valentines looked more like guns on tracks than tanks and, to counter their old age, required a considerable amount of maintenance. My troop sergeant was older than most, drank too much and lacked the enthusiasm and efficiency shown by others of his rank. I struggled with my work, making many mistakes, and from a military point of view I had a bad start with the regiment. At least I learnt from the experience, so that later, when I was in charge of a squadron, I ensured that any newly joined officer was paired with the best sergeant. Luckily the horse came to my rescue to boost my morale and protect my personal standing, because the regimental stables contained many horses, including privately owned and German ones, which had been commandeered by the British army, at the end of the war. Prior to my arrival the Regiment had followed up their pre-war equestrian fame with considerable success at racing, cross-country and show jumping. A group of officers were involved in what had become a well-known racing syndicate. All the officers contributed monthly to a stables fund to pay for the horse food, while the stables came with the barracks free and a few soldiers worked as grooms. Throughout my army career these valuable perks helped me, in a fantastic way, to participate in many enjoyable horse activities.

I remember many mornings, getting up at 6 a.m., to be taken by a three-ton truck, feeling cold and sleepy, to the stables in the barracks, to ride with a group of other officers in a riding school. This led to a welcome opportunity for me to compete at the hunter trials, run by the 3rd Hussars. There was an enormous entry and I found myself riding a German horse, regarded as a moderate animal, in the novice event. To the amazement of all, including myself, because my horse had been a novice for many years, I had the fastest clear round, to become the winner. As a result I became a candidate for a place in the regimental hunter trial and show jumping team and my confidence rose considerably.

Something to look forward to is a wonderful morale booster and the thought of going on leave, to ride in a military steeplechase at Sandown, in England, in March '53, provided this for me. But I had a big problem in that, before then, I had to lose a stone, in order not to be overweight for that race. Luckily the officers' mess cooks co-operated by giving me my own special non fattening food and, with the additional help of cigarettes, I reduced my consumption at meals, survived the inevitable ridicule and lost weight according to plan. To get fit, every day, whenever possible, I rode a horse round and round the riding school, with shortened stirrups feeling like a monkey.

Suddenly I encountered an extraordinary small world situation, which I found to be, at the same time, quite entertaining and extremely sad. A military doctor introduced himself to me, as the son of a near neighbour, to my home in Waterford, Ireland. I immediately liked him and we went out together for a drink. When he had drunk a few beers he told me that he only had, at the most, a year to live and soon afterwards he became drunk. After that he would often appear in our officers' mess to see or go out with me and get drunk, a condition in which he was harmless and very amusing. I always enjoyed his company despite the sad situation of his health and the embarrassment of being with a man who behaved erratically after imbibing.

I went on my first exercise with my troop of Valentine tanks and remember that two things left an impression with me. Firstly the stylish way the squadron officers' mess, in the field, served delicious food, which we ate with silver off good china. Secondly the difficulty of map reading in a strange countryside and how easily I could become lost. March 1953 arrived and to my relief my diet had worked. Thinner than ever before, I set off to England, full of expectancy and excitement about what lay in store for me during my first leave from the Regiment. Rendez-Vous had been entered for the Military Hunters' Chase at Sandown and only a week later at Aintree in the Fox-hunters' Chase, which included all those enormous Grand National fences. Government House at Sandhurst provided a luxury base for finishing my preparation for the exciting racing programme. Rendez-Vous was stabled behind the house and it was wonderful to renew my acquaintance with him, during some sharp gallops and fast schools over practice fences. I had to pinch myself that I alone had this privilege to ride such a magnificent horse, who could jump so fluently, giving me a thrill at each and every fence.

The first Saturday, as a warm up for Sandown, we were entered in a point-to-point at Tweseldown. I think that Rendez-Vous won this race for me so easily, that I realised that he was extremely fit, as once again I experienced that excitement and emotion as he imperiously increased the length of his stride, to stretch in to even more exhilarating leaps over the final three fences. My expectancy and excitement for Sandown, on the following Saturday, increased even more than before. The annual military race meeting started on the Friday and I was surprised at the pomp and ceremony of the occasion. But this, together with the sheer thrill of knowing that I would be participating on the following day, helped to curb my fear when I walked the course and saw the big fences in front of me. They were considerably higher than point-to-point fences and much more imposing. In the back straight the proximity of the seven fences to each other was frightening, but did not prevent me from looking forward to the next day.

On the Saturday the drive to Sandown will always be remembered by me. The mixture of fear and excitement gripped me and stayed with me during the early races. I had to wait until 4.45, according to my mother's diary, for my race, the last of the day, to take place. I had only just made the weight and therefore could not wear even a light vest under the maroon and Eton blue jersey (family colours). I felt the frost was setting in as I walked to the paddock in my overcoat. To my surprise I found myself being led across the middle of the paddock to meet Queen Elizabeth, the Queen Mother, and to hear her say 'good luck'. Then off with the coat, a leg up onto Rendez-Vous and I was led, shivering with cold and fear, down that long path from the paddock to the course, in front of the grandstand. But after a smart gallop to the start I felt warm and determined. Rendez-Vous sailed majestically over those seven fences in the back straight, giving me a wonderful thrill, as we kept nicely in touch with the leaders. I employed the tactics, fortuitously learnt the previous year, and approaching the third last fence raised my whip to feel, once again, that glorious acceleration followed by an enormous stretch as we stormed over that next jump. We came flying into the second last, sharing the lead with one other horse, in the firm belief and excitement that the race was between the two of us. The next thing I remember, clearly, is being in my bed at Government House at Sandhurst. Then I learnt that Rendez-Vous had been knocked over, at the second last fence, by the other horse, as it crashed to the ground, knocking me unconscious.

Anyone who has ridden in races, for more than one season, will know that any jubilation will inevitably be matched by major disappointments. To have come so close, after losing so much weight, during many months of training and expectancy, was bad enough, but on top of this we were soon told by the vet that Rendez-Vous was injured so badly, that he would not be able to race again that year. Hence the extra thrilling trip to Aintree was cancelled plus two or three more point-to-points. Now I realise that I should have thanked my lucky stars that I had not been badly injured but, at the time, I was miserable and my poor parents found it hard to console me. Then they came up with the best solution by sending me to our beautiful home in Ireland for a week. There I relaxed while appreciating the beauty of the countryside, and the friendship of the local people.

On my return to Germany, out of the blue, I was handed an opportunity to race again. At a place called Bad Lippspringe, where the British Army maintained a large area of playing fields, for all sports, which in later years would provide excellent polo grounds, a steeplechase course had been laid out for two race meetings in consecutive weeks. The Regiment was due to move to England in June/July (1953) to be stationed at Tidworth and Warminster. Because of this the renowned regimental racing syndicate had been terminated and dispersed, so that it appeared that no suitable horses remained to compete in these races. However Peter Jackson, second in command of 10H, had distinguished himself in combined training events and show jumping, with his big black headstrong horse, called Zulu. He suddenly decided that 10H must be represented and that his horse, although not a thoroughbred, was fast enough to give a good account of himself. But Peter was a big man, who would be far too heavy to ride in any race and hence he asked the three experienced regimental jockeys, 'Who wants to ride Zulu for me?' To my delight they all refused, in the belief that the horse lacked real racing speed and probably might run away and kill any jockey, stupid enough to ride him. Then he turned to me and I quickly volunteered because, after my debacle in England, I was looking for any chance to ride in another race. For the next few days I was frequently attacked verbally, being told that I had made a terrible mistake and would, at the least, make a fool of myself, if not be badly injured. But I was impetuous and wished to continue my racing career, especially after my recent bad luck. Then when I much enjoyed the training gallops and schooling over fences on Zulu, despite the way he pulled so hard, I was determined to take part in the races.

The day came for the first race meeting and, while changing clothes for the race, I was wishing that I had taken the other jockeys' advice. Cantering down to the starting post Zulu went faster, than I had intended, and suddenly I found that I could not stop with the other horses. I managed to make Zulu go in a large circle around the starting post and then, to reduce the circle gradually, until it was quite small, but I still could not bring Zulu to a halt. Rowley Gibbs, the Brigade Major at Munster, who was a good friend of my parents and destined to be a senior general, was the starter. He suddenly threw himself towards me in order to catch hold of my reins. He succeeded but then was unceremoniously dragged at least fifty yards before Zulu finally came to a halt. I have for ever retained a picture in my mind of a bowler-hatted man beneath me in a horizontal position, hanging on to my reins. There must be very few starters at race meetings, who would risk life and limb, in this manner. Temporarily I was immensely relieved to be static, but a few moments later the race was under way and once more I was struggling to control Zulu. Luckily each jump made him check and helped me to have some control over our speed. In fact he leapt so magnificently, giving me that same thrill I had experienced with Rendez-Vous. I began enjoying the race and even thought we might win. But then over the last three fences he jumped badly to the left, giving away vital ground, and we finished a close second. I was delighted to have finished safely and with the realisation that I was no longer a one horse racing jockey. The following week, at the second Lippspringe race meeting, I walked Zulu to the start and then, in our race, had a carbon copy ride of the previous one, jumping to the left over the last three fences and finishing second to the same winner. I felt that I gained valuable experience and had represented the 10th Hussars well, as their sole competitor. Also I was happy to know that I had survived the enmity and criticism of the other regimental jockeys.

My next big excitement was purchasing a German car from a 10th Hussar sergeant. It was a black 1936 Mercedes. During a trial drive of the car, I was worried about being able to stay on the right-hand side of the road, because I had never tried this before. Initially my heart was in my mouth, but once I realised that I was in full control, I felt like a king. I relished the feeling of independence, given me by the car, but over the next few months I had more than one adventure with this old Merck. Punctures happened fairly frequently, together with a few breakdowns, in awkward places, most of them caused by an endless generator problem. Once I had an alarming experience, when to prevent the engine from stalling in the middle of flowing traffic, I had to keep driving at 80 k.p.h. or put the gearbox in neutral and rev like hell with the accelerator.

On the sporting front I swam quite well in the inter-squadron competition, that consisted of relay races, and was selected as a reserve for the regimental team, which was renowned in Germany from previous years. This involved some intensive training and on the day of the big championships I stood in terror as the long freestyle race relay took place, because it was planned that if there was a big enough lead I would swim the final two hundred leg. To my relief I was not required to participate and the day ended in jubilation when the Regiment won the championship.

On the military side of life I continued to struggle to be an effective troop leader in C Squadron and I knew that my squadron leader was not happy with me. In hindsight he should have tried to give me guidance or arrange for some assistance from another experienced officer. Even better he ought to have changed around the troop sergeants to give me one, who was able to advise and teach me. But he seemed to be more concerned with other matters including his two spoilt pets, known as sausage dogs. During days, spent in the barracks, there was a mixed programme, of instruction for some soldiers and maintenance on the vehicles done by the remainder. I was not involved with the former and was still ignorant and inexperienced with the latter, so I used to hide in the office allotted to junior officers. Luckily for me the horse again relieved the pressure, because I was suddenly told, by Peter Jackson, that I had been selected for the regimental show jumping team, which would compete in the big annual inter-regimental competition, held at Lippspringe. Even better I would be riding a brilliant old pre-war German international horse called Pascha with my hunter trial winning horse as my reserve. The down side of this was that I had to become part of the regimental rear party for the move to England, which delayed my return home by two weeks. However the training started well in advance of the move by the main party and I much enjoyed getting to know Pascha, together with the schooling sessions on both horses.

When jumping Pascha I experienced both thrill and fear, while trying to adapt to his tearaway style. As we approached any fence he would accelerate rapidly, as if he wanted to bolt into the distance, and as long as I kept absolutely still and avoided interfering in any way, he would check his speed, only one stride away from take off, before jumping perfectly. If I tried to slow him down he would further increase speed and crash through the fence. There were days when courage failed me and everything went wrong with the cry of timber, ringing around the schooling arena. Peter Jackson nearly lost his patience with me and threatened to take me out of the team. One day he ordered me to get down on the floor to be the horse, while he sat on me and demonstrated the squeeze of the grip and the different applications for acceleration and slowing. At the time, to have such a big man on top of me was humiliating and uncomfortable, but not only did I learn from it then, but in my next career forty years later, I suddenly remembered it and applied the same treatment to a difficult client with success. Since then I have helped many people with this treatment and explanation.

The main party of 10th Hussars duly left for England and the handover to our successors had to be completed by the few of us left behind, in the rear party. The day for the big horse show arrived and I awoke in quite a nervous state. In the morning I jumped both horses in individual competitions. First the reserve horse went well but not good enough to get a rosette. Next Pascha went into the arena in an overexcited condition and proceeded to go faster than ever, at fences, which were much smaller than we had been schooling over. Whatever I did to soothe him must have been wrong, because we knocked most of the jumps down. Peter Jackson was furious, threatening me with a fate worse than death, if I did not have a good round in the team event. Early in the afternoon we walked the course to find the jumps much bigger than anything that I had ever ridden over before, and there were so many of them. So while I rode Pascha around, waiting for our turn to jump, I felt more fear than at any other time on a horse in my life. However when we entered the ring Pascha pricked his ears and felt so much calmer than in the morning that I became a little more confident. As we crossed the start line I reminded myself to stay still, whatever happened, and Pascha hurtled towards the first fence, checked one stride from take off and jumped perfectly. The further we went the more I began to enjoy the thrill of these enormous fences, which he sailed over effortlessly. I remained as still as a mouse, in disbelief that we were clearing jump after jump, while travelling so fast between them. Pascha was clearly remembering his pre-war international life and enjoying these large obstacles, which he obviously respected far more than those little ones in the morning. Then I remember that wonderful feeling, as we went past the finishing flag, with a clear round safely completed. A few minutes later Peter Jackson also went clear, making our team total the lowest and we had won the Regimental Championship. It was a moment to savour for a long time and even now, after sixty years, I still tingle at the memory of that momentous victory. This was my first personal involvement in a team win, of any significance, for eight years, when at the age of twelve, I had played wing forward in the Stonehouse School rugby team.

My last few days in Germany were hectic. Our small rear party had to complete the handover of the barracks and vehicles, while packing all our clothes and belongings, besides selling or ridding ourselves of any possessions that we could not take with us. For me the latter included my beloved old Mercedes car and, for a while, I thought I was going to have to leave it abandoned in a dump. Luckily on the day before we left a sergeant, from the incoming regiment, paid me a small amount for the car and I sadly handed over the keys of the first vehicle that I ever bought. The next day I caught the train and my first foreign tour in the army was over.

CHAPTER 5

Return to England 1953

ON 29 JULY 1953 I WAS delighted to be back in England, to begin three weeks leave. I was also happy to be staying in the comfort of Government House, Sandhurst. To my surprise Prince Henry, the Duke of Gloucester, was a guest for one night before the Sovereign's Parade on the following day, when he was taking the salute, as the VIP, after inspecting all the cadets. In his well known style, the Prince talked and laughed until the early hours of the morning, keeping my poor Dad up, together with several other dismayed people, who had been invited to dinner. The next morning there was a rush to get the Duke dressed and fed in time for the parade. It was wonderful for me to be relaxed in a chair, watching the cadets perform, as I had done one year before, in this long demanding parade. At the lunch that followed, I celebrated that already I had been an officer for one whole year.

August was to be a month with and an incredible mix of fun and tragedy. My sister Rachel was in Greece with the British Embassy in Athens and my brother Peter was serving his national service with the Irish Fusiliers in Egypt. So Mum, Dad, sister Blanche and myself went home to Ireland. After a couple of days in the luxury of Whitfield Court, my parents and Blanche set off for a few days in Dublin, to see the famous horse show, while I moved locally to Tramore to play in a tennis tournament. All plans were disrupted on 5 August by the sudden death of my maternal grandmother. Daughter of Lord Lansdowne, who had been a Viceroy in India, she had married the 6th Marquis of Waterford and was then widowed in December 1911, after giving birth to six children. Granny 'Bertie' had so distinguished herself in that war, with her nursing and organisation for the wounded, that she had been created a Dame. Then to everyone's surprise she was remarried to the 12th Duke of St Albans in 1918, whose home was Newtown Anner, near Clonmel in County Tipperary. Thereby Granny rose from Marchioness to Duchess to join her sister Eve, who was the Duchess of Devonshire, and never used the Dame title, which she had gallantly earned, and that explains why, we, her grandchildren never knew anything about her valid claim to fame, until many years after her death. We all met up for the funeral, which I can only vaguely remember, but I did record how brave my mother was in the way she gracefully accepted her big loss. She died on 5 August 1953 aged 76.

In the following week I went to all the four days of the local Tramore race meeting, and enjoyed several good post race parties. Then I said goodbye to Blanche as she left us to travel to Denmark, where she had been invited to stay with a friend, who worked there in the British Embassy. For the weekend Mum, Dad and I set off on a wonderful scenic drive through counties Cork and Kerry. We stayed two nights in Kerry at a beautiful place called Derreen, which had once belonged to my mother's family. Then on the way home we called on Claud and Emma Pert at their house near Mallow in Cork. A retired general, Claud had also been a pre-war international 9 goal polo player. I remember him complaining bitterly that his life was being ruined by having to listen, on the radio, to England being defeated at cricket by the Australians while Emma, with her fabulous sense of humour, told him to switch it off. Several years later Claud came out of retirement, to become the manager of the renowned Guards Polo Club at Windsor, in England, and gave great service there for close to twenty years.

At the end of my leave I returned to my regiment, at Tidworth in England, to be told that I had been transferred to B Squadron and was now leading their 4th Troop. I was delighted to find that now I had an experienced and efficient troop sergeant and a cheerful group of men under me. My new squadron leader gave me a pleasant welcome and I felt relieved that my military future was being given a new opportunity. Then I set off for my first weekend from Tidworth to stay with an uncle and aunt, Peter and Angela. He was an admiral who was about to take over command of the Royal Yacht and his sense of humour was most entertaining. But that weekend there was only a short time for laughter, before a telephone call informed us that Blanche had been killed, in a car crash, in Denmark. If ever fate played a part, it was in this tragedy. Her friend had an English right-hand drive car, exported to avoid tax, for the roads of Denmark, where the traffic drives on the right. A caravan had become unhinged, from an oncoming car, and had crashed directly into their left-hand front door, instantly killing Blanche and only slightly injuring her friend, in the driving seat. At Sandhurst, the next week, Dad organised a funeral service at the beautiful Academy Church, followed by cremation and the spreading of ashes in a lovely garden. Rachel had come home from Greece and some cousins, including David Miller, son of Lady Patricia Beresford also attended. It was a very sad day, during which I felt deeply for Mum, who had lost two close kin in less than a month. I found it hard to accept that Blanche had actually died and longed to open the coffin to see that it really was true and, if it was, to have a last view of her.

On returning to Tidworth I discovered that A Squadron had moved to Warminster to become the demonstration squadron for the School of Infantry. This meant that there were many more duties for the soldiers in my troop and we, the junior officers, had to take on an increased number of days as orderly officer, to cover the absence of a whole squadron. We were now equipped with Centurion tanks, which were vastly superior to the old Valentines, left behind in Germany, but naturally I had difficulty adapting to the different technology. This was underlined when we went out on Salisbury Plain to participate in an exercise for a few days. I shared the limited space in the turret of my tank with a radio operator and a gunner. Maintaining control of all the equipment at the same time, while preventing them from interfering with each other, was not easy. Within the turret I had the map, a compass and the written orders for the day. While referring to these, as necessary, I had to talk on the radio through a hand mike, with headsets balanced on my head. The wires connecting these together could easily become entangled round my body, in the gun or some part of the many controls. The whole turret and gun could be traversed 360 degrees very quickly, either by myself or the gunner, and in doing so items of clothing, equipment, mugs, plates or food could fall to the floor, sometimes to places that were inextricable. Ideally food and refreshment was taken outside the tank on the ground, but on many occasions this was not possible and there was a kettle that could be boiled, inside the turret, to make tea or coffee to go with sandwiches and packet chips. There was a control switch for the radio, which would connect me, as required to my driver, to the other two tanks of my troop or on a different network to the squadron leader. Without good concentration, it was easy to become confused and switch incorrectly to give instructions to the wrong person. So there was great scope for a comedy of errors, at any time, but especially when I was struggling to understand a tricky route on the map. Luckily there were no one taking photographs to record some of the situations, which I muddled through.

There was only one night of the exercise left and, in mid-afternoon, I was beginning to think that I was going to survive my first escapade, on Salisbury Plain, without getting into any trouble. Then suddenly I received orders to advance with all three tanks across a steep valley, to take up a defensive position, as quickly as possible. I led the way in my tank and the other two Centurions followed, fairly close behind, on the same narrow path. As we were approaching the top of the hill my driver hit something solid with one of the tank tracks, which came clean off the sprocket. Behind us the next driver, while changing down to halt smoothly, missed his gear and hurtled backwards into the third tank. In a flash all three tanks were immobilised and out of action. Naturally I immediately called up on the radio to report the disaster, but could not raise an answer from Mark Fleming, our squadron leader. I tried with all the available radios to get through to somebody, but failed to raise any reply. So we took out our cookers and made ourselves a really healthy meal and then settled down to sleep. The next morning I was again trying to make radio contact when a scout car appeared, with Mark Fleming in it. He looked unshaved and furious, but hardly said a word, other than we must wait for the fitters to arrive, as he departed to find and despatch them to us. When all the damage had been repaired sufficiently, we rejoined the rest of the Squadron. A short time later the exercise ended and we limped home. On arrival in the barracks I nervously waited for a summons to be reprimanded, even punished, and all through the following week I expected to receive a lecture about all the sins that I had committed. Unbelievably I never heard another word said about the incident, and my life continued, as if nothing had happened. However I learnt several valuable lessons from the experience and became determined to repay Mark Fleming by working extra hard.

Yet again horse competitions came to my rescue. This was heralded by the good news from Sandhurst, which told me that Rendez-Vous was fully recovered from injury and was fit for action. During autumn '53 there were a number of hunter trials events, at weekends, for which my parents and I had three horses to share and compete with. The Commandant's charger, a big black horse called Perfect Knight, a novice bay mare, Rockall, and the incredible Rendez-Vous. We had much enjoyment with little success at various events, until in November we went for a finale to Tweseldown, where we had already enjoyed point-to-point successes. Here Rendez-Vous showed what a versatile horse he was by jumping a brilliant round, over a long difficult course, that included many rails, which could be knocked down by the slightest touch. He seemed to think that the rails were all absolutely solid and he lifted high and well clear over each and every one, even when we made a bad approach, on three or four occasions. The result was the only clear round, in a very fast time, from sixty entries, and we had won first prize. The exhilaration was magic and I felt so grateful and lucky that we owned this fabulous horse. That night we returned home to Government House, Sandhurst, as a happy family and enjoyed our celebration.

My military life was now diverted towards some serious hard work. I started a ten week D&M instructors' course at Bovington Camp, in Dorset. This covered how to teach the mechanical function and maintenance of wheeled vehicles and tanks, together with the method of being a driving instructor for both. Little did I realise that this training would have such an influence on my second career, twenty years later, although I was immediately impressed by the instruction techniques and the system of applying questions. I was able to practise both, during the many teaching practices (TPs), which we had to give throughout the course. These TPs required us to treat the other officers, on the course, as if they were students, and it produced some amusing incidents caused by one officer. He tried to be too clever with questions, when the rest of us gave our TPs, and so he became a sorry victim of all our questions, on the day his turn came to give one, which he was unable to finish.

My twenty-first birthday arrived and my parents gave me a small Morris car and a good party. I was thrilled to have reached such a responsible age and to have been given the means of independence for moving around. The following week the Bovington course broke up for Christmas. We had reached the halfway stage and had completed the driving stage with the lorries, having been introduced to the system of commentary driving. Initially I thought it was ridiculous and embarrassing, making me stutter and stammer, feeling really stupid talking out loud to myself, while driving. Then suddenly I realised that it was incredibly effective, in the way it improved my attention to detail. Verbalising every action, not only made me carry out the correct actions, but also helped me to remember them for the future. So after some persistent pushing by my instructor, I fully accepted it and took in a lesson, that would come to be extremely useful twenty years later. My Christmas leave in Ireland was much enhanced by a visit from my new girl friend, Margaret Grenfell, who came over for ten days. She was one of the sweetest girls I ever met. A petite blonde, with a wonderful smile and a quiet sense of humour. Her father had been in the 10th Hussars with my Dad, before being killed in the Second World War. I was clearly not her man of the future, because she was intensely artistic, but I enormously enjoyed her company and we had great fun together. We went to three good dances, the Waterford and West Waterford hunts balls, followed by the annual dance at my home in aid of the local Jubilee nurse. Once again I revelled in the pure pleasure of the Irish hunt balls. On the way home from the second one, attempting a short cut, we found ourselves lost in the mountains. This must have added to the amusement, because my mother's diary records that it was 6 a.m., when we returned to Whitfield Court in great form. During this leave I had three days wonderful hunting. Jumping a large variety of banks and walls, I was as usual excited by the atmosphere, generated by the cry of the hounds and the sound of the horn, and this was a valuable preparation for my next racing season in the coming spring.

Back at Bovington we started studying and doing TPs on the more complicated engine of the Centurion tank. After a couple of weeks I began feeling ill with flu symptoms, but I battled through the lessons, the maintenance work on our tank and the driving, because I did not want to miss any days of the course. Then a sharp pain in my side began to attack me, from time to time, and I presumed that I had pulled a muscle. This was followed, a few days later, with problems when passing water, which felt like being tortured. I became extremely worried that I had caught an unfashionable disease. Despite suffering from these three problems I was foolish enough to accept a lift to London one night, to attend a smart party in a hotel. Inevitably, at some stage, I had to answer the call of nature and when I went to the gentlemen's it was quite full of people. To my horror, as I did my business, I could not stop myself from emitting some yells of agony, in front of many gawping spectators. For the next weekend I went to Government House, Sandhurst, where my father was starting his last term as Commandant of the Military Academy. On the Sunday morning I was finally forced by a screaming headache and violent pains in my side, besides excruciating agony when using the throne, to throw in the towel and retire to bed. A doctor was called and announced that my temperature was 103 and then, to my immense relief, he diagnosed that I had a pyelitis of the kidney. This explained all three symptoms and clarified that I had nothing to be ashamed of, so I quietly submitted to being taken to the Cambridge military hospital in Aldershot.

The hospital ward was enormous with twenty-four beds. Here I learnt several new dimensions of life, from watching and listening to all that happened and what was said by the many patients. It was confirmed that all three problems were all part of the kidney problem, for which the cure involved three daily painful penicillin injections in my bottom. But it seemed to work remarkably quickly, because I was back at home in one week and then, after a further week's convalescing I returned to

Bovington. Sadly, although I finished the remaining two weeks, it was deemed that I had missed too many TPs and too much driving, and I was not allowed to qualify as a D&M instructor. However I did appreciate having the extra knowledge about vehicles and the method of instruction.

Back with my troop of tanks in B squadron at Tidworth I started to look forward to the coming point-to-point and hunter chase season, with great excitement. Rendez-Vous was reported to be very fit and had been entered, again, for hunter chases both at Sandown and Aintree. As a warm up he would hopefully start by running at Larkhill and Tweseldown, in point-to-points. Three days before Larkhill I had another kidney attack and to my intense dismay had to return to the same hospital. Not only did I have to suffer another course of those horrible injections, but then I was told the disappointing news that Rendez-Vous, in the hands of a substitute jockey, had finished unplaced, showing signs of being unfit. In fact hindsight revealed that he was simply short of one fast pre-race gallop, because the following week at Tweseldown, just after my release from hospital, I watched him, clearly close to his best, run extremely well. But unfortunately at the third last fence he jumped so big that the jockey fell off. Because he was much smaller and lighter than me, he had to carry an amount of heavy lead under his saddle, which therefore became difficult to stay on. However I was thrilled to see Rendez-Vous prove his fitness and happy to know that he should now be ready in time, to run at Sandown in the same race as the previous year, at the March military meeting.

After various discussions, to my relief, it was decided that I was fit enough to ride at Sandown, but to my horror, when I weighed myself, four days before the race, I was well over the race weight. I went on a banana and milk diet which was so successful that I made the weight on the day. Rendez-Vous jumped brilliantly again and in repeat style of the previous year, a half mile from the finish, produced a glorious extension of stride to join the leader, giving the appearance that the race was between the two of us. At the second last fence it felt as if he had jumped extra well and I had just said to myself, 'we are safely over', when he crumpled and fell, bringing down the other leader. Later I was told that the landing is higher than the take off, an unusual feature for a steeplechase fence, and clearly this had surprised him causing him to pitch and fall. A nurse on duty at the fence said to me, 'Don't I recognise you from last year, when you were concussed and babbling rubbish in a terrible state. Glad to see you are unhurt this year.'

Initially this identical repeat of bad luck at Sandown did not depress me too much, because Rendez-Vous appeared to be none the worse. This of course meant that we could continue to race him, but luckily Dad decided to withdraw from the race at Aintree and enter instead for a point-to-point, to allow him to recover his confidence over smaller fences. So we returned to Hackwood Park, near Basingstoke, where Rendez-Vous and I had had a thrilling win two years previously. This time he jumped appallingly badly and, as we were pulling up unplaced, I thanked my lucky stars that we had not tried to take on the Grand National fences. Then later I was told that poor Rendez-Vous's tail had been carried high throughout the race, which I could not see from his back, and sure enough the next day he was diagnosed with an injured back.

Now I was depressed by facing the possibility that my racing season was, for the second year, probably prematurely over. Then someone advised me to telephone the secretary for the next point-to-point, scheduled at Tweseldown, to inquire if any horses had been entered without a declared jockey. To my delight Mrs Mitchell, MFH of the Vine Hunt, had double entered her horse, Tudor Court, for the Ladies' Race as well as the Adjacent Hunts' Maiden Race and liked the idea, of standing down, to let me give the horse a good school for her. Even better when Tudor Court jumped brilliantly for me and won the race in great style. It was great to win, on a horse that I had never sat on before and for a strange owner, especially as I had only hoped for a spare ride, without any thought of glory. Another bonus was that I had discovered the wonderful privilege accorded to army officers, which allowed us to represent any hunt, without having followed their hounds, when riding in point-to-points. This seemed to be real justice, because it gave members of the British forces the opportunity to catch up on the time lost while abroad.

Further excitement ensued when Dad decided that, after treatment, Rendez-Vous was sufficiently recovered to run in a hunters' chase at the famous Cheltenham. But it was false hope because, although he, in cavalier form at the start, broke the tapes, with a spectacular rear, he ran poorly to finish last. The only mitigation was that he had jumped well enough to complete this renowned course and I could now boast that I had been round three miles of the one and only Cheltenham. Rendez-Vous was now roughed off for a summer's rest with a special charge treatment on his back. I was kept cheerful by an invite from Mrs Mitchell to ride Tudor Court again. She had followed up Tudor Court's Tweseldown win, by riding him herself to victory in a Ladies' Race. But at the coming Easter Monday Vine point-to-point she badly wanted to win the Members' Race and hence my opportunity for another ride and an almost certain winner, as there were only two other horses in the race and they had a poor reputation. In the paddock Mrs Mitchell warned me to be extra careful coming to the first fence, because her horse had started a habit of trying to run out at it. So I set off for the middle of the first jump, but about fifty yards from it Tudor Court seized the bridle bit with his left jaw, and made it impossible for me to counteract him, as he ran out to the left of the fence. I managed to turn round quickly and we were safely over at the second attempt, but by then the other two were sailing over the second obstacle. Nevertheless we gradually closed the gap without going too fast, and were only five lengths behind, as we came to a bend little more than a half mile from the finish. I noticed that both the other horses were hanging away from the rail, and stupidly could not resist taking advantage by joining them, next to the rail, on their inside. A look of amazement came on the face of the leader who immediately increased his pace to his fastest. We then had a thrilling neck and neck battle over the last three fences and were still level at the finishing post, but I lost the race by a nose. If I had waited behind the leader until coming to the last fence, I would surely have won comfortably, but I had to face an owner, furious because she thought that I had not listened to her warning about Tudor Court running out at the first fence, which was totally incorrect, as explained above.

After Easter, to my dismay, the symptoms of another kidney attack returned and I was rushed, once again, to the Cambridge Military Hospital in Aldershot. To my surprise, after a couple of days, the doctors informed me that I had appendicitis and would be operated on the next day. The extraction of my appendix appeared to be a very simple and harmless procedure, but I was given an enormous shock on the following day, when told to get out of bed. I felt hopelessly weak and had presumed that I would be given at least two days bed rest, before having to stand. I soon learnt to accept feeling fragile, but I could not cope with the laughing, caused by some of the antics of a few characters in the ward. The effect was a ripping pain in the area of my ribs, which increased to unbearable proportions, when I stupidly sat down to watch a comedy show on television. Unbelievably I had difficulty making myself stop watching, even though the pain was killing me.

One of the patients in the ward was challenging most of us to work out solutions to a variety of problems and tricks. I became enthralled with these and, to this day, I have been able to remember three of them. Frequently I have enjoyed producing them in front of groups of people who, without fail, have turned into bubbling enthusiasts, attempting to find the answers. At that time this man was suffering from a badly cut finger, as a result of an accident with a broken glass at an officers' mess party, and he knew that he was in danger of losing that finger by amputation. The result was amazing mood swings, from being in incredibly good form with his tricks, to being depressed to a point of thinking he was about to die. One morning, early at around 6 a.m. he announced that he was dying and then requested another patient, who was a close friend, to tell his wife that he had left this world in a brave and calm way. Eventually we found a night nurse to attend to him and she quickly gave him a drop of brandy, which brought him back to being cheerful and laughing at himself. I wondered if his friend would have been prepared to lie with the message to the wife, if events had turned out differently.

After yet another spell of convalescing, fully fit, I returned to my regiment at Tidworth, wondering what the summer had in store for me and received a nasty shock. We were going to have to move from the comfort of the barracks to a tented camp, on Salisbury Plain, near a village called Tilshead. We had been given the task of taking over hundreds of tanks, which we would have to maintain and issue, from time to time, to different regiments of the Territorial Army, throughout the summer. The move out there and the settling in at the camp was not helped by the horrific rain, which caused our tents, at times, to be filled with mud. Then the collection of the tanks, from a nearby railway station, produced a mixture of excitement and stress. Inevitably from a period of five to six days of non-stop ferrying of so many tanks, through a village, there had to be a few collisions with walls and even houses. With all the noise and damage made by convoy after convoy of tanks, passing through their village, the poor inhabitants of Tilshead must have felt that they were being invaded.

When the tank collection was finished, I found that my tank troop had suddenly become responsible for 50 tanks, besides the 3 we already had. Then the first territorial regiment arrived and took most of them from us, for use during their two-week training camp. This started a cycle of handing out, taking back, intensive maintenance and handing out again. In between the work on these extra tanks we continued to maintain our own 3 and do various training exercises. The appalling weather naturally increased the problems of the job, besides giving us unpleasant nights in our damp tents.

My morale was restored by finding that I was on a guest list for debutantes' parties in London. Many invitations arrived by post for cocktail parties and dances. This provided a welcome opportunity for me to escape from the Tilshead mud to enjoy some fabulous entertainment and meet many lovely young ladies. I learnt to exist on little sleep, over quite a long period, sometimes going to work without having been to bed. In hindsight I must have taken more than a few risks, when driving back from London, in the early hours of the morning. Yet because of these festivities I met a very special lady called Diana Blacker, who was beautiful in looks and character and was to make me happy for several months.

I received another shock at Tilshead when I was appointed 'food officer' for the officers' mess. Planning the menu for lunch and dinner, every day, was a no win job, because if I organised good food the messing funds would be over-spent, and if I did not I would be the butt for many complaints. To compensate for this I had an introduction to polo at Cowdray Park, near Midhurst in Sussex. Several other officers

Hugh and Peter Dawnay's christening day on 9 April 1933 at Whitfield Court

Hugh Dawnay's grandfather, Hugh Dawnay, second son of Viscount Downe.
Killed in action during the First World War

Hugh Dawnay's father, David Dawnay with his three brothers

Lady Katherine Beresford, Hugh Dawnay's mother

David Dawnay and Lady Katherine Beresford when engaged, at Curraghmore

The Duchess of St Alban's, formerly the Marchioness of Waterford, with her family in 1922

Hugh and Peter Dawnay with their mother at Newtown Anner, Co. Tipperary

David Dawnay receiving the laurel wreath at the 1936 Olympics

Hugh Dawnay's grandmother, Susan Dawnay, at Whitfield Court

Hugh Dawnay on Pickles, 1938

Blanche, Rachel and Peter Dawnay with their mother at Newtown Anner, Co. Tipperary in August 1943

LEFT: *Hugh and Peter Dawnay at Newtown Anner in August 1943*
RIGHT: *Hugh Dawnay on Dolly at Whitfield Court in August 1943*

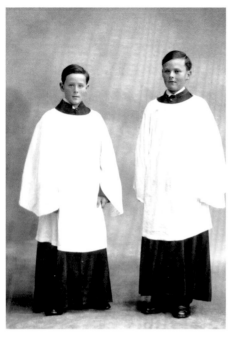

Hugh and Peter Dawnay dressed for
Lower Chapel Choir, Eton

Hugh Dawnay at Eton

Eton – Hugh Dawnay is second from right and
Peter Dawnay second from left in the second row.

in the regiment had been playing, once a week, for a month or more, and were preparing to form a team. My kidney illness and appendicitis had prevented me from joining them earlier. I learnt how to hit a ball and played my first chukka. I enjoyed it, but not knowing where polo would eventually lead me, and at the time being literally crazy about steeplechasing, I did not subscribe to play regularly.

Dad had left Sandhurst to take up his last military job as commander of the London Territorial Division. The house allotted to him, for his final three years in the Army, was the Old Parsonage in Fleet, Hampshire. Much of his work was now at weekends and evenings and this freed him up to restart playing polo, on week-day afternoons, after a fifteen years out of the sport. With his pre-war reputation as an international 7 goal player, he was immediately in demand, especially as his handicap had been reduced to 4. At Cowdray he was asked to play high goal with their club side, to be in the medium goal team of Billy Whitbread, the owner of the beer of that name, and my regiment invited him to be the pivot of their low goal team. Dad had a dream beginning, playing good polo, in several excellent games, at all three levels. But then he had an unlucky fall, broke his ankle and had to rest for a few weeks. He was playing again, before the end of the season, with mixed success with his teams and clearly suffering from the effects of the long interruption.

Meanwhile my regiment had happily returned to Tidworth, having completed our task for the Territorial Army. All the extra tanks had been safely delivered back to the railway station, without incident. My barrack regimental routine was, with little warning, suddenly given a dramatic, unexpected change. I was sent off on an independent mission, for which I took one tank and crew to join a recruiting circus that went to three locations. I grasped the challenge to be better than all the other elements of the circus, which included an artillery gun, a signals vehicle and an infantry section plus representatives of the administrative corps. By coincidence the officer in charge of the infantry section was my second cousin, John Dawnay, who would soon inherit the title, Viscount Downe, and become the head of our Dawnay clan. I much enjoyed the chance to chat with John and together we met a wonderful mix and variety of people as we travelled from place to place. Also my tank crew were very efficient, so that we appeared to acquit ourselves extremely well, until we were about to finish in the third and final location in Norfolk.

The majority of the visitors to the circus had been school cadets. Gradually they had been wearing down my patience, by asking hundreds of questions and being disobedient about sitting in safe positions, as directed, during tank rides. Rather than appear ignorant about complicated technical tank matters I often cited the secret list, as my excuse for not answering their queries. So when the last group, which was the largest we had ever had, swarmed all over the tank, I noticed that it would be difficult to keep all of them safe during the tank ride. Hence to ensure against an accident I came out of my cupola to insist that all the cadets had their feet securely placed. The result was that the little beasts filled my cupola and the only place, left for me to sit, was on the cupola lid, with my legs outside. As I instructed the tank driver to move off, a mischievous feeling pervaded my body to do something different for this final ride, tempting me to try to give these demanding little rascals a bit of a fright. Hence I decided to pretend that we were going to drive straight into the lake, which was about three hundred yards away. While we headed towards the lake, over the intercom, I explained my plan to the driver. I had to presume that he had understood because, for some reason, the equipment of that day did not provide the driver with a mike, with which to acknowledge directions. I repeatedly told the driver ' speed up, change up' and by the time we reached the shore of the lake, the tank was travelling at close to full speed. 'Driver right' I ordered and at the same time I leant my body to the right. He thought I said 'halt' and braked violently. For a moment I felt the sensation of flying, but then I hit the ground with a resounding thud and all the wind left my body. I was temporarily unable to move or speak, although luckily I was not injured in any other way, possibly helped by the experience of having had so many falls from ponies and horses previously, especially as a child.

If ever, in my life, I have felt foolish and incapable of doing anything to change my situation, it was then, as lying on the ground, I realised that all the cadets had surrounded me and some of them were unbuttoning my clothes. For a while I was unable to stop them, but suddenly my breathing became normal and I struggled to my feet. Luckily nobody of any authority saw the incident and I was able to return to the Regiment at Tidworth without another blemish on my record. In later years I have dined out on this story and in competitions for recounting embarrassing moments, I have been hard to beat, when describing what happened.

After only one week, back in barracks, I set off happily to spend the month of August on leave in Ireland. Dad was also on holiday and our beautiful home, Whitfield Court, was prepared to be used to good advantage. The highlight of this month was the prestigious twenty-first birthday of my first cousin, the 8th Marquis of Waterford, who was head of the Beresford clan, my mother's family. Lady Juliet, his mother, a widow since the early thirties, was a wonderful organiser and she liked to give stylish parties. To celebrate this coming of age of her beloved first born, she arranged three days of festivities at Curraghmore, the family estate, with fireworks on the first night, a cocktail party on the second and a magnificent ball as a finale. To support these events my parents were prepared to have a very large house party. My brother Peter, who was then at Oxford University, had invited two undergraduate friends together with two young ladies and I had persuaded three lovely debutantes and an army friend to come and stay, making us a young group of ten. I was thrilled that Diana Blacker was coming as well as another beauty called Sheara Grant-Ferris who was renowned for wearing elegant clothes.

I will never forget that house party. Whitfield was filled with life, laughter and fun. The three parties at Curraghmore were sensational and we also enjoyed two days of horse racing at nearby Tramore. As a group we became quite mischievous, doing some daring, possibly stupid, deeds, which amused our little minds. One of these was to jump out of our cars, when driving along a small side road, and spread empty milk churns across it. An incredible week ended with a dance for Ann Dawnay, another first cousin, who had also reached the magic age of twenty one. Although all our guests left, the rest of August continued to be highly entertaining with many parties, including tennis, tea and drink invitations. At these I could not resist challenging people to try and fathom the games and problems, which I had learnt from my fellow patient in hospital. The result was that not only did some guests overstay their welcome at parties, while attempting to work out the solutions, but others continued, for days afterwards, seeking the answers by inviting me, on the telephone, to play with them by asking questions like 'if I do this what will be your reply etc., etc'.

CHAPTER 6

My Third Lottery – a Significant Boss

I RETURNED TO TIDWORTH AFTER MY leave, wondering what kind of shock might be waiting for me, this time. Sure enough there was more than one surprise in store, which involved the future of B Squadron. We had a new squadron leader called Graham Pilsbury and in two-weeks' time we had been designated to replace A Squadron at Warminster, as the armoured demonstration squadron for the School of Infantry. Wrongly I thought this news spelled disaster. Going to a strange place, just as I had become accustomed to life at Tidworth, temporarily having to lose some regimental friends, not knowing what to expect from Graham and realising that Warminster was even further from London, all combined to depress me. I packed up and moved there with a heavy heart, but in a very short time I was beginning to enjoy a totally new kind of military life. For the first time, as a regimental officer, I could see a clear end product to the work we did, and I quickly became aware that, in Graham, we were being led by a good and understanding leader. The demonstrations, which we had to give, could not be done properly unless our tanks were in perfect working order, after some serious rehearsals, often involving the use of live ammunition. Hence maintenance and preparation of the tanks' engines, tracks, radios, main guns and machine guns had to be permanently excellent or else bad results would be inevitable. My soldiers in 4th Troop highly enjoyed participating in these demonstrations and appreciated having a real reason for working hard.

My morale received a further boost when Dad informed me that he had bought a new racehorse. She was a mare called Flying Rosette who, the previous year, had won an amateur flat race in Ireland and was thought to have a good potential as a steeplechaser, possibly good enough for the Grand Military Gold Cup at Sandown. She was being immediately put into training with the veteran trainer, Alec Kilpatrick, known as the soldier's friend, who had stables and gallops near Collinbourne Ducis. For the first time this gave me an opportunity to ride with professionals during exercise and schooling over fences early some mornings, whenever allowed to escape from Warminster. From this I gained valuable experience, learnt new race riding skills and had an amount of fun.

At Warminster I was also adding to my knowledge, but here it was military expertise, that I was acquiring from Graham Pilsbury, our new squadron leader. You could not call him a typical cavalry officer, but he was the best squadron leader that I ever had and my confidence as a troop leader was increasing daily in many dimensions. Graham clearly provided me with my third lottery win. Not only did he give me pride in myself, but he taught me priceless leadership tips, which I gratefully applied when, years later, I commanded a combat squadron of the Regiment. Best of all he possessed a depth of kindness that warmed our hearts but in no way interfered with the very high standards, which he set for himself and us. The result was a very happy and efficient squadron, which for the first infantry course produced a row of excellent demonstrations.

We had problems, including some injuries, but somehow Graham always came up with suitable adjustments, while maintaining a lovely quiet sense of humour. Perhaps the worst event, of those early Warminster days, happened when a senior officer was accidentally blown into the air by a blank round, fired from one of the Squadron tanks, but luckily Graham fended off the blame and no charges were made. Definitely the most amusing day was brought about by a young corporal, in command of the reserve tank, for one demonstration, blocking our squadron radio frequency throughout the proceedings. He was singing and whistling into his mike, in the belief that he was switched to the intercom and that only his driver could hear him. As a result Graham was unable to direct the action with the orders as rehearsed, became inarticulate with rage, yet miraculously, we managed to complete all the manoeuvres without a hitch.

While I was heavily involved with the first round of demonstrations at Warminster, with an occasional early morning on the training gallops with Flying Rosette, my parents were giving intensive training to three horses for the coming session of autumn hunter trials. They reported that not only was the faithful Perfect Knight, the retired charger from Sandhurst, jumping like a young horse, but that Rendez-Vous seemed to be fully recovered and the new young mare, Rockall, was enjoying being schooled with them. Hence on an October Saturday I went to the first event at Larkhill with great expectations, but found that they were too fresh to be controlled properly, although Rockall came fourth in the novice class.

The following weekend my parents went to Germany, where Dad acted as judge at the British Army hunter trials out there. So I went to Aldershot, where our three horses were stabled, to give them a thorough work out. A week later, highly excited for two reasons, I returned to Tweseldown for the big annual army event in England. Firstly I had three rounds to ride and felt confident that, win or lose, Rendez-Vous, no longer a novice, should give a thrilling performance over the bigger fences in the open competition. Secondly the lovely Diana Blacker would be watching and then staying with us at Fleet. Rockall gave me an enjoyable ride in the novices, but hit a couple of rails. Then Rendez-Vous was unbelievable in the open, clearly still believing that the rails were solid, he gave me a fast clear round. We were nearly deprived by bad luck, because another competitor jumped the last fence parallel with us and, although Rendez-Vous did not touch the jump, when I looked back I saw both top rails fall down. Fortunately I yelled at the fence judge 'I did not hit it'. Later he told me that he would have penalised me if I had not shouted, making him realise that the other horse had caused both rails to fall. So Rendez-Vous had achieved another Tweseldown clear round, and after sixty horses had competed, it was announced that he had also clocked the fastest time and was the winner. I was thrilled and even more delighted when told that we had beaten two famous three-day event horses. Obviously I was extra pleased to have won in front of Diana, who did seem to be quite impressed but not overawed. I still had one round left as part of the family team, in the inter-hunt competition. Mum rode Rendez-Vous, Dad was on Perfect Knight and I took Rockall, for the second time that day. It was wonderful to perform, this one and only time, as a family team and I much enjoyed the experience, although we did not earn a rosette. But Rendez-Vous carried my 54-year-old mother to yet another fault free round. Hence we took Diana home to the Old Parsonage, to share a joyful celebratory dinner with us.

The following week heralded yet another new adventure for me, when all of the three horses were taken by lorry to the Mecca of English fox-hunting in Leicestershire. Their temporary home was the military stables in Melton Mowbray. From there they were in easy reach of the three famous hunts, the Quorn, Belvoir and Cottesmore, and it was hoped that Dad, Mum and I would have a wonderful taste of the best hunting in England during November and December while, at the same time, qualifying the three horses for the next point-to-point season in the spring.

To be allowed to take whole days off for hunting in Leicestershire necessitated ensuring that my tanks were all kept in good working order for the demonstrations. This included the enormous engine, the main gun, the machine gun together with all the sighting equipment, the radios, the turret traversing system and the tracks with so many individual steel links which could so easily be damaged. I had a strong troop of men, who knew what work was required, and a knowledgeable sergeant to direct them, but he was not that good at keeping them happy at the same time. I discovered that the secret for covering this dimension was to let the men clearly know that I cared about what happened to them. Inevitably, for different reasons, most of them, from time to time, would commit some minor indiscretion and be summoned to what was known as squadron orders. Here they would be marched in to face Graham, who duly handed out punishments, suitable to their crime. I was the only troop leader to arrive a few minutes before this confrontation, in order to talk to Graham with a plea for a light sentence, because of their satisfactory work. This normally worked and the men were so pleasantly surprised by the result, that they responded with harder work on the tanks. Luckily Graham firmly believed that hunting was good training for the battlefield, and that an officer seen participating in this well known area, was providing good publicity for the 10th Hussars. Even so I had to choose days that were free of demonstrations.

However there was a shock in store, because we soon discovered that we had picked the wettest two months of the decade, as we encountered heavy rain every day that we hunted in Leicestershire. I remember the misery at the end of most of those days hunting when, not only, was I soaked to the skin, but I felt that I was sitting and standing in water. But I did get a feel of how good it could be to fly across that countryside when enjoying a few short hunts and I appreciated meeting a new group of people, despite the terrible weather. On the racing front, there was another disappointment, when Flying Rosette went lame and her trainer, Alec Kilpatrick, decided that she should be rested for a year. My steeplechasing aspirations appeared to be shattered, until I received a telephone call from Dad, who had sensational news for me. Determined to have a runner in the Military Gold Cup he had just bought another horse called No Law who was well bred by the renowned stallion Within the Law. Dear Dad told me he had sold some shares to fund the purchase of the new horse, but when I went to Kilpatrick's to get acquainted, I quickly came to suspect that the price had not been too expensive. No Law was small and more than a little crazy on the gallops, where I often thought that we were about to disappear into the far distance. He would throw his head up and down and sideways in an uncontrollable fashion, while gathering speed with every stride. Somehow with great difficulty I always found a way to get him in to a circle, in which he would finally stop.

Luckily No Law was racing fit, when bought, and he could be immediately entered in races. The first was scheduled for mid-November at Leicester racecourse, on a Monday. Late on the Sunday night I started to drive to Melton Mowbray, where I intended to stay the night. On the passenger's seat of my little car I placed a portable radio next to me, and after every corner I had to move it, so that I could continue to hear music and hourly news headlines. This helped to keep me calm about the exciting prospect on the following day of, for the first time, riding against professional jockeys and experiencing the extra speed of a two-mile chase. Around halfway to my destination, the heavens opened with a heavy downpour of rain, and when close to Melton the news headlines, on the radio, announced that the races had been cancelled. In frustration I accelerated with the result that I failed to negotiate the next right-hand bend and went down a minor road to the left. Like a fool, instead of turning back to rejoin the main road, I continued and took the next right turn, expecting this to correct the error. Suddenly I found myself on what turned out to be a disused airfield. Round and round I went until, through the rain, I saw a gap in a hedge that resembled an exit and headed for it. Then an ominous noise of a wheel spinning told me that my little car was becoming stuck in the mud. Shivering with cold I tried to sleep in the back seat for the rest of the night. Soon after 7 a.m. I walked to look for help and luckily met a man on a tractor, who agreed to pull my car out of the mud and then told me the quickest route to Melton Mowbray. When I arrived there I was given a message which suggested that I took Rendez-Vous out for a day's hunting with the Quorn. Naturally I jumped at the opportunity, as it provided some compensation for losing the race ride. To my surprise I did not feel too tired and was able to enjoy the day, even though the wet conditions, once again, limited the length of the hunts.

Life at Warminster continued to be highly active and I began to realise that we were involved in a very fulfilling job. It was lovely to see that morale throughout B Squadron was high and from the satisfactory performance of our tanks, in the demonstrations, it was clear that the men of my troop were maintaining them conscientiously. My memory for names has suffered from age, but I do recall that in 4th Troop we had at least three great characters, including the driver of my tank, who I think was called Mountain. His repartee to situations, as they happened, was most entertaining and the other two thrived on his wit to embellish their own jokes.

The most thrilling of all the demonstrations was the Firepower display. We made the beginning look extra spectacular by what could be called a little cheating. Before the spectators arrived we would zero in on the first target by firing, until we hit it fair and square. Then we would carefully register the settings on the sighting equipment, before withdrawing to be positioned totally out of view, behind a hill. There we would switch off all the engines and patiently wait for the crowd to draw up, in their buses, and take their seats. Graham then gave the dual order to start up and move off, which produced an enormous roar as at least twelve Centurion tanks appeared over the hill, halted and within seconds had all fired, with one hundred percent accuracy, to obliterate the dejected remains of tank hulks. Naturally the spectators were highly impressed and showed it with loud applause, which gave the demonstration an effective start. We were watched by a mixture of infantry officers on the various courses and foreign visitors, with an eye on purchasing for their governments. Hence we felt pleased that we might be helping to sell Centurion tanks to our allies.

Night time demonstrations added an extra dimension, of having to make some blind approaches, to exact destinations in the tanks. This was equally nerve wracking for us, in these armoured giants, as it was for members of the infantry, who participated on foot, in rehearsals and in the actual demonstration. Unbelievably when we went at the slowest possible speed, people on foot nearby could not hear us arriving. If we suddenly accelerated or fired a main armament blank we could impart the fear of God into them. On the vital night, in the demonstration proper, I would feel that our approach was taking three times longer than in the rehearsals, and I would start to worry that we had gone past the crucial marker and might be putting innocent bystanders in danger.

In the hunting world the sport continued to be spoilt by the relentless wet winter. Hence in mid-December, when Rendez-Vous and Rockall had qualified for the point-to-point season by obtaining their hunt certificates, Dad decided that it was pointless keeping the three horses in Leicestershire any longer. This disappointment was well compensated for by our racing plans for No Law, who was now entered for three races over a short period of time. The first was at Birmingham and when I arrived at the racecourse, I was still pondering the same questions, which had worried me on that wet night en route to Leicester; how would I manage against the professional jockeys in my first ever two-mile steeplechase.

However a far bigger problem arose on the way to the start, when No Law threw his little head in a manner even more crazy than on the gallops. For a moment I thought we would never stop, just the same as my experience on Zulu in Germany in '53, but somehow I managed to regain control some distance beyond the race starting point. When we rejoined the other horses, I was in terror of what would happen in the race itself. To my enormous relief, after the tapes went up, he became the easiest horse I had ever sat on in a race, jumping brilliantly and galloping calmly under total control. With six fences left to jump I thought we might win as we were cruising in fifth place. Then suddenly the four in front of me accelerated so quickly that we were left behind before I could react. I tried to catch up, but in vain, although No Law was still jumping perfectly, and we finished fifth behind the winner called Tripleplatz. To use racing jargon, I had failed to see the pace go on and thereby lost any possibility of being able to contest the finish. So my worries were justified as the pros had fooled me and the shorter distance of two miles had confused me.

Our next race was even more awe inspiring, because it was part of the famous St Stephen's Day (26 December) meeting at Kempton where a vast crowd always go to watch the renowned King George VI Steeplechase. To make all considerations fit together, I volunteered to be the orderly officer at Warminster on Christmas Day and requested two weeks' leave immediately after that. This allowed me to go to Ireland after the race, have twelve days there for hunting and hunt balls and then return in time to get to Leicester, for race number three with No Law. The extra excitement for me in Ireland was that Diana Blacker had accepted my invitation to come to Ireland again and even agreed to travel over with me.

My race was after the big race, the King George, and the Birmingham winner Tripleplatz was one of the runners. Kilpatrick had arranged that I was allowed to take No Law early to the start and without the excitement of other horses I arrived safely having avoided a repeat of the Birmingham terror. But in the race I failed to prevent a carbon copy of the previous outing and with No Law jumping perfectly I could not understand how I again missed the moment when the pace went on. I cursed myself for letting it happen, especially when I dismounted and saw that No Law looked so fresh, as if he had not been in a race. The consolation was that clearly we had a good steeplechaser, although a bit crazy at times, and all that was required was for me to ride a two-mile chase correctly. I made a resolution there and then that, before we went to Leicester for the next race, I would find the right tactic to employ in order to keep us with the leaders at the crucial moment.

Diana Blacker travelled with me to Ireland, where I enjoyed two wonderful weeks and, for once, everything went according to plan, except on one hunting day. Under pressure Diana agreed to ride my mother's horse with me to the meet, while I rode my hunter and led one for my father. When we had reached the halfway point, it began to snow, very unusual for Waterford, causing the day's sport to be cancelled and nearly freezing Diana into immobility. Otherwise, at night, we immensely enjoyed two hunt balls and the annual dance for the district nurse at my home while, during daylight, I had several good days' hunting. Fortuitously most of the countryside we encountered was wire free, which not only greatly improved the sport but also provided me with some excellent pre-race training before Leicester.

I took Diana to catch the boat from Cork for Wales, a few days before my leave ended, but arranged that she would come with me, to give support at Leicester races, the following Monday, for No Law's next race. On the Saturday I had an extra good final day's hunting and crossed back to England that same night. After a restful sleep on Sunday night, I met Diana in London, where we boarded a train for Leicester. At the racecourse I was horrified to find that Tripleplatz was again running in my race. Because he had been entered, before winning those two chases, he was still allowed to take part in a novice chase, although naturally he had to carry a penalty. Yet as I walked around the racecourse, while the first three races were happening, an idea of how to change the situation to my advantage, which could prevent a repeat of being left behind in the middle of the race, came to me. Hence in the changing room I summoned all my courage to speak to Tripleplatz's rider and ask him if he would mind me riding alongside him at the front during the early part of the race. He was a really famous jockey, called Dave Dick, who had won Gold Cups and many other races and in later years married the sister of a fellow cavalry officer. He replied in crude cockney, 'Certainly young man as long as you stay on the f———g outside and never come on my f———g inside.' I was thrilled as this completed the plan with which I had been struggling with, ever since the race at Kempton. In the paddock I told our trainer, Alex Kilpatrick, about my proposed strategy, to which he indifferently answered, 'If you like but get up quickly to go to the start early to keep No Law calm'. This had again been pre-arranged with the authorities and naturally it helped me to be first in the line up and next to Dave Dick on Tripleplatz.

The memory of this race has never left me and I have relived it hundreds of times, while talking to others and when on my own. Together we led the field over the first ten fences with both horses jumping beautifully. Then suddenly with five jumps left to be negotiated, two other horses joined us, on my left, and the pace increased so much that I said to myself, 'It cannot be possible to jump at this speed'. But it was too late to slow down and, four abreast, we swept into the obstacle. There was a loud crash on my left as one horse fell heavily, while I marvelled at the brilliant fast leap of No Law. At the next fence the other horse on my left, with a sickening thud, turned head over heels. My exhilaration was already unbelievable but further increased at the following jump which Tripleplatz hit hard and all but toppled over, allowing No Law to take the lead by about ten lengths. He then sailed over the last two fences and cruised to victory by six lengths, although Dave Dick started to catch us up after Tripleplatz recovered his wind.

What an incredible thrill to come into the winners' enclosure with Diana smiling and many people congratulating me, including the trainer. Like an idiot I slightly spoilt the glory when the famous champion jockey, Tim Moloney, shook my hand and for the sake of something to say I blurted out, 'But we were twenty to one and I didn't bet a penny'. Quite rightly he immediately slapped my face, as betting by jockeys is illegal and winning a steeplechase, against professional jockeys, was obviously more important than money. It was a lesson well taken and when Fred

Winter, equally renowned, came up to me in the dining car of the train returning to London, I said little besides 'thank you'.

At Warminster the demonstrations continued successfully, but I was made to worry more than usual during one night march in the tanks. I was terrified that we might knock over or even kill someone and when the marker, where my tank was due to stop, failed to appear this fear increased. Even I did not realise just how slow we were going, yet eventually we halted correctly at the right place to the great relief of my crew and myself.

The next race for No Law was in late January at Newbury, where there were only four runners. I employed the same tactics as at Leicester and this was working well when the four of us, in a row, came to the fourth last at break neck speed. For the first time in a race No Law took off too close to a fence, put his head on the ground and almost fell, before making a spectacular recovery. Somehow I stayed on, after thinking I would fall off, and we came to the last fence in third but well behind the two leaders. Like an ass I did not see that the fourth horse had pulled up and ruined the glory of my survival by riding an unnecessary finish for third place, thereby learning another important lesson the hard way. As a matter of fact that was my last ever two-mile race as, for the rest of my racing career, I only rode over three or more miles, but the velocity of the jumping at the end of Leicester and Newbury races will live with me for ever. In February we went to Windsor to try No Law in his first three-mile steeplechase. Realising that I had to change the racing tactics for the longer distance, in the changing room I started talking to a very experienced older jockey called Jackie Dowdeswell. He was charming and insisted, that I should stay close to him during the race so that he could wave me on at the right moment to go for home. No Law jumped brilliantly as we followed Jackie until, as promised, he gave me the signal. For a vital moment I could not find a gap, between the horses in front of us, and when I did accelerate to join the leaders I found that we were in a thrilling finish of four horses abreast over the final two fences. We were still locked together at the finishing line but sadly I was judged to be fourth. If I could have obeyed the signal earlier we might have won, but it had been an exciting experience and we now knew that, despite his little size, No Law could stay three miles, which gave us good hope for the Sandown Military Gold Cup in March. The next day I went to Tidworth for a conference and was delighted to find that many of the Sergeants had watched my race on TV and had cheered me on over those last two jumps.

Suddenly the weather became foul with heavy snow, followed by hard frosts, bringing chaos to our racing plans. Firstly the early part of the point-to-point season was cancelled, impeding the preparation of Rendez-Vous and Rockall for the hunter chases, at the Sandown military meeting. The weekends became miserable anti-climaxes, even though ice skating on frozen lakes provided some fun. Meanwhile I ate rather more than usual, to counter the cold, and my weight increased, although I needed to be extra light in a week's time, for No Law's next race, on Friday at Kempton. Hence for two days I went back to my strict diet, but then I heard a weather forecast, which predicted more snow for the rest of the week and deciding that there was no chance of racing at Kempton, I returned to enjoying good healthy meals. Sure enough the countryside was still white on Friday morning and it was announced that Friday's racing was postponed to Saturday, which in turn was cancelled. Then unbelievably late on Friday night an unexpected thaw set in and I awoke Saturday morning to be told that Kempton was on. I will not forget the conversation with my father on the telephone explaining my weight problem. Despite my suggestion that a substitute jockey should be found, No Law was withdrawn and instead a race, ten days later, at the famous March Cheltenham Festival, was selected.

The Broadway Novices was the name of our Cheltenham steeplechase. It was a great privilege for me to ride there, especially as all the famous professional jockeys of that era were sitting on the other twenty-two runners. Who could forget lining up behind the tapes between Pat Taaffe and Fred Winter? As we approached the first fence I could not see it through the haze of other horses, but somehow No Law jumped it well. Basically the same happened at the next four obstacles and it was with much relief, as we rounded a bend to come downhill towards the sixth, that I was able to say to myself 'What could be better, I can see the fence, we are lying eighth, I am on the rails and we are meeting it right?' Then there was a sickening crash and I found myself somersaulting and luckily ending up lying under the rails. I looked up to see poor No Law stuck in the middle of the jump having been struck by several horses. In hindsight he clearly must have thought he would leap into a quarry or oblivion, because a few years later that fence was deemed to be dangerous, for that very reason, and was removed from the course, after too many horses had fallen there. No Law never recovered fully from this unfortunate experience and obviously I rue the day before Kempton, when I ceased my diet as who knows how many races he might have won for us? On the other hand how many people, who would absolutely love to ride at the famous Cheltenham festival, never actually have such an opportunity?

Two weeks before my third military Sandown race meeting the weather finally improved sufficiently to allow the point-to-points to resume. But that weekend the only near meeting was the Hursley, where our horses were not qualified for any other race except the Open. So reluctantly I had to accept that Rendez-Vous and Rockall would have to be in the same race and I agonised over which to ride. Rockall had been leaving Rendez-Vous behind on the gallops, so eventually I chose her and allowed my cousin, Patrick Beresford, to be Rendez-Vous's jockey. Uncharacteristically Rendez-Vous fell at the halfway point, but Patrick claimed that he put his foot in a hole and that he had felt like a winner at the time. Rockall flew for most of the race and only tired, close to the end, to finish a good fifth in a big field, which was very promising as we knew she needed a race, to reach full fitness. Then the following Saturday at Tweseldown Rendez-Vous was lame and I rode Rockall overconfidently, by joining the leaders at the start of the second circuit to finish sixth, after tiring up the last hill. Dad scolded me severely for going too fast too early, instead of waiting until near the end.

The two-day Sandown meeting on 18, 19 March beckoned, with extra excitement, as for the first time we had three runners. On the Friday Rockall was in the Past and Present Hunters' Chase and No Law in the coveted Gold Cup, while Saturday would give Rendez-Vous, we hoped, a third time lucky chance to win the Military Hunters' Chase.

But for what occurred 'disaster' would be an understatement. Rockall fell at the third and never raced again, No Law lost lengths at every fence by show jumping them all to finish fourth, which showed that, without the Cheltenham fall, he should have won and Rendez-Vous fell exhausted at the last fence. Clearly I should have pulled up and I was very unpopular at home because, having failed to finish the previous two years, I stupidly wanted to pass the finishing post this time.

Suddenly my luck changed for the better. We returned to Tweseldown where Rendez-Vous won a point-to-point in his old devastating style by storming over the last three fences. This was watched by Alistair Tuck, the new Colonel of the 10th Hussars, who was suitably impressed, which was fortunate, because in the future he would be needed to collude in our racing plans. Then out of the blue I was offered a ride in the Meynell hunt race in Derbyshire. This was on the second horse of Brigadier Roscoe Harvey, a famous old 10th Hussar and pre-war jockey. His first horse, ridden by another 10th Hussar officer, who was older and more experienced, was also in my race. We stayed with the parents of another officer, called Ian Lee, in a glorious house party atmosphere. Never before had I met so many fun loving young ladies in one place and I was enthralled to hear that, in that area, they were known as he local 'bitch pack'. So when Roscoe's little horse unexpectedly responded to my whip, by hurtling me over the last two fences to win by a nose I was mobbed by these lovely creatures and life was temporarily too good to be true. I returned to Warminster in a happy state with the words 'bitch pack' indelibly recorded in my vocabulary, for use in a story should I ever write one.

The following Saturday Rendez-Vous was entered in a race at the Hampshire Hunt, known as the HH point-to-point, held at Hackwood Park, near Basingstoke. I had had mixed luck there in the past, winning once and losing once from a stupid mistake. On arrival at the course I was thrilled to be told that I had a second ride, in the open race, on a horse called The Rag. He had won this open the previous year and would be favourite to repeat the victory this time, but his normal jockey had been retained to ride at a different race meeting. First I had to prepare for Rendez-Vous with the excitement that I was probably heading for two winners on a day. Sadly he went badly from the start and jumped, without his normal prowess, awkwardly, and realising something was amiss I pulled him up before the last circuit. Then I had to rush to change colours and weigh in for The Rag's race. At the scales I met the owner Captain (retired navy) Courage, an imposing man who gave me clear instructions. There was a large field and we stayed around 5th and 6th position for two circuits with The Rag jumping superbly. At the second last we jumped in to the lead and stayed there to win comfortably. As always a win was a wonderful thrill and the praise from the Captain made it even better. The following day more good news was received in that Rendez-Vous was found only to have a minor injury, which the vet forecasted would clear up in a few days.

Once again a racing season was over but, now for the first time, I could look forward to a summer in England, full of equestrian action, together with the many parties and debutante dances. This was because we had decided to see what Rendez-Vous could do as a show jumper, as a result of noticing his incredible spring when hunting and during those hunter trials, which he had won. So during a weekend I exchanged my car for the family land rover and trailer, loaded the great horse into it and drove him down to Warminster, where we trained together under a good coach, before competing in the first show.

CHAPTER 7

My Fourth Lottery –
My Sporting Career

ALDERSHOT WAS THE SETTING FOR my show jumping debut with Rendez-Vous. The occasion became more frightening than I had expected, when I realised that I would be watched by several Generals, including my father and many other senior officers. I looked for advice about how to tackle the tricky course and listened intently to one pretty young lady, who gave me a good suggestion about how to be quick around the corners. Rendez-Vous set off brilliantly, leaping effortlessly over the first few jumps. I was beginning to feel that we were heading for a clear round, when a nasty bell rang out, to tell the world that I had jumped a wrong fence. I had taken the advice too literally, by turning a corner so sharply, that it brought Rendez-Vous into a fence, already jumped. I was furious with myself, but on top of that I had to face my father, who complained bitterly that he felt humiliated in front of his fellow Generals. Furthermore he unfairly accused me of preferring to talk to attractive ladies instead of learning the route round the course.

Our next jumping venture took me to London, to the Military Tattoo, at Earls Court. Getting there, driving a land rover, pulling a large horse in a trailer, was an adventure in itself. Navigating through London and negotiating the roads of those days was not simple and, frequently, I thought I was lost and I took much abuse from angry taxi drivers. Then Rendez-Vous gave me a fright, when I tried to enter the indoor stadium, to jump in the first competition. As the giant doors opened the noise of the enormous enthusiastic crowd terrified him. He refused to enter and stood, very erect, on his hind legs. The announcer had repeated my name at least three times before, with the help of several kind people, we eventually made an awkward arrival and commenced jumping the big course. We had some success, jumping on three nights and being placed at least twice, but besides this, I much enjoyed watching all the other magnificent events at the Tattoo, especially the naval teams, who raced with guns over obstacles. Their disciplined teamwork and fitness was amazing.

The summer of 1955 must have raced by. The Warminster demonstration programme was hectic and busy, the debutantes' dances were numerous and every weekend I took Rendez-Vous to jump, in a horseshow, somewhere in Wiltshire or Hampshire. He continually performed brilliantly, but I always made one mistake on his back, normally at the easiest fence, while we sailed effortlessly over the bigger ones. Then my luck changed, probably because of a hangover, when I went to Salisbury Show, after being up all night at a dance. The result was that in the Fox-hunter Competition, in fear of inflicting further pain on my head, I sat as still as a mouse and wonderful Rendez-Vous jumped a perfect clear round without any interference from me. Then before the jump off, I gulped a gin and tonic, shortened my leathers, by two holes, and went into the ring with a do or die attitude. To my surprise it worked and Rendez-Vous flew the course with a brilliant clear round, which was faster than all the others. I could not believe that Rendez-Vous and I had qualified for the Fox-hunter final, which was scheduled for the Horse of the Year Show, in October, at Harringay Arena, in London.

In hindsight, this is when I should have realised, that the privilege of riding such a super, good-looking and flexible horse, as Rendez-Vous, who was brilliant enough to win, at three dimensions of equestrian competitions – racing, hunter trials and now show jumping, was itself another glorious lottery. Hence as young as 23 years old I had already had the incredible good fortune of winning 4 lotteries. While I was show jumping my Dad was distinguishing himself, once again, in the polo field, at both Windsor and Cowdray. I wondered if I was stupidly missing an early opportunity to learn the game, but realised that it is impossible to do everything and that my experiences with Rendez-Vous were valuable. Also it was possible that I might never again be in a situation to participate in show jumping. Ironically my parents, one day in July, missed possibly injury by a few minutes, while visiting, unknown to them at the time, what would later become their future working home. They watched three races on Ascot Heath from the middle of the racecourse, and then returned to Fleet, intending to see three more on television. Instead they heard from a news flash, that Ascot racing had been cancelled. Lightning had killed one lady and injured thirty people on the Heath, where they had been standing.

Meanwhile I made a real ass of myself at a regimental dinner in London. My double mistake was to miss lunch and go to a cocktail party before the dinner. At the table I was unable to handle the food and had to escape out of a side door to be sick. However I avoided the wrath of authority by going on leave to Ireland for most of August. There I attended several wonderful parties and spent a week in the wilds of Galway with the Harvey family, who were fishing in lakes and streams. The latter provided a dramatic change to my lifestyle and a welcome relaxation, which I much appreciated.

In September B Squadron finished the rewarding work at Warminster allowing us to rejoin the Regiment at Tidworth. The winter was to be used as a preparation for the move of the 10th Hussars, early in 1956, to Jordan. At that time we had been posted to Aqaba for one year, which was to be followed by two years in Libya. I was designated to become the regimental gunnery officer and therefore had to go on a tank gunnery course at Lulworth, Dorset, in October, to become qualified. Before departing for the South West, I took Rendez-Vous to the Fox-hunter final at the Horse of the Year Show. This involved another difficult drive to and through London in order to reach Harringay. It was a memorable day as, before my competition, I had the opportunity to mix and talk with many of the stars of British show jumping, besides watching some famous horses and riders perform. When my turn came I walked the course and was horrified by the size of the jumps. Then Rendez-Vous did his usual antics of refusing to enter the arena for a few minutes, before we hurtled over the massive fences. My memory tells me that we hit most of the jumps, although my mother's diary records only eleven faults. At least we did complete the course, but it was a very long day for me, with only one horse, that jumped just a single round. Yet I was happy to have added this daunting experience to my show jumping career to be added to my racing and hunter trial endeavours, mostly on the great Rendez-Vous, my fourth lottery.

I now had to return to some serious work to do the ten-week tank gunnery course at Lulworth in Dorset, near the sea. However I received a pleasant surprise, which gave me great pleasure. Our staff sergeant instructor was excellent and the subject, for me, was relatively understandable, so that I enjoyed most of the work and found the results rewarding. Stripping and assembling machine guns, after practice, became surprisingly easy and the TPs (teaching practices) were constructive and fun, because of a good atmosphere in our group. The days on the range were tiring but exhilarating, as we had to perform a demanding mix of duties, including handling many rounds of heavy ammunition, commanding a shoot, loading and being the actual gunner. Simon Walford, from County Meath in Ireland, was also on the course. Son of a famous polo player, who had been killed in the Second World War, his friendship added enjoyment to my time at Lulworth. The spot where we had to wait for the transport to take us out to the ranges contained a large patch of brambles. Childishly we tried to catch each other unaware and then, after a run and a push, one of us would find himself, upside down, in this prickly assembly of weeds, roaring with laughter.

One weekend I returned to the Regiment in Tidworth for a big reunion as a spectator, for a spectacular parade and march past of the Centurion tanks. One 10th Hussar troop leader, Nigel Budd, added an amusing dimension by hiding a pretty young lady in his tank throughout the proceedings. Many of us had a good laugh at his audacity, but luckily this did not include the hierarchy, who remained blissfully ignorant of the lady's presence.

The following weekend I went to Tweseldown with Rendez-Vous, to defend our title, from the previous year, as the Army hunter trial champions. Early on we hit one fence, but my disappointment was swept away when, at the end of the competition, the announcer said that, over this tough course, not only had there been no clear rounds, but that Rendez-Vous was the fastest, with one fence down. The thrill of retaining the cup was increased when I was told that, behind us, in second place, was the famous Olympic horse, Kilbarry, ridden by the renowned Olympic international rider, Colonel Frank Weldon. In November and first half of December our four horses, Rendez-Vous, Rockall, Flying Rosette and No Law were taken out with the Hampshire Hunt, to be qualified for point-to-points and hunter chases. Most of this was done by my mother and my father's new ADC, Christopher Gaisford St Lawrence. He was from Howth Castle in Dublin, and showed incredible patience in the hunting field with No Law, when he behaved in his mad manner. My family called him 'Vewy vewy' because he could not say his 'Rs' and always used the double adjective to describe good and bad things. As three of our horses had names beginning with 'R', it was amusing to hear him talk about them. I was only able to assist occasionally, at weekends, because of the distance from Lulworth and the availability of suitable hunting meets. Added to this I temporarily lost the use of my car, from a minor crash, when returning to Lulworth in a thick fog. I was rescued by Ronald Ferguson, a friend and a great character, whose daughter Sarah later married Prince Andrew, thus becoming the Duchess of York. Ronald was already famous for a variety of reasons. He kindly collected me, took me to his home in Dummer before delivering me to Basingstoke station to catch a train to Dorset.

I received a welcome Christmas present in the form of a 'B' grade for my gunnery course, which was the best result I had ever achieved from any course. This sent me home, in great form, for yet another wonderful Christmas leave, which included enjoyable hunt balls and dances, plus some good hunting in Waterford, Kilkenny and Limerick. I clearly remember one day in Kilkenny, when I was lent a big black horse by a dealer with a very good reputation. He was fast and a wonderful bold jumper, but difficult to stop. To my chagrin Victor McCalmont, the renowned Master and Huntsman, more than once, yelled across the field. 'The man on the black horse behave yourself'. The day was quite an adventure and luckily ended with Victor being very understanding about my difficulties with the borrowed black horse.

I returned to Tidworth to find everyone occupied by preparations for the move to Jordan. To my relief I was informed by Colonel Alistair Tuck that I could remain in England until early May, in order to represent the Regiment in the military races at Sandown, and at point-to-points across the country. To justify this I had to attend a four-week physical training course for instructors, in March, and privately study furiously for the promotion exam. However, from enquiries, I was horrified to hear that that the course was expected to be intensive and extremely tough. I was told that it included several long cross-country runs, wearing full battle order, and that I would have to box opponents, in order to learn how to judge boxing contests. During January I frequently drove from Tidworth to Aldershot to assist with basic exercise and gallops for the four race horses. Rendez-Vous, Rockall and Flying Rosette were all jumping out of their skins, ready to do battle on the racecourse. At the same time I received good news from Captain Courage about the condition of his horse, The Rag, whom I expected to ride in some hunter chases, including the Past and Present at Sandown.

Two memorable social events temporarily took my attention away from the horses. Ronald Ferguson, my saviour from the car crash, married Susan Wright on 17 January at a smart London wedding. To my surprise, I was asked to be an usher. There was a lavish reception and I believe I did my duties correctly, while immensely enjoying a wonderful afternoon. The following weekend I went all the way to Yorkshire to attend the twenty-first party, a dance for my cousin John, the future head of the Dawnay Clan. I stayed at the elegant Wykeham Abbey, Viscount Downe's ancestral home, near Scarborough, where the ball took place. I remember being captivated for most of the night by a petite blonde, only to discover later on that she was promised to another. Nevertheless I really enjoyed the night and appreciated being complimented by many people for dancing so much with the prettiest girl on the floor.

I returned to be with the horses throughout the next and last weekend of January. We carried out an intensive schooling programme with all the horses, including The Rag, whom I was due to ride at Hurst Park the coming Wednesday. At the Old Parsonage, Dad's army house in Fleet, we were well looked after by Roualt, the soldier servant, and our Polish chef. They gave us not only comfort and good food but also considerable humour. The repartee between them was priceless and, together with the chef's funny accent, there was much cause for laughter. At that moment life was fantastic and the racing outlook appeared to be wonderful. But around the corner, on Tuesday, there was a shock in the form of the coldest night for nine years, causing Hurst Park to be cancelled. Then Wednesday night was registered as the coldest night of the century and any possibility of racing in the next few weeks seemed to be remote. I kept myself occupied by packing my heavy luggage in a crate that had to go with the regimental main party, which was leaving Southhampton by boat on 14 February and by working for the promotion exam.

There was a temporary improvement in the weather allowing us to resume the galloping and schooling of the horses and I had a thrilling ride on The Rag, in a Hunters' Chase at Wincanton. We came third, but I felt we could have won, if I had ridden a perfect race. I went to two enjoyable dances, one given by the Wiggins, of 11th Hussar fame, in Hampshire and the other in London, hosted by the Halls, who in Bath had been good friends during my Warminster days. Then on 14 February the 10th Hussar main party set sail for Aqaba in Jordan via the Suez Canal, and I went to Southampton to wave goodbye to the ship. I returned to the Old Parsonage for two weeks' leave in the hope of riding several races, but for the rest of February the cold weather intervened and all race meetings were cancelled or postponed. My deep disappointment was increased by the situation creating a clash, on the first Saturday in March, between The Rag's hunter chase at Newbury and our four horses at the postponed Tweseldown meeting. Our horses would never be ready for Sandown if they did not run at Tweseldown and Dad would not entertain having a substitute for me. To add to my sorrows my legs became painfully chapped from riding so much in the freezing conditions. Yet my morale was sharply revived by meeting, at a dinner party, given by the widow of a famous wartime general, called Straffer Gott, the fun-loving Drew twins.

Flicky and Penny, who were about to begin their debutante season, lived close to us in Fleet and we became almost inseparable at weekends, going skating, dancing and playing tennis. They were glorious mimics and we laughed endlessly copying the characters from the 'Goon Show', which included Peter Sellers, Harry Secombe, Spike Milligan and Kenneth Williams, the funniest comedians of the day, in the most amusing radio show of the era. For the dancing we loved to go to a local nightclub, called Mimosa, and my weekly task was to find another man to make up a foursome there. Expecting that soon I would disappear to the Middle East for three years I reckoned that it was better to go there unattached and the twins provided the perfect prescription for this.

March beckoned and I had to report for the physical training course in Aldershot. Two events decreased my worries about what I would have to face. Firstly I managed to arrange that I could live at home (The Old Parsonage in Fleet) throughout the course and secondly, on my first day, the new chief instructor introduced himself with the good news, saying that he had changed the contents of our programme, which thereby would be far more civilised than expected. We did not have to box or run and the main emphasis was on organisation and sports refereeing. The time flew by as I got up at six every morning, so that I could ride the racehorses, before driving rapidly to Aldershot for the course. Finally the cold weather abated and the postponed Tweseldown point-to-point took place. I had to accept that on the same day The Rag would run at Newbury, ridden by the famous John Oaksey. My situation worsened when No Law and Rendez-Vous were deemed not fit enough to run and Rockall went lame, after only jumping two fences. So only Flying Rosette gave me a complete race to ride and she went poorly, to finish well behind the main group in the Open race. Then the news from Newbury was that The Rag finished second and John Oaksey would partner him for the rest of the season. However another enjoyable Saturday evening with the Drews in the Mimosa did much to dissipate my disappointment.

I thought my luck might be changing when I received a telephone call about riding a horse belonging to a Major Nathan, but little did I know what I was letting myself in for. The Garth Hunt were short of runners for their members' race, on the following Saturday at Tweseldown. In fact if I did not ride for Major Nathan, there would probably be no members' race. So on Sunday I went to school the horse to find that he was not only rather ordinary, but also slightly fat for racing. Nevertheless I accepted the ride for the next Saturday, in the hope that the other runner would also be a poor racehorse, and because I would be there anyway to ride our horse. On arrival at the racecourse I discovered that my single opponent in the members' race belonged to and was being ridden by Charlie Smith, the brother of the well-known flat race jockeys, Doug and Eph Smith. He told me that this was also the first race for his horse, who was a complete novice. So I jumped at the opportunity to suggest that we should ride upsides together, until three fences from home, when we could then make a race of it. Charlie appeared to be delighted with the idea and I fully believed that he had agreed with my plan. However when the starter dropped his flag Charlie was facing in the wrong direction, giving me no option, but to head for the first fence on my own. We arrived in the wings going a decent gallop and I lent forward for what seemed to be a perfect take off. But my horse suddenly stopped and I flew over his head, to land on top of the fence. Very quickly I slid off the fence on to the ground, caught the rogue and remounted. As I did this Charlie arrived, jumped the fence fluently and continued towards the second one. I then managed to beat my horse over the first and then, in disbelief, saw that Charlie was lying across the second obstacle, which I then safely jumped, before proceeding towards the third, an open ditch. Once again my horse stopped dead on the take off stride and I landed in the ditch, while Charlie overtook me once more. But Charlie was then spreadeagled across the fourth and I jumped it successfully, only to run out at the fifth giving back the lead for the third time to Charlie. We then continued without any further problems to finish in that order, with Charlie a fairly easy winner.

Waiting for my second ride I walked to the Tweseldown hill to watch the next race. An old friend rushed up to me to say 'Did you see those two idiots in the first race.' I could only reply 'Yes' while thinking 'If only Charlie Smith had carried out our agreed plan'. And my morale was not improved by Flying Rosette jumping poorly in the following race to finish fourth, behind the winner Cardinal's Drum, owned and ridden by Ronald Ferguson. The realisation that our next race together was over the bigger fences at Sandown was a little frightening, to put it mildly. However I ended the day in my third race on my beloved Rendez-Vous, who cheered me up by jumping superbly although not fit enough to contest the finish.

Our visits to the Mimosa on Saturday nights now took an eventful and funny turn. Christopher Gaisford St Lawrence, my father's ADC, had frequently said to me 'How can you go out with those ghastly Dwew twins?' His inability to say his Rs added much amusement to his stated opinion of the Drews, which even varied to include 'those dwedful Dwews'. Suddenly one Saturday the man, who was expected to join us, had to cancel at the last minute. After trying four or five other men unsuccessfully I resorted to calling Christopher. Before I could even ask him he had replied, 'No way will I go out with those dwedful Dwews'. In jest I threatened him with a negative report from the General and that he would lose his job if he failed me. After much complaining he, eventually, with great reluctance, agreed to join us. Because Flicky appeared to have established that I was her property, Christopher found himself paired off with Penny for the first dance. To my amazement he was instantly captivated and never even tried to change partners. Two months later they became engaged and, a year later, they were married. I wondered if I should challenge him to rescind publicly, his defamation of his loved one's family, with those memorable words, 'dwedful Dwews'.

I spent the week before Sandown races on a diet, limiting myself to a lunch of a boiled egg and an orange, which I took with me to the PT course at Aldershot. Combining some gallops and schools over fences with the PT course daily schedule, made the days extremely hectic. Up to the last minute we were hoping to run No Law on Friday, in the Military Gold Cup, and Flying Rosette in Saturday's Hunters' Chase, although the latter was doubled entered in both races, to cover all eventualities. No Law raised our hopes early in the week by going well, but at the last hour, appeared to be off colour, and had to be withdrawn. Hence

93

on the Friday, when my father decreed that the 10th Hussars must be represented, I found a very thin version of myself, riding Flying Rosette down to the start at Sandown. As expected the pace was too fast, she hit most of the fences and by the second circuit we were tailed of, together with Ronnie Ferguson on Cardinal's Drum. Both of us pulled up coming to the third last fence and I felt relieved and lucky to be still alive. Also I started to look forward to a good meal that night, before riding a good jumping horse for another owner, carrying a much heavier weight, the next day in a point-to-point.

My pleasant dream was interrupted when my father came running to meet Flying Rosette, while calling out to me, 'We run tomorrow . . . we definitely run here tomorrow'. 'I do not want to ride this bitch again. Today we have done our bit by representing the 10th Hussars, so tomorrow please let me be free, to take a good point-to-point ride,' I replied, in a desperate plea for him to change what I regarded to be a disastrous decision. 'Do not waste my time arguing. Having got this far, I will not abandon my plans now. Without any doubt we are bringing Flying Rosette here to represent the Regiment in the Hunters' Chase tomorrow.' he said in a very dominating manner.

In the Sandown changing room Ronald and I mutually consoled one another, while discussing future racing plans for our respective horses. We examined the possibilities of declaring for Saturday's race, as he was also entered, and a little cunningly l insinuated that it would be ridiculous for us to repeat such a bad experience. I was thinking 'If I have to starve for another night, at the least I do not want to race against Cardinal's Drum, who finished well ahead of us, in a recent point-to-point at Tweseldown, even though we clearly have no chance of success, whatever happens.' On the Saturday, after arriving at the Sandown racecourse, I was in a miserable state, while I waited for the Hunters' Chase, which was the last race at five o'clock. I could only wear our coloured jersey, because of the light weight, and when I took off my coat in the paddock, I shivered with cold and hunger. It was 17 March, St Patrick's Day, so Dad had covered the bridle with shamrocks, which amused me and cheered me up a little bit, although it appeared to be a waste of time, especially as we were number 13 of twenty-three runners. In the race we made a good start to arrive at the first fence in the second row of horses. To my amazement Flying Rosette stood off with an enormous jump, which put us in the lead as we rounded that first bend. Instead of being delighted, I thought 'This is terrible, now she will fall in front of all the horses and I will be trampled on'. This seemed likely, because the back straight at Sandown has seven fences, so close together that once in front, between fences, it is difficult to relinquish the lead. But Flying Rosette proceeded to jump all of them in fabulous style and when we reached the bend, which is known as the Railway Turning, we were well in the lead and I was beginning to gain confidence. Three more big leaps and we passed the stands, comfortably in front, which allowed me to give Flying Rosette an easy ride, just before the top of the hill, followed by a decisive acceleration downhill, which thereby maintained our surprising lead at the start of the second circuit. Yet despite our considerable advantage over the other surviving runners, I reflected that soon she would blow up and give me a hell of a fall. This fear was reinforced, when she suddenly took an enormous breath, which threw my legs off the saddle. This happened because, as an experiment, my father had, for the first time ever, put elastic girths on my racing saddle. In fact Flying Rosette continued to jump incredibly well and when, for the second time, we rounded the Railway Turning, I gave her a slap of the whip, and to my amazement and delight, she accelerated effortlessly. The last three jumps were soon consumed and unbelievably we were the very easy winner, as the outsider of the race at 33 to 1. The exhilaration was unforgettable, as my mother led us in to the winners' enclosure.

With hindsight it appears that four separate pieces of fate, completely unplanned, gave us this wonderful victory. First the race on Friday had unwittingly brought Flying Rosette to peak fitness. Second she preferred jumping in front of other horses, which happened totally unexpectedly, after that enormous leap, over the first fence. Third the elastic girths assisted her wind. And fourth, most important of all, she was on the day the best of a very bad lot! The latter only came to light five years later, when it was explained to me by her previous trainer, Toby Balding, who in search of vindication for his lack of success with her, had studied the history of the other twenty-two horses, to find that none of them had ever won another race! Flying Rosette only ran one more race, in which she was hot favourite, but she went lame at halfway and had to be pulled up. After that she was retired to stud and we bred a useful hunter from her.

The rest of March was hectic and enjoyable. I completed the PT course without injury and thankful for a good report, which declared that I was qualified to organise and referee many different sports including boxing. I did several practice papers for the promotion exam, rode some gallops and schools over fences and on every Saturday was active at point-to-points. My best day was at Larkhill where I had two winners, one in the members' race for the Duchess of Newcastle and one on the faithful Rendez-Vous in the Military race. April was probably the best month of leave that I ever had. It started with an enjoyable Easter with the Drew twins with whom, as already explained, I also had several entertaining evenings. On seven days I rode in point-to-points, including four Saturdays and three Wednesdays, which amounted to ten rides, that gave me three winners, a second, a third and one fall. The memorable winner was for an old rogue called Len Colville. His Sea Rover had previously come second for me after almost falling at an open ditch. Hence the next time I rode him I succeeded in covering him up behind other horses at the ditches and then released him, three fences from home, to win easily. A slightly embarrassing victory happened at the New Forest where the lady owner's colours were shocking pink. The fall was from another horse belonging to Len Colville, who had told me that she was brilliant when in fact it later transpired that she had a reputation for diving through fences.

On 3 May I took the dreaded promotion exam at Bulford and felt reasonably confident that I had passed. Then during my final weekend of my leave I rode in a race at Tweseldown, before rushing to London for the 10th Hussars Old Comrades' dinner, after which I tried to date two young ladies, one after the other, with little success, because both were offended. Then I returned to Fleet to prepare for my journey, to join the Regiment in Aqaba, Jordan. The Drews helped me to finalise my affairs, including settling outstanding bills, and I rewarded them with a wonderful evening in London seeing the famous musical play, *Salad*

Hugh and Peter Dawnay at Whitfield Court

Whitfield Court

David Dawnay in a Churchill tank going uphill in Tunisia. He received a DSO medal for his victories with the North Irish Horse there in the Second World War.

David Dawnay in jeep with US and Russian generals

*Lady Katherine Dawnay, Hugh Dawnay's mother,
with his sister Rachel Dawnay, at Monte Cassino, 17 May 1947*

Catterick Camp, 1951

Catterick Camp, 1951

David Dawnay, Royal Military Academy, Sandhurst, 1951

Burma Company Junior Steeplechase, 2 April 1951

Hugh Dawnay with all his family in October 1952

Cadet's Race at Army point-to-point, 19 April 1952

Hugh Dawnay and his father at the Staff College, Royal Military Academy, Sandhurst point-to-point 22 March 1959

Hugh Dawnay and his father, Major General David Dawnay

Sovereign's Parade, Royal Military Academy, Sandhurst

Bovington, Lulworth, 1952

Days. The next day I flew in an RAF plane to Cyprus, where I stayed in a transit camp before continuing to Jordan.

Aqaba gave me my first experience of soldiering in a hot climate. My bedroom was a tent with a concrete floor and a mosquito net draped over my bed. I soon discovered that I had a choice of being too hot under the net or of being eaten by mosquitoes without it. Gradually I learnt how to use the net and stay reasonably cool. The daily work programme was refreshingly different to Europe with a 6.30 a.m. start followed by an 8.30 breakfast and finishing at 1 p.m. After lunch most people went to the beach to cool off in the sea, which provided the best swimming I had ever had. Because the water quickly became deep it was a glorious, not too hot temperature and I enjoyed swimming out to rafts which were strategically placed.

At work initially I received a shock when appointed to be MTO, the Motor Transport Officer. This meant that I was in charge of all the B vehicles, those with wheels instead of tracks. It was like organising a combined taxi and lorry service. To keep everybody happy I had to make many telephone calls to confirm or tactfully refuse vehicle bookings. My task was complicated by the fact that the average quality of the MT drivers was lower than that of the tank drivers. This presented me with an extra challenge of achieving good man management results, which I relished and after a few weeks I started to enjoy the job. In the officers' mess the evenings were brightened by drinks in peoples' tents before dinner. Alcohol was incredibly cheap and nearly every night someone gave a party. Inevitably consumption increased and I had to learn a lesson of how much I could drink the hard way. One night I passed out at the dinner table and for my sins I was given twenty-eight extra orderly officer duties. This coincided with a multiplication of my military duties, which happened because of my extra qualifications from the courses, which I had recently taken. I became Gunnery, Sports and Swimming Officer. I surprised myself by thriving on and enjoying the results of working harder than I had ever done before. I organised gunnery courses which included my lectures, ran the inter-squadron swimming gala, fulfilled all the requests for transport and did three orderly officers every week.

Our Colonel, Alistair Tuck, produced the most wonderful initiative, which changed the lives of many of us. He went to Baghdad in Iraq and bought twelve Arab stallions from the racecourse. With difficulty he transported them to Aqaba where he organised a programme to teach them to play polo. It took time to get them well enough and fit but suddenly we found ourselves enjoying chukkas three times a week. To avoid the heat of the day we played before breakfast on the sand next to the beach and had the most incredible fun. Little did I know that this would have such an impression on my future life. In fact I was probably the best of a bad bunch and I found myself instructing at the same time as learning the skills and the rules.

Meanwhile in England my mother had a horrific accident. She was in a field feeding our race horses, when one took a kick at another, missed, but caught her in the face. Both the top and bottom jaw were broken besides a cheek bone and all her teeth were crushed. At first my father thought that she was dead, but after a spell in hospital she made an incredible recovery. My sister Rachel was a big comfort to her by making frequent visits. After returning home my mother needed a big amount of dental treatment. Years later she realised that an ill wind had literally blown good. Appalling headaches, which were the result of a racing fall when she was young, had ceased to trouble her after this accident. My mother's misfortune was largely compensated for by some wonderful news for my father. He was due to retire from the army the following year, 1957, and had been appointed Clerk of the Course at the famous Ascot Racecourse. This would considerably help my life for the next twelve years in several different ways.

Suddenly at the end of October there was a dramatic change to our lives in Aqaba. The saga of the Israel Egypt war unfolded very close to us. Because of the British treaty with Jordan my regiment not only could not join in but had to be prepared to repel the Israelites if they invaded Aqaba. Geographically we were in a strange situation in that we could see into Israel, Egypt and Saudi Arabia. The Jewish holiday resort of Eilat was on the other side of the bay of Aqaba and in daylight we could see and hear planes landing and taking off from the airport there. One night all the lights in Eilat went out and we listened to intensive aircraft activity followed by the sound of bombs exploding in Egypt. The next day the radio told us that the war had started. We were then cut off completely from our usual line of communications to Cyprus and became one hundred percent reliant on reserve rations. Hence corn beef was served in more than ten different ways. At first and last light the whole regiment had to stand to in tactically defensive positions as protection for the possibility of attacks from either Israel or the local Arabs, who mostly supported Egypt. Contrary to expectation, instead of a depression among the soldiers, there was an incredible lift in morale, which must have been caused by the possibility of being involved in the war.

This state of emergency lasted several months during which our air link to Cyprus remained closed and was only partially replaced by a much longer route via Habbaniyah in Iraq. Christmas passed by and with it the exchange parties between the officers' and sergeants' mess. These included a play to be done by the hosts. While rehearsing for the officers' play I discovered that I had an ability to dance. Initially I had a very small part but needed a drink or two to give me courage which lit me up to dance, I thought unseen, to the music being played for the introduction. Suddenly I was surrounded by the director and others who all insisted that my dance routine should become a part of the play. The result was a further increase in my drink intake and in front of the sergeants I was almost drunk. However it appeared to be a success and ever since at dances and hunt balls I found I had great confidence when on the floor.

1957 arrived and with it a big adventure for me. I had an open invitation to stay with the Governor of Kenya, Sir Evelyn Baring and his wife Molly, a relation through marriage, but because of the Suez War I has almost given up hope of going. Then the Middle East became peaceful again and I applied for leave. Humphrey Wakefield, a newly joined lieutenant, who lived in Northumberland, near the Barings, persuaded me to take him with me. Our plan was to hitch a lift with the Royal Air Force, all the way to Nairobi, via Habbaniyah in Iraq and Aden in Yemen. Technically this method of transport was called 'indulging' and those, who did it, were given the lowest priority by the RAF and could be offloaded, at any place or at the last moment, if anyone on official duty appeared, looking for a seat. Before leaving I went to the regimental medical centre to have a variety of injections and vaccinations and I trusted that Humphrey would take my advice to do the same. We had little difficulty getting seats on a plane to Habbaniyah where we stayed in a transit camp. After applying a few times we were reluctantly allotted two seats to Aden, but on the understanding that we could be thrown off en route. We landed somewhere on the east coast of Arabia where our medical documents were inspected and Humphrey was found to have no certificates. I left him to argue his case and had interesting conversations with various RAF officers. While talking to one senior officer Humphrey arrived saying 'I have to talk to the commanding officer of this terrible place.' 'You are talking to him,' replied the officer. Humphrey, taken by surprise, stuttered through an explanation that he had all the necessary injections but forgotten to bring the certificates and expected his word to be accepted, instead of being offloaded, which was threatened. The commanding officer was surprisingly patient but very firm in insisting that he had a choice of having all the injections there and then or of losing his seat. As we flew on Humphrey resembled a sore pin cushion and I could not help laughing at him.

In Aden we were taken to a horrible tented transit camp, which was most uncomfortable, very hot and humid. We were up early, the next day, to go to the movements office where, to our horror, we were met by some rather unpleasant gentlemen. In those days, the Movers, as we called them, were apt to be disgruntled officers, jealous of their brother pilots, who also resented others flying round the world. They said that, although there was a plane going to Nairobi soon, it was impossible for us to fly on it, because there was no way we could be guaranteed a return flight, when we required it. We begged and pleaded that we would take the risk to no avail and feigned sympathy. We were walking towards our vehicle discussing what to do when, incredibly, round a corner appeared a jeep, containing a General, and Air Marshal and two other army officers. The General, who had lost an arm in the Second World War, was Commander in Chief Middle East Forces and had recently visited Aqaba, where he had talked to me about my father.

'Dawnay, what on earth are you doing here?' asked General Bourne.

'We are trying to get to Nairobi but the RAF will not take us,' I replied.

'Leave it to me,' interrupted the Air Marshal. 'Both of you report back here tomorrow.'

'Where are you staying?' asked another officer from behind the General.

'The transit camp,' I replied.

'That is ridiculous,' he said. 'It is not fit for a beast. You can move immediately to the civilised cavalry camp. Also if you like to play polo this evening go down to the polo club at 4 o'clock.'

Suddenly life was close to being perfect. We were now living in comfortable surroundings amongst friends, we played in a game of polo and the chance of a flight to Nairobi was extremely hopeful. The next day the chagrined officer, in charge of air movements, told us that we had seats on a flight to Kenya the following day, but we had to sign an agreement that the RAF were not responsible for our return to Aden.

After a pleasant flight to Nairobi, we were soon ensconced in the luxury of Government House. Our hosts the Barings were charming and we enjoyed an excellent dinner, although the head waiter had very shaky hands and I feared that he would spill drink over me. The next day I experienced an amazing coincidence, when another couple arrived as guests and turned out to be my ex close girlfriend, Diana Blacker with her newly married husband. What a small world, but I had to put up with it and make polite chat for a day before Diana and husband moved on to visit other places in Kenya during their honeymoon.

Humphrey and I had a memorable two weeks in Kenya. We were taken on some day safaris and were sent to stay three nights with a distant spinster cousin, called Pam Scott, who arranged for us to play some more polo. Then when the time came to return to Aden there was absolutely no sign of any RAF plane to take us. In desperation we went to the Governor for help and he, slightly reluctantly, found a solution. A chartered Hermes aircraft was due to arrive in Nairobi, full of troops, before going empty to collect another load from an unnamed destination, but via Aden.

Somehow the Captain was persuaded, on condition that we were discreet, to bend the rules and take us at no charge. I will always remember that flight because, on this fairly large plane, Humphrey and I were the only two passengers being looked after by four lovely air hostesses. At Aden we met the movements officers, who very insincerely apologised that we had had to fly civil at our own expense. We grunted something inaudible and asked for a flight to Habbaniyah, Iraq, as soon as possible. He replied that there was one in three days' time but that it was unlikely we would get seats. So we stayed again in the comfortable cavalry camp, had yet another game of polo and, with our hearts in our mouths, reported to the airport at 5 a.m. on the appointed morning. After waiting two hours a nasty corporal told us that we were not on the passenger list. Humphrey and I walked away in a shocked state, because we were now in danger of being recorded, in Aqaba, as absent without leave. 'If only we could meet the Air Marshal,' we both said at the same time. Five minutes later around the corner came a jeep, carrying the Air Marshal with a group of senior officers, destined for a flight to visit troops upstate in the Yemen.

'What are you boys up to now?' yelled the Air Marshal.

'Unsuccessfully trying to get to Habbaniyah and becoming absentees,' we replied.

'Go back to the movements office, I will see what I can do,' he answered.

We could not believe our luck and forty minutes later we were taking our seats on the plane. Soon afterwards we were airborne for Habbaniyah. Then on arrival we discovered we had to wait two nights for the final flight to Aqaba, which would mean reaching the Regiment on the last day of our leave. But a hiccup was threatened, when an angry transit Camp Commandant burst in to the lounge, in front of everybody, demanding to know how we had arrived, because our names were not on the manifest of the plane from Aden. Hence it was clear that the Air Marshal had ordered that we be put on the plane, above the allowed cargo weight. The Commandant seemed at a loss, in how to deal with us, and amused us enormously, when promising to report the whole affair to the Air Marshal in Aden. Thus we duly returned to the Regiment two days later, unable to believe how lucky we had been on so many occasions.

Back with my regiment I learnt that the plans for the 10th Hussars had been dramatically changed, because of the recent Suez War. Our move to Libya, where we should have completed the three-year tour in the Middle East, had been cancelled and instead the Regiment was, once again, going to be stationed in Tidworth, England.

The rest of my time in Aqaba was probably the busiest I have ever been in my whole life. As Sports Officer I organised the regimental athletics meeting besides becoming Soccer Officer in charge of the regimental team. As MTO I was responsible for the annual inspection of all the wheeled vehicles and I continued to control many Gunnery courses. I was playing polo three times a week, cricket for my squadron team and swimming every day. So much work and sport made me be more conscientious than ever before, and this was recognised by our new Colonel, Peter Jackson, and rewarded in two unexpected ways. Firstly he announced that I was to be promoted to captain and appointed Adjutant of the Wiltshire Yeomanry in England. Secondly I was to leave Aqaba a month earlier than the regimental main party in order to take part in a four-week riding course at Melton Mowbray, Leicestershire, in England. I took the regimental soccer team to play against an RAF team near Amman, the capital of Jordan. It was quite an adventure. I was given a flight in a dual control trainer jet fighter, during which the plane flew incredibly low, near the ground, several times. In the officers' mess I played liar dice and was clearly allowed to win before money entered the proceedings and then I was first out; a valuable lesson. The football game was close and exciting, although we lost narrowly. However a few weeks later, at return match in Aqaba, we had our revenge, helped by home support.

The advance party for the regimental move, of thirty men, were specially selected, to include all those, who had compassionate reasons to return early to England. We waved them goodbye saying 'lucky devils' but later that day we heard that the plane had crashed, killing all of them. I will never forget the collective sorrow and misery that night and during the next few days. Never, before or since, have so many people, whom I knew, died at the same time. My journey home was via Cyprus and when I landed there I was sent to another uncomfortable transit camp to wait at least four days. Luckily I remembered that Michael Allenby, whom I knew, was ADC to the Governor, Field Marshal Harding, and I telephoned him. Half an hour later a large car arrived and took me to Government House, Nicosia. I then had four wonderful days as a guest of the Hardings. The Field Marshal in a charming, humble way told me to be totally relaxed and enjoy myself, because I deserved a restful time after being in close to war conditions in Jordan. Despite the terrorist threat in Cyprus, Government House was full of fun people and everything we did was done in a party spirit. Lady Harding was a very jovial character and it was great fun, accompanying her, on some of her official outings. It was hard to believe that there were any terrorists in Cyprus.

CHAPTER 8

New Job – My Polo Career as Player and Coach

THE COURSE AT MELTON MOWBRAY turned out to be an extremely valuable experience, both for the rest of my time in the Regiment, especially when I became stables officer, and for what would become my second career as a polo coach and instructor. It reconfirmed all the basics within the equestrian world and taught me many useful new things, especially the way to control a large group inside a riding school, and suitable exercises for them. The chief instructor was an aggressive Major, called Richie, who demanded high standards. Luckily for me my cousin, Lord Patrick Beresford, had told me about a civilian groom, called Ted, who would clean tack in return for a tip. He was so good that, much to the annoyance of all my fellow students, my saddle, bridle and other tack always looked the best and I was frequently congratulated by Major Richie.

I had three horses to ride and look after and found the grooming and stable cleaning to be really hard work. However the riding was most enjoyable as we did much jumping over cross-country fences and show jumps. One day, while exercising by myself, I could not resist going down a long lane of jumps and suddenly found myself on the ground in a heap under the horse. Luckily nobody saw what had happened and I finished the course with a good report. After a short leave I went to take over my new job with the Wiltshire Yeomanry. I had arranged to live at the Bowood Estate near Calne in Wiltshire. This belonged to a distant cousin, Lord Landsdowne, who allowed me to share a flat with his Estate Manager. Luckily he was a good cook and fed me well. The main office of the Yeomanry was twenty minutes away in Trowbridge, where Mr Hill, the civilian chief clerk, worked. He was a great character and very efficient, but had a grumpy demeanour whenever anyone dared to disagree with him. I learnt much from him and was often amused by his criticisms of my superiors.

The majority of my yeomanry work was in the evenings when I visited the squadrons at Devizes, Salisbury, Swindon and Trowbridge. Different nights were allotted to them to do their weekly training and I went to watch and try to help with any administrative problems. This gave me some wonderful freedom in the daytime and I used it for hunting and riding. Our brilliant horse Rendez-Vous was stabled at Badminton, the magnificent home of the Duke and Duchess of Beaufort, known as Master and Mary. This was too far for daily riding, but handy for hunting, especially as I had an open invitation to stay at weekends. When I did I had to pinch myself to see that I really was staying in such a wonderful house in a great estate. There was an incredible mixture of grandeur and luxury mixed with gloriously relaxed comfort.

Close to Bowood lived George and Beryl Maundrell, on a big farm, where they had bred many fine horses for hunting and racing. We met in the hunting field and I was invited to ride with them, early in the mornings, whenever I wanted. Of course I could not refuse such an offer, which was extended to sumptuous breakfasts afterwards, when I was treated to many memorable stories from George, who had had incredible experiences with horses. Because I knew Rendez-Vous so well after all his endeavours, which I had shared with him on the racecourse, cross-country and show jumping we made a good partnership in the Beaufort hunting field, so that we were always close to the front of any hunt, reminding me of my fourth lottery win. On Saturdays with three hundred horse followers out it was important, early in a hunt, to jump a big fence, while the majority were queuing for a small one. I also developed a successful system for the relatively few occasions that circumstances made everyone have to go through one gate after a check, which had allowed all the followers to be in the one field. Gerald Gundry, the renowned MFH and

Field Master, would suddenly drop his hand and lead the way to the gate. Many tried to canter alongside or behind him. I brought Rendez-Vous, in the third or fourth row in a highly collected canter and, as those in front, inevitably, had to slow up violently near the gate, I allowed Rendez-Vous to accelerate through them, to be close behind Gerald, as he entered the gateway. Alternatively I located Mary (Duchess of Beaufort), riding side-saddle and arrived behind her at the gate, while others respectfully gave way to her. The overall result was that the Maundrells and I were close together at the front of many good hunts, which gave us plenty to talk about, when riding on their farm or at breakfast in their house. It also gave the George the welcome idea to ask me to become his point-to-point jockey, which I gladly accepted with happy anticipation, because he was a renowned owner, who had had many winners in the past.

Another piece of luck came my way, when I was introduced to Bryan Marshall, a horse trainer who had been a very famous steeplechase jockey, winning two consecutive Grand Nationals at Aintree, and had had many other big race winners. He invited me, twice a week, to ride out with his early morning string of racehorses, on the two schooling days. So on most Tuesdays and Fridays I was out of bed at 6 a.m. in order to drive to Bryan's training stables at Lambourne. Under his critical eye I would first ride exercise, which means walking and trotting amongst a string of more than ten horses, then a fast gallop and finish by schooling at speed over three fences. It was an enjoyable and valuable experience, because I learnt so much, kept fit riding good horses and at breakfast, afterwards, listened to some fascinating stories by Bryan. His wife had been a successful show jumper and had much to add to the conversation. At Badminton I had the privilege of meeting another great character. He was known as Chatty Hilton Green and had been a famous Master and Huntsman before and after the Second World War. He kept several horses at Badminton and when unwell asked me to hunt them. Besides giving me extra hunting it allowed me to rest Rendez-Vous, whenever he had any kind of injury, and I learnt from the experience of hunting different horses.

It was wonderful to find myself at home in Ireland for Christmas 1957. My parents were in residence, as my father had finally left the British

Army, having finished his second job as a Major-General. As previously explained he had been appointed Clerk of the Course at Ascot racecourse and for this job a lovely house, pompously called Royal Enclosure Lodge, had been provided, but at that time Ascot only had flat race meetings in the summer and autumn, with no winter fixtures. Therefore, as he could spend most of the winter in Waterford, he had become Joint Master of the Waterford foxhounds, together with his friend Robin Hunt, who had quickly developed into a fantastic huntsman.

I took advantage of the situation to have ten days' hunting in three weeks. Besides two days a week with the Waterford, I rented hirelings with other hunts for another four days. One of these was in Kilkenny and gave me the most memorable hunt of my life. For this I rode a broken-winded grey horse called the Shiverer. He was well known for his jumping ability, although not the fastest, and we finished among the only 6 out of 60 who finished a straight six-mile hunt. It was such a good hunt that Victor McCalmont, the famous Master and Huntsman, took hounds home immediately afterwards. At the meet a married couple, from England, whom I knew, had extolled their delight to be present. Sadly they had both fallen in to the first big ditch and missed this amazing hunt.

I returned to Bowood and my Wiltshire Yeomanry duties. The work was mundane, but my life highly enjoyable, as I continued to hunt with the Beaufort, ride with the Maundrells and twice weekly visit Bryan Marshall on the schooling days. To my intense excitement the point-to-point season opened in February, especially as I had more potential rides than I had ever previously experienced. This produced the unusual problem, for me, of conflicting engagements on several Saturdays. Brigadier Roscoe Harvey, who had moved to live in Gloucestershire, had two brilliant horses but one broke down in his first race with me, when landing over the second last and feeling like a winner. Then at Larkhill I was given a chance ride on a very good-looking young horse with great potential. Initially I had a shock when, in the paddock, as I was being thrown up on the horse, the owner said 'Give him a strong kick at the first fence because he has never seen one before.' Although the horse tried to run out at the first few jumps his confirmation was so good, that it was easy to hold him straight. He jumped high into the sky at the first and then at every succeeding fence a little less high, until at halfway I knew he would be a star. As instructed I pulled him up six fences from home, to protect his confidence and prevent injury. Three races later, against some good horses, he won for me, at the Berkeley point-to-point in sensational fashion. The owner talked about the Grand National for the future but sadly, out at grass that summer, he galloped into a rail and hurt his back so badly that he could never be cured.

That point-to-point season turned out to be the best and most enjoyable that I ever had. I rode seventeen horses in thirty-six races, having three winners and only three falls. The only disappointing dimension was that Bryan Marshall, who had previously given me great praise for my school riding, insisted that the point-to-points made my style worse. I never discovered why that was, but the thrill of three rides every Saturday kept my morale high. Also the knowledge that in six months from racing, hunting and schooling I had ridden fifty horses was very pleasing and extremely valuable for future experience.

To my great surprise in April 1958, I was invited by the Beauforts to be part of the Badminton house party, for the famous three-day event. I was told that Queen Elizabeth, Princess Margaret and the Queen Mother would be staying and I had difficulty putting together enough smart clothes for the three days. The best part was being in the VIP locations to watch the cross-country day. The achievement by horse and rider in completing that course, must be second to none, and such a close view of many of them, in action over so many fences was memorable. In Badminton House for me every meal was an occasion and I tried to be on my very best behaviour, although it seemed to be easier than I had expected. On the last night I was placed next to the Queen at dinner and was pleasantly surprised how relaxed she was, and it was relatively simple to talk to her. Also in the house party I enjoyed meeting the blind Colonel Ansell, who was then the supremo of British show jumping. He had lost his sight, when wounded in the

Second World War, and while a prisoner of the Germans, had thought out the plan, which had so successfully revolutionised the show jumping programme in Britain after the war.

The next excitement was the summer polo season at Tidworth. The twelve Arab stallions had been brought home from Jordan and a few old ponies had been bought in England. My father who was also playing at the Guards Club, Windsor, kept some ponies at Ascot and sent two for me to play at Tidworth. Driving over from Wiltshire was time consuming and playing against experienced players was difficult, but it was valuable experience. Then the tournaments started and previous lack of match play was a clear disadvantage, but we were on a learning curve. As the 10th Hussars team, in the inter-regimental, we were murdered and we fared little better in other matches until near the end of the season. I took over the No. 3 position for the Captains and Subalterns team and our luck started to change. Miraculously we reached the final where we played the hot favourites, the Queen's Bays. The ball ran in our favour most of the time and, to our surprise, we won by one goal. Suddenly polo was a big part of my life, my handicap was raised to one and I became ambitious for the future.

The summer had been made even more enjoyable by the race meetings at Ascot. My father was thriving in his new job and used his perks to give lunch parties on race days. Guests included many old friends, officers and wives from my regiment, the 10th Hussars, and the majority of our relations, who appeared to be really delighted to be invited. Also we were able to participate in a horse show which took place on the racecourse. Our Arabs had been taught to jump and we acquitted ourselves reasonably well in a novice team event. When autumn came my pleasant easy life with the Wiltshire Yeomanry came to an abrupt end. There had been, out of the blue, an establishment change, which meant that the two jobs of training major and adjutant had to be combined and I duly returned to regimental duty at Tidworth.

The regiment was preparing for the next move, which was to Munster in Germany and this was scheduled for early summer in 1959. I became second captain to a tank squadron, with surprisingly little work to do.

This enabled me to continue hunting Rendez-Vous with the Beaufort and to have many enjoyable weekends at Badminton. Then once again I took over the regimental soccer team. To have all the better players released and available, when required, was not easy, but I battled away at it. In the first round of the Army Cup the team had to play extra time and I drove back to the barracks to collect extra support.

Another Christmas in Ireland was highly enjoyable, with hunting and dances. There had been a dramatic change to my father's situation in that steeplechasing was being introduced at Ascot in the winter. Hence he was only able to come to Ireland every second week, for an extended weekend, to have two days' hunting. This was unfortunate and the extra travelling probably affected his long term health.

My 1959 point-to-point season started with good prospects as I expected that at least five good horses would be given to me to ride by three owners. Yet bad luck persisted as one after another went lame. I enjoyed plenty of rides but most of them were on undistinguished horses. For the second consecutive year I was invited to Badminton for the three-day event. It was completely similar to the previous year and equally appreciated by me. For a short time I was in the same land rover together with the Queen and Queen Mother. They amusingly mimicked the people in the admiring crowd, with words like 'Isn't she lovely' showing that they clearly knew what was being said about them.

Suddenly in the Regiment we encountered a shock, in the form of a new Colonel, who had come from another regiment, like an aggressive new broom. He demanded improvements all round. Then came the move to Germany, which added to our discomfort, because Munster, which was the nearest British base to Holland, was situated in a very boring flat area. The saving grace for me was that we had brought our horses with us and I enjoyed riding alongside a canal, in which colourful German barges transported a variety of goods. Even better some of the horses, who were there to race, were put in a syndicate, which would share all expenses and winnings. My representative had been bred by my father and I was happy to let him be a part of it. On most free weekends, we set off to a distant racecourse, to try our luck and had a number of adventures. One little mare called Perequita was soon a winner and our morale rose high. Piers Bengough, who was a accomplished jockey and successful owner in England, was the trainer and I learnt from him and his experiences. He and his wife Bridget made sure our racing days were enjoyable and light hearted, although a disciplined procedure for each day was followed. A delicious picnic lunch was produced and on the way home we stopped at a restaurant for a good German steak for supper. To train the racehorses properly necessitated an early start to the day. We woke at 6 a.m., so as to be at the stables by 6.30 to go out as a proper racing string on exercise. Cold water sometimes had to be used to get one member of syndicate out of bed, but we all agreed that once on a horse in the early morning we were enjoying the best part of the day.

Suddenly my simple life as a second captain was violently changed when, for the second time, I was again appointed MTO in charge of transport. The incumbent had been sacked from the Army and had left a mess behind him, which required hard work to rectify. Luckily a very efficient sergeant, called Ludlow, was posted to the troop to assist me and, despite some nightmarish problems, we soon had matters running smoothly.

After a while we started to play polo, which I had to organise, at a local ground called Dalbaum. We had arrived too late with too few ponies to compete in the 1959 inter-regimental tournaments, but towards the end of the summer I managed to play in some quite good polo at Bad Lippspringe, where the best of the Army polo was played. I was also asked to umpire some important matches and learnt much from the experience.

In the autumn we had to take part in a Brigade and Divisional Exercise. I found myself in charge of massive wheeled convoys, which had to travel long distances through the night. I never found the map reading easy and had to extract myself from some dramatic errors. The worst of these happened, when I led a hundred vehicles up a cul-de-sac and had to turn them round, one by one, before returning to the main road. After the manoeuvres came the dreaded annual inspection, known as the Admin. Besides painting the barrack rooms, all the vehicles had to face a rigorous inspection, carried out by a team from outside the regiment. Sergeant Ludlow designed a brilliant system of teams, rather than individuals, working on the lorries and jeeps. One team cleaned, another lubricated and a third painted the bodywork and the signs. On Admin day it was announced that MT troop had been given a distinction, the highest possible result. Then the inspecting General walked up to me and said 'Inspectors can make mistakes, let us make one last check, turn on the front and rear lights of all your vehicles.' That morning one driver had found a rear light bulb missing and had pinched one from another vehicle, causing a chain reaction, during which two bulbs had been broken. Hence on inspection three rear lights were missing and somehow we extracted these vehicles to the far end of the line where bulbs were fitted, before the General reached them. It was a short-lived triumph because I was soon sent to England for a ten-week Driving and Maintenance Course, followed by six weeks' leave, during which time Sergeant Ludlow left and the caretaker MTO allowed the old chaos to return to the troop.

During the sixteen weeks I had much fun in the 1960 point-to-point season. The base at Ascot was most helpful for the weekends, from the D&M course, and throughout my leave. I drove all over England, taking full advantage of the rule, which allowed Army officers to be qualified for almost all the races at point-to-points. Hence I won members' races at the New Forest and Larkhill and gained a third winner at a truly memorable day at the Warwickshire meeting. This adventure started in the members' race, in which my horse turned a somersault at the second fence. Miraculously I did not break a bone, although the skin of one of my shoulders was lacerated. I was wondering if I would seize up with stiffness, before my ride in the last race, when I was requested to take the place of an injured jockey in the open race. This horse had run in the Grand National and was the most incredible jumper that I had ever ridden. He took off a long way from every fence to land far out on the other side. With half a mile left to run he dropped back from the leaders, but continued to jump the remaining fences brilliantly. The thrill of that jumping made me forget my shoulder, so that I felt strong and confident when going to the paddock for the last race. To my horror we again arrived wrong for the second fence and there was a sickening noise, as my horse ploughed through it. His head hit the ground, but, somehow, he did not fall and I stayed aboard, only to find I had lost the reins. They had gone over his head and the buckle was bouncing on the ground, looking as if it was impossible to retrieve them. Then I saw the next fence looming and desperately reached forward with my right hand to recover the reins, only two strides from it. He then started to jump brilliantly, but I thought the two leaders were too far in front to catch. His jump at the last was extra big and after it I began swinging my whip at speed. To my amazement he changed up a gear and charged past the two to win by a length. During the long drive back to Ascot I reminisced over my day, unable to believe that I had had such wonderful experiences in two of the three races. The next day it was difficult getting out of bed and hard to move about, because of a stiff shoulder, but I did not complain.

In April I returned to the Regiment to find that it had moved seventy miles east to Paderborn, a much more pleasant area, with hills and valleys. I was now a qualified D&M instructor for tanks and wheeled vehicles. This meant that I had to organise courses, give lectures on vehicle operational systems and take driving tests. The latter added to the risks of life, but I welcomed the opportunity to escape out of barracks, in order to avoid the chaos in MT troop. In hindsight I should have reported my temporary replacement for the mess handed back to me, but I think a touch of conceit told me that I would be able to correct the situation. Many vehicles had not had monthly inspections and their documents were not correctly completed. The only way to rectify matters was to report the loss of the some papers, but we received a poor report at the next regimental inspection and my reputation was tarnished. Paderborn was close to Bad Lippsringe where the British Army had control of 50 acres of open ground, which provided playing fields for many sports including polo. When not on exercises we went there to play chukkas three times a week. We had a week team for the inter-regimental tournament and in the first round we were humiliated by a strong QDG team led by their Colonel, a very experienced player, Colonel Jackie Harman. However we learnt lessons and applied them, two months later, in the Captains and Subalterns, which to our great joy we won.

1961 was another eventful year. I moved to A squadron to be second in command to a super efficient Australian, who was on secondment to the 10th Hussars for two years. I learnt much from him and remember his expression about having a tight ship. In the summer I continued to improve my polo while enjoying some tournaments with the Germans in Düsseldorf and Hamburg. This was the year of the Guidon parade and Prince Henry, Duke of Gloucester, Colonel in Chief of the 10th Hussars, came out to Germany to present the new Guidon. The preparation required much hard work, including many hours on the drill square, under a guards drill sergeant. I was excused the marching because of a recurrence of pain from my verrucas, which had originated in my prep school, Stonehouse. Instead I was appointed ADC to the Prince for the weekend. I had dreamt of being an ADC to a Governor or the like and this was a chance to prove I could be good at it. I had to cajole and push the Prince and his entourage from one event to another and had some anxious moments, when worried that we would arrive too early for the big parade. But I enjoyed the weekend and the Colonel, not known for being complimentary, congratulated me on a job well done. The high pitched laugh of the Prince and some of his unintelligible jokes were not attractive, but he was pleasantly approachable and I appreciated the royal aura. The parade itself was an enormous success, all the social events went well and, when it was all over, there was a feeling of pride and high morale amongst all ranks.

In August I was selected for and went with the BAOR polo team to play at Cowdray for a month. I stayed with the Hawker family at Midhurst, Sussex and was made very welcome. I played number two and although we were given quite good ponies, I found that the opposition were always mounted a little better than us. But we had no right to complain, because the experience and lessons learnt were of immense value and the polo enjoyable. I returned to Germany to find that my handicap had been raised to 3 goals.

Also in Germany the time had come for a change in Colonel. Bill Lithgow who had commanded the renowned King's Troop, Royal Horse Artillery, took over as our Commanding Officer. It was a welcome change as his predecessor had ruled us in a rather aggressive and selfish manner. At the same time Piers Bengough went to England to be an instructor at RMA Sandhurst thereby causing quite a move around within the regimental structure. I found myself commanding HQ Squadron and in charge of all the horses, including responsibilities for training the racehorses and polo ponies. This experience was to have a big influence on my future, because it taught me a considerable amount about stable and horse management and gave me extra time to study polo and team building. On the negative side I was not able to increase my knowledge of military subjects, which might have affected my career as a soldier. For two years I stayed in barracks when everyone else went on exercises and at the time I had no regrets.

As a racehorse trainer I was quickly misled into thinking it was much easier than it actually is. Nick Gaselee, of the Life Guards, who later became a leading amateur jockey and then a successful trainer, had given a horse to Piers Bengough to train. This horse had won good races in England before becoming sire and what is termed a 'dog'. Nevertheless because of the English wins, he would automatically be high in the German handicap, unless he ran badly in conditioned races first. So I prepared him for conditioned races, with very little galloping, expecting him to be last. Ridden by Nick, he came second in his first race and won his second proving that a 'dog' needs special treatment and misleading me in to believing I might be a gifted trainer! However the other racehorses, in the regiment, were not of such quality and their initial results were so disastrous, that I had to restart their whole training process from the beginning.

In April 1962 I went on my first ever foreign polo trip which turned out to be memorable and of great influence to my future. I captained the British Army of the Rhine Team in the Rome Polo Tournament. The present Duke of Wellington, then Brigadier Marquis of Douro, as chairman of our military polo in Germany, had accepted the invitation and included himself in the team. This meant we were only an 8 goal team up against 12 goal teams which included players worth 6 goals. The drive to Rome was wonderful and I was a passenger in the comfortable

Mercedes of Hugh and Rosemary Pitman. I was thrilled to see famous places in Switzerland and Italy, especially Lake Como and the bridge with houses on it in Florence. Finding our way into Rome was not easy and not helped by Hugh Pitman saying 'Surely to god most Italians can speak English'. We stayed at the Sporting Hotel, which was also hosting the players for the Rome tennis tournament. Our morale was raised by an amusing incident that happened to our bold Brigadier Marquis. He had made what could be called a grand arrival. He had landed in one plane, his wife in another and their Bentley with driver had coincided with their arrival at the hotel. But in the Italian army Brigadier means Corporal and the hotel receptionist had shown the Douro couple to a staff room, in the back of the building. He was outraged and throughout dinner, that first night, we were frequently told how many Italians he had captured in Africa during the Second World War.

Our first polo match was disastrous and I am happy that I do not remember the score. But the positive result was that afterwards I talked with the Pakistani Brigadier Heskey Baig. What a character as well as a brilliant polo mind. His first words are lodged in my brain for life 'Don't panic remember we are British'. He then offered to coach us and the next day we had a session with him in the practice field. What he taught us that day became the main basis for all my tactical coaching of the future. It also improved our team enormously and, although we did not win any of the remaining matches we acquitted ourselves well enough to leave Rome with our heads held high.

Besides the polo we had a fascinating social programme, seeing much of Rome, throwing a coin in a fountain and eating incredible meals in private houses and restaurants. Heskey Baig continually kept us amused with his wit and charm and once danced on the table where we were sitting. We challenged him that a good Muslim should not be drinking to which he replied, 'I have so much faith that I trust Allah to change whiskey into water as it touches my lips'. Later he added 'I must admit there are times that I feel a little tipsy and begin to think that Allah is letting me down.' One day we had a buffet lunch outdoors in the midst of a display of lovely old carriages. With a plate over full, as usual, I sat down on a two-wheeled carriage, just as Hugh Pitman got up and it tipped over backwards. I was covered from head to foot in pasta, vegetables, sauce and other food, but the owner of the antique carriage was much more upset about his property than my condition. Luckily a kind lady came to my rescue by cleaning me all over and comforting me, in such an embarrassing situation.

I returned to Paderborn for a summer that was not too eventful. My responsibilities with HQ Squadron were mainly covered by Sergeant-major Reddish, a man with attention to detail. I tried to handle the morale factor of an entity of men, who were split into a variety of administrative groups, with little structure for *esprit de corps*, like there was in a tank squadron. The horses took most of my time in one way or another. The racehorses in the early morning and the polo ponies later on. The former were in better condition and were acquitting themselves reasonable well on the German race courses, without actually winning. In the polo there was a big disappointment in the inter-regimental, when we narrowly lost in the semi final. Other tournaments were enjoyed.

In October 1962 I received incredibly exciting news. I had been selected to be in the British Army polo team, to play for a month, in India, during January '63. I had had no idea that this tour was planned or that I was good enough to be picked and I had never dreamt of returning to the land, where I was born. The cynic might have said I was only in the team, because my father was Chairman of Army Polo, but later events demonstrated that the best four had been chosen.

My father had already completed five years in his Ascot job. The steeplechase course had been built and was in action during the winters and the massive new grandstand for the Royal Enclosure had been completed. In addition to his Ascot work he was honorary Colonel of the 10th Hussars and the North Irish Horse, besides being Chairman of the Army saddle club and the polo. Then at home in Ireland he was building a dairy herd and piggery, as well as being Master of Hounds. Of course he was a good delegator and was greatly assisted by Mr Butt, his highly able chief clerk at Ascot, but later events showed that he had taken on more than was good for his health to stand the strain.

Approaching Christmas brought the dreaded Admin inspection and with it the barrack block inspection and competition. Sergeant Major Reddish organised the painting and cleaning, while I set out to create pride, together with will to win atmosphere. I must have succeeded because HQ Squadron won, which gave me enormous pleasure and fulfilment. One day the second in command of the regiment appeared at my morning squadron parade, demanding to inspect every man. He failed to find anything wrong and his face looked more and more surprised, while I watched his reactions. It was pleasing to know that my standards were acceptable to my seniors.

In preparation for India I went to the regimental gymnasium for daily circuit training. This comprised a mixture of floor exercises, skipping and weight lifting. The latter made my forearms very strong and when we arrived in India I was the fittest in the team. The downside was that later that year, for the first time ever, I developed tennis elbow and I was troubled by it for several years.

The team for India was Major Ronald Ferguson, Life Guards (5), Captain Lord Patrick Beresford, Horse Guards (4), Captain Michael Fraser, QOH (3), myself, 10H (3) and reserve Captain Tim Ritson, QOH (2). We flew out in an RAF plane, provided for Admiral Lord Louis Mountbatten, the last Viceroy of India and at that time, head of all the British Armed Forces. The plane had been divided into two halves, the front just for the great man and the back for his entourage and us. Soon after take off Patrick and I were invited to have lunch with the noble Earl, because our late mutual uncle, Hugh Beresford, had died under his command when HMS *Kelly* had been sunk near Crete in the war. So we left Ronald, Michael and Tim, crushed in their seats, while we sat at a large round table with our host. After several attempts to ask questions I realised that Mountbatten did not want us to talk unless he questioned us. This incredibly distinguished man looked at the ceiling rather than answer me.

We lived most of the time while in India in the officers' mess for the President's bodyguard. The first night we went to an Indian Cavalry Reunion Dinner, where we were split up on to separate tables. I will never forget the exuberance, enthusiasm and joy of the Indians, as they re-met each other and talked of the old days. For a short while I thought they were all imitating Peter Sellers before I realised they were just being themselves. The second day we were introduced to all the polo ponies, that were being lent to us. There were forty ponies, each held by a smartly dressed groom, known as a syce. It seemed too good to be true that we each had eight ponies, for four chukka matches. We spent several mornings, trying and practising on our ponies, and went sightseeing in the afternoons. Ronald was impressive with his team planning and briefing, so that we keenly looked forward to playing as a team in three Test Matches against the Indian Army team and in one weekend tournament.

The three Test Matches were fast, furious and thrilling, against the Indian Army, but sadly we lost them all, although Ronald's strategy was successful, in that we normally held our own in every chukka, until the last minute, when everything went wrong and many goals were scored against us. It took an Indian to point out the reason, when admitting, that in protecting the forty ponies before our arrival, they had all missed the previous tournament and had lost vital fitness. Hindsight would have told us to play two ponies in every chukka. A non playing coach would probably have advised this to us, but we did not have one. However we did win two games in the weekend tournament. But I realised that polo was not the only important part of our visit, because there was so much else to appreciate and enjoy. The Independence Day parade was as moving as anything I have ever witnessed. We had VIP seats and the colour, pageantry, variety including elephants and camels, and pure numbers was all an overwhelming sight. It ended as darkness arrived and the farewell notes from a Bugler, high up on a roof, were proof of perfect timing which made it so emotional.

Our sightseeing included Agra, the Taj Mahal and Fatehpur Sikri, where they had played human chess before deserting the place when the water had gone bad. We saw the Taj Mahal in sunlight and moonlight and were amused by a guide, who on both occasions claimed that the shadow, in the water, only happened at that specific time. One weekend we drove to Jaipur, returning by train, to be guests of the Maharajah and Maharani of Jaipur, in their mini palace, because the large palace had become a hotel.

For a day I flew to Lucknow to find where I had been born. A Sikh major, wearing a fine turban, was my guide for the day and we found the house, where my family had lived, then occupied by three Indian Army families, whose husbands were far away near the Chinese border. I had a fascinating tour of a historic city and felt quite emotional.

I spent a day watching England play India in a cricket test match and saw Colin Cowdrey score a century. The performance by spectators was often more entertaining than the cricket. The colour of dress all round the stadium was fabulous and the cries of encouragement, including 'good shot' were hilarious. Frequently in varying parts of the crowd a fight would break out, often ending in one unfortunate person being ejected from the top to the bottom of the stand. The general noise level was fascinating and this was added to by the many transistor radios listening to the commentary. Rao Rajah Hanut Singh, whose title meant bastard son of a majarajah—it was better to be recognised as such than to hide it—was probably the best ever Indian polo player, when 9 goals pre-war. In England as a post-war 4 goal player, he had again distinguished himself by leading a team to win many of the best British tournaments. That year he was playing in some of the Delhi tournaments and often came round to talk to us, at the officers' mess. He was one of the few conceited men that I have met and had to like. He spoke about himself in the third person 'Hanut did this---Hanut said that'. From him we heard some incredible stories and learnt many helpful points, about every dimension of polo. He loved to say that polo was the Sport of Kings and not for peasants and it was amusing to hear him try to justify this controversial concept. One of his stories told how when a syce, pre-war, had to substitute for an injured maharajah in a big match, he had wet his pants and Hanut added, 'That proves polo is not for peasants'.

As the tour drew to a close Ronald Ferguson, who had contributed much to polo on and off the polo field, was unwittingly digging his own grave for the coming summer season in British polo. He continually told us that his life was unbelievably perfect, because here he was having the best possible preparation for the English season, in which he was due to play with Juan Carlos Harriott, the best player in the world, and

Prince Philip. He had also started to undermine our admiration for him, by making the same joke, every time our post was brought in by an Indian orderly, on a silver plate. 'Bad luck Patrick you have been recalled to Cyprus'. Against some strong objections Lord Patrick Beresford had been allowed to leave the emergency situation in Cyprus to join our team. One day Patrick opened his letter and then collapsed in hysterical laughter. We all tried to help him up and to enquire, what was so funny. Finally he said 'I am not recalled, but Ronny your squadron is going to Cyprus next month'. To be fair Ronald took the news extremely well and even started making plans for his mission to Cyprus before leaving India.

CHAPTER 9

Return to Germany and my Promotion to Major

In summer '63 at Paderborn I was very hopeful of success for 10H in the inter-regimental polo. Nigel Budd had come back from Malaysia to add extra strength if I could keep him disciplined. But there had been a rule change that allowed officers, stationed in England, to come out to Germany to play. Hence in the semi-final we played the Horse Guards (the Blues) which included Patrick Beresford. At half time we led by two goals, but overconfidence by Nigel allowed the Blues' number one to score an unnecessary goal, which brought them back in the game and allowed them to go on to win. Nigel Budd had also behaved erratically away from the polo field and he was confined to barracks just as he hoped to be married. The result was a marriage in the barracks and I was asked to be best man. Hence I found myself looking after the most enchanting American couple, called McMillan, who had come to give away Biddy the Bride. Not only did I have a delightful weekend with new friends but I also received a wonderful invitation to the United States.

With the polo I enjoyed some good tournaments at Düsseldorf and Hamburg and finished the season by going to St Moritz in Switzerland. The height was quite unsettling, leaving me short of breath but I gradually became accustomed to it. My team won one match and I was asked to umpire the final in which a funny event happened. Two old rivals were marking each other far away from the ball when one of them, a very tall player, suddenly crashed to the ground. I had not seen the incident and therefore could not give a penalty although the big man insisted that he had been ejected by the boot of his opponent. Initially he refused to move unless I gave a penalty and it took a long time to persuade him to get up for a throw in.

That autumn I finally had to go out on one large Brigade exercise to control the re-supply of petrol and ammunition. We lived relatively comfortably in a mobile officers' mess and one day the Brigadier, Hugh Davis, ate with us. In conversation I recalled a race at the Beaufort point-to-point in which his horse had beaten mine. In jest I complained that I had requested his jockey to go an easy pace but he had done the opposite. The Brigadier replied, 'Actually I told my jockey that whatever Dawnay says to you, do the opposite.' The whole table, especially Bill Lithgow, laughed with great gusto.

For Christmas '63 I planned an incredible three-week hunting leave in Ireland. I intended to visit many other packs of hounds besides the Waterford. But as I stepped ashore in Ireland it started to snow and for the first time in several decades hunting in Ireland was stopped for a month.

1964 was an action packed year. 10H returned to England to be stationed once again at Tidworth, where we were converted from tanks to armoured cars while preparing to go to Aden for possible active service. I attended yet another course at Bovington in a group of officers and sergeants. We were trained on the Saladin armoured car and Ferret scout car so that we could pass the knowledge on to the rest of the regiment at Tidworth.

The polo season started and I spent much time on the road between Tidworth and Windsor trying to play in both places. In Windsor I played my father's ponies in some good polo and I took the opportunity to listen and learn both from my experiences and the conversation of those around me. I detected an incredible mixture of knowledge and ignorance and the latter was demonstrated by remarks at the bar. For example a player was saying 'I don't understand how I could play so badly today when I had a good game yesterday.' A quick look at the programme showed me that this gentleman had been one of the stronger players on the field on Saturday but on Sunday had been the lowest in handicap. He clearly did not understand that you play as well as you are allowed to.

At Tidworth I encountered an unexpected problem in that there was no opposition for our 7 goal regimental team to practise against. This forced me to plan two away games. The first at Cirencester against a medium goal team which had won at Windsor the previous year and which included Eduardo Moore the up and rising superstar. We had a four goal start and unbelievably won by a goal. I had to pinch myself to believe we had won. Then the second was at Cowdray where the opposition included the old timer Peter Dollar and a strong Kenyan 4 goal player. Again to everyone's surprise we won by one goal and we returned to Tidworth full of confidence.

'Pride comes before a fall' was never better highlighted by what happened in the regimental tournament at Tidworth. We played a low goal Gunner team who only shot at goal three times to score twice while we had twenty shots at goal to score only once having hit the goal post many times. It was hard to accept but a great leveller and my pride was temporarily restored at Windsor where I joined a team, including a 4 goal Argentine for a medium goal tournament. We won the first round against Juan Carlos Harriott, the world's greatest player, who was supporting a weak team. But in the second round the 4 goaler arrived on the ground boasting that he had danced all night and not gone to bed. The result was that he played appallingly and we were easily beaten.

Before going to Aden, which is now in Yemen, we had two months' leave to cover embarkation and annual leave. I had planned to spend most of this time with my girl friend, a lovely redhead, by taking her with me to Ireland and other places. Just as the leave started she telephoned to say that it was all too much and we had better part as friends. I was devastated and spent my leave in a state of depression. My parents took me to stay with friends for the York race week and there was good racing at Ascot. I also retreated to my Irish home for much of the time. My father was upset with me for being depressed and tried to rally my spirits unsuccessfully. But good did emerge from it in that I became determined to have a good year in Aden and went out there with no distractions at home to interfere with my healthy intentions.

After we landed on the tarmac of Aden's international airport somebody commented on the purposeful manner in which I strode to reach the transport that was waiting for us. Indeed it turned to be an incredible year during which I saw more of the world than in any other twelve months of my life. The regiment was divided between four locations, with headquarters in Little Aden some distance from Aden itself, one squadron in the Beihan area, another in the Radfan, where the most intense fighting had been, and the third far away in Sharjah which was a garrison town in the country of Oman. This third squadron was itself divided into two having to send a captain and two troops to defend an airport in the Kingdom of Salalah. I was now second in command of A squadron with Robin Wilson as my squadron leader.

A squadron started in Beihan but I had to be based in Aden in order to supervise all the administration. This involved a twice daily talk on the radio to Beihan and a weekly trip in a little plane to deliver the many requirements. This was known as going Up Country and I had to be landed on a very bumpy small runway. I learnt to ignore the danger and this stood to me later in life when flying to many countries I always told myself that nothing could be worse than landing in Beihan. In Aden it was refreshing and pleasant to swim in the sea and when I not travelling up country I swum every day. Also the polo season was just starting. The polo club was in Big Aden close to the international airport. To get there involved a drive of forty minutes via a long causeway which connected the two Adens. The polo was low standard but competitive and enjoyable and was followed by a welcome drink at the club bar. It was of course important to replace all the liquid lost from playing in such heat. After one month I was told to stay a few days in Beihan in charge of the squadron while Robin Wilson rested in Aden. During this I witnessed a fatal shooting accident when a soldier in a small artillery attachment was cleaning a weapon and unintentionally shot a friend. On the pleasant side I spent a night as guest of the local political resident. We stayed on a flat roof under the moon and stars listening to Tchaikovsky and drinking whiskey. It was closest that I have ever been to Utopia.

1965

At the end of four months there was a change round of the three combat squadrons. The larger half of A squadron went to Sharjah in Oman and I took the remaining two troops to Salalah. This was my first independent command so I was both excited and a little nervous when an RAF plane delivered us there. It was an important refuelling location for the RAF who had a small detachment to administer this and a traffic control team for the landings and take offs. Recently it had been attacked by terrorists and we were there to guard and protect it from a repeat offensive.

I had a memorable six weeks in Salalah. The surrounding countryside was rich with colour and there were several scenic views. The most onerous work was at night when a scout car guard had to patrol the large perimeter of the airfield throughout the hours of darkness. The only unusual incident happened one day as we arrived at a beach for a swim. We saw an Arab disembark from a boat which then went back out to sea. We surrounded him quickly but he lay down in the praying position and was difficult to approach. Finally we apprehended him and delivered him to the local police.

As Colonel of the Regiment my father visited all the squadrons in every location. He came with Bill Lithgow, who was still our commanding officer, to Salalah for two days. It was quite strange showing him, in an official manner, round the accommodation, the vehicles and the general area.

During the whole year I was defeated by the temptation to drink too much whiskey. However it did produce one big bonus. One morning in Salalah my hangover was so bad that, when offered a cigarette, I exclaimed 'I will never smoke again'. Another officer grabbed my hand and said 'Neither will I'. We proceeded to treat it like a bet, between us, with both of us determined not to be the first to break the resolution. Every time we met we both offered the other a cigarette. I expected him to give in soon and then probably would have restarted burning my money and my lungs. Incredibly two weeks passed and my determination increased with the realisation that after fourteen days the worst was over and I would now be able to do without nicotine for ever.

When the six weeks ended we flew to Sharjah where we immediately embarked on a flag-raising drive round the whole of Oman. Robin Wilson had already left with his group, in a clockwise direction, leaving me orders to go in an anti-clockwise route, with a plan to meet up eventually in Muscat, the capital of Oman. It was a wonderful experience with some breathtaking views and several amusing incidents. Our last vehicle was an enormous Scammell which was there to pull scout cars out of deep sand. In fact it was in regular demand to help Arab trucks and cars which had either skidded off the road or become stuck in sand. The Arabs appeared to be most grateful and we enjoyed their joyful reactions to be saved from a long walk to find help.

There were long tracks of desert which could only be navigated by using a compass and a speedometer. I expected to become lost but somehow we kept close to the correct route. Twice we stayed the night together with an Arab regiment that had British officers. Our fellow countrymen were delightful hosts producing delicious dinners and clearly enjoying an exchange of conversation. I was relieved when we successfully met up with Robin Wilson and his group in Muscat, which was an intriguing place and I was fascinated by some of the architecture. Then as one large group we crossed the countryside to return to Sharjah.

I had just one month in the camp and town of Sharjah. It was the only place that I ever attempted the ancient sport of tent pegging. The horses appeared to be even more excited than ourselves as they literally tore across the sand towards the pegs. I learnt a little bit about the technique required and picked up a few pegs with my lance. It was a delight to experience some part of the old cavalry warfare. One day we received the shock news that my cousin Ian Scott had been killed when his scout car was blown up by a mine in the Radfan. His driver was badly injured but made a full recovery a year later. The sadness felt by all of us was acute but this tragedy did at least bring about the replacement of scout cars by the Saladin armoured car, which could better withstand the explosion of a mine under it. As a result further deaths and casualties were prevented.

We shared the officers' mess with the local headquarters staff. A few of them were big drinkers and attracted me to join their group in the

Prince Henry, Duke of Gloucester at the Sovereign's Parade in 1952

Hugh Dawnay with his first squadron, 1955

(LEFT–RIGHT) *David Dawnay on Perfect Knight, Lady Katherine Dawnay on Rendez-Vous and Hugh Dawnay on Rockall at the Army Hunter Trials at Tweseldown, October 1954*

Hugh Dawnay with Diana Blacker at a hunt ball in Ireland

Hugh Dawnay on No Law at Leicester in 1954

Hugh Dawnay on Rendez-Vous at Army Hunter Trials, Tweseldown, in 1955

David Dawnay as Clerk of the Course at Ascot Racecourse in 1957

Hugh Dawnay at Whitfield Court

Hugh Dawnay on Larry at Opening Lawn Meet in November 1957

Badminton, April 1958
(LEFT–RIGHT) *Hugh Dawnay, The Queen, Princess Margaret, Duke of Beaufort*

Captains and Subalterns Cup 1961

India, January 1963

India, January 1963

David and Hugh Dawnay in Oman, 1965

Sharjah, Oman

Berlin Polo Tournament 1966

evenings. This was not good for my long term health and my indiscipline that month probably caused some liver problems later in my life.

I left Sharjah a little earlier than the rest of the squadron to join up in Aden with the regimental polo team, which was going to Kenya. The reader may remember that I had been to Kenya before in 1957 so that I was thrilled to return and overjoyed to be combining this with several polo matches. However we experienced a humiliating start when playing against a team of two old men and two young ladies at a place called Gill Gill. Our host, a wild Dane called Fin Ross, had stitched us up at the meal, before the game, with spiked drinks which he had called harmless. During the match I saw two balls instead of one and was unable to play effectively. Yet it was a useful experience and in the future I tried to ensure it did not happen again.

Our second port of call was Kitale in the North. Our host there was a great character who drove us all the way at incredible speed in his old car. We won our two matches and, with confidence restored, arrived at the capital city Nairobi. Here we were well entertained with some good dinner parties and sightseeing, including a fascinating trip round the local game park. In the polo we acquitted ourselves well in two matches although I forget the results. By the time I returned to Aden I had benefitted from a useful polo experience, an enhancement to my cultural education and an extremely enjoyable two weeks, during which we met many kind people and amusing characters.

A squadron was now in the one area which had experienced regular combat. Squadron HQ and two troops were in the Radfan, sharing the defensive duties of a long peninsular within a valley, with a battalion of infantry. The Coldstream Guards and the Marines alternated in this location and their styles were in total contrast, although both were effective in their own way. The two other troops of A squadron were in independent outposts supported by so called friendly Arab soldiers. Once again I was based in Little Aden, making weekly trips by helicopter to the combat posts. The time came for me to relieve Robin Wilson for a few days and be in command. One night the trip flares outside the perimeter wire went off twice. The first time was just before dark while I was having a shower that had run out of water leaving me covered in soap. After a struggle to put clothes on in that condition the conclusion was a false alarm caused by animals, but even so we went to bed a little uneasy with guards and patrols strengthened. The second time I was woken at 2 a.m. by trip flares outside the perimeter next to my tent. We were all quickly in our stand to positions, but initially there was nothing to report. Thirty minutes later half a mile away there was a noise that suggested a person or people stumbling over an obstacle but then silence resumed.

The next morning there was much discussion as to what had set off the trip flares. The majority thought that it was animals or birds. Then we discovered that our field telephone was not working and a signals repair technician was despatched to find and cure the fault. Later he invited me to walk outside the perimeter fence next to my tent. There he showed me where the field telephone line had been cleanly cut and my heart almost stopped, when I looked up to register that the top three strands of the perimeter wire had also been severed. It then seemed to be logical that an intruder had intended to enter the camp next to my tent. He must have then reached the area from which we heard the noise thirty minutes later. Without the trip flare I would have been the first victim of an attack.

The other clear memory of the Radfan was that contrast in attitudes between the officers of the Coldstream Guards and the Royal Marines. Both were highly proficient professionals but the former combined their standards in the field with extra comfort in the base whenever possible while the latter despised it and revelled in rough living. I dined with both at different times and admired the table laid out with silver and the gourmet dishes produced by the Coldstream, while I was amused by the criticism of this by the Marines as we ate plain food from their dull table.

In Aden the polo season was lit up by a visit from a Scots Guards team led by Mark Vestey. He and his brother owned an enormous business empire including a fleet of ships. One of the ships happened to be in the port of Aden and a few of us accompanied Mark on a surprise visit. It was amusing to watch the face of the captain when he suddenly realised that such an honoured guest was aboard. The Scots Guards polo team played the civilian team on one day and the military on the next and won them both. John Willis took over from Bill Lithgow as Colonel commanding 10th Hussars. Inevitably he made a few changes in the chain of command including sending me to be second in command of C squadron and therefore back to where I had started the tour administering Beihan. Timothy Hope was my new squadron leader and it was not easy to adjust to the system and whims of a new boss, even though I received an outstanding report from Robin Wilson. However soon our year in the Middle East was over and we were packing up to go home. Independence for the Aden Protectorate, soon to become South Yemen and later to be united with the North as one Yemen country, was approaching. The terrorist group were becoming increasingly brave in their actions against us. So it was with much relief that I felt the RAF VC 10, which was taking me home, lift off the tarmac of Aden airport.

The Regiment stayed in England while all ranks took their leave, before heading once more for Germany. I had set my heart on obtaining a military job in England for two main reasons. I wanted to look for a wife and I hoped to play high goal polo, which I reasoned was a vital step if I was to achieve further improvement in my game. All my scheming and planning was cruelly terminated when Colonel John Willis told me that he wanted me to take over command of B squadron six months after we arrived in Germany. I was devastated but I did realise that nobody with any military ambition can refuse the opportunity to command a combat (sabre) squadron. In fact hindsight has shown that this was an ill wind that blew good. I duly went to Munster in Germany with a strong determination to find a new dimension in my life that would compensate for this drastic change in my plans. I had no idea what it might be but I did not have to wait long before something happened which would change my life and put me on the road to a truly incredible new career. In April 1966 I was sent by the Rhine army polo association to play in Düsseldorf so that I could assess the handicaps of the twelve German players.

With great respect to the German players, although they were courageous with a varying degree of polo ability, they had no idea of the requirements for basic positioning by a team in a game of polo. Also their riding and hitting techniques were not of a high standard. Hence after playing some chukkas with them and having consumed an amount of schnapps and beer in the local pub, I had to tell them that they should all be rated with a minus handicap.

'How can this be?' echoed from all in the room. For a moment I was lost for an answer and then suddenly a simple explanation came to me with great clarity. I picked up four salt and pepper pots and put them in a line down the table with an equal gap between each one saying 'Polo should be played like this – einz, zwei, drei, vier, but you play it like this', and I moved the pots to be four abreast across the table. One of them said, 'Very interesting, tell us more.' I nearly fell off my chair because this was, at that time, the best known line from the famous American comedy 'The Laugh In'. Instead I summoned all my self-control and proceeded to explain a few more points about basic polo tactics. 'Why don't you become our trainer and teach us to play correctly at the weekends?' 'Bingo,' I thought, 'this is my new dimension' and I accepted the offer. In further discussion I requested that I be given somewhere to stay and that I would be well entertained at the weekends but did not look for money. The Germans became careful and promised to telephone me with their final decision. I drove back to Munster fearful that I had asked too much and spoilt my opportunity. But within the week they duly called and confirmed the arrangement.

Meanwhile at Munster I was responsible for the organisation of polo at Dalbaum, which was half an hour in a car from our barracks. The 9/12 Lancers, stationed at Osnabrück, came over to play with us at least once a week and we had enjoyable chukkas with them. I was determined to win the 1966 inter-regimental tournament in Germany. The team was clearly going to be Piers Bengough, John Willis, Peter Dwerryhouse and myself. The main problem was the ponies for Peter who was a super athlete but not a good horseman. He owned two small ponies and in previous years they had become increasingly harder for him to stop as the season progressed. In a discussion with my father, at Ascot, he had suggested that if the two little ponies were always limited to one chukka, except on match days, they should stay at their best and be still under control for the inter-regimental. I had said that Peter would object and probably not comply. He replied that I would have to put up with it and come up with a different reason on each polo day.

On the first day at Dalbaum I pinned up the chukka list showing Peter with only two chukkas. He arrived in his Mercedes and with a big smile said ' How wonderful, lad, to have polo today . . . what only two chukkas for me? Why the hell?' I said that they were not fit enough and Peter had little time to create a fuss before the chukkas were under way. The same scene took place on every polo day, but somehow I managed to produce an acceptable reason each time. With the 9/12 Lancers as a strong opposition I was able to give our regimental team an amount of opportunities to play and practice together. I experimented tactically by playing, myself, at No. 2, with John at 3, Piers at 1 and Peter at back. We started to meld effectively and I decided to keep the team playing with that line up.

I had commenced my third tour in Germany by remaining second in command of C Squadron, then led by Piers Bengough. In the next door barrack block on the other side of a square B Squadron, which I was due to take over within six months, was located. With some trepidation I watched their performance from a distance and began to realise that their standards, in most dimensions, were lower than the other squadrons and simply not acceptable. Gradually a plan formed in my mind, which I knew would give me an unusual advantage, of being prepared to make changes immediately when I started my term as squadron leader. I had already been promoted to Major and it was strange wearing a crown on each shoulder and being called Major instead of Captain. Little did I know that thirty years later the title would still be applied to me by people in many different places.

I had become friendly and close to an Irish nurse in the local military hospital. This together with my visits to Düsseldorf at weekends enormously increased my happiness and confidence, which in turn galvanised my enthusiasm to achieve great results with B squadron. Meanwhile at Düsseldorf my system of polo instruction, structured for the German standard, seemed to be reaping rapid success. I tried to temper the inevitable excitement and danger of conceit by telling myself that low standards are easy to improve. Then with delight I began to feel that the same should apply when I took over the reins at B squadron.

The big day arrived and I walked from C squadron barrack block across to a similar building in which B squadron lived. My predecessor had left a letter with a few points in it and had found an excuse not to be present for the handover. Initially this was a shock but in hindsight it actually helped me as it prevented any delay for me to put my ideas into action. A great compensation was the enthusiasm and support of SSM Tod Hunter who was my squadron sergeant-major. He helped me in all the details of the squadron organisation and appeared to be delighted with it.

The next few weeks were possibly the most exhilarating of my time in the army. My aim was to raise the morale of all the one hundred and twenty men under my command. They were divided into eight troops of which five were armoured car troops, one the HQ troop, one the troop of lorries and one the fitters' troop, who repaired vehicles as required. I tried to make them proud of themselves, their own troop and of B squadron. I carefully prepared my first squadron address, remembering the wisdom of Graham Pilsbury, who had been B squadron leader in the days when we were the demonstration squadron at Warminster. I told them B for Best, which meant high standards, and that all complaints must come direct to me and not be covered up. I encouraged them to salute all officers in a manner that demonstrated pride in being 'B' while reminding them that officers, by replying to all salutes, had to work harder than they did. I challenged them to achieve far better results in the inter-squadron sports and promised time for training and my full support.

There was an immediate result in that an atmosphere of enthusiasm emanated from all ranks. SSM Tod Hunter told me that he could not believe the improvement in saluting and we won the first inter-squadron sports event. Every day I studied my office wall chart, which gave the list of men in each troop and I talked to all my officers and sergeants about strengths, weaknesses and problems of the men under them. Then I made five inter-troop postings and reckoned that I had levelled the overall troop abilities as close as was possible to achieve.

I remembered that in the past at concerts given by the regimental band, with supporting acts by other soldiers, there had been no representative from B squadron and made a plan to change that situation. I told all eight troops that there would be a competition between them for the best 'act', in which they had to perform and invited the Bandmaster to come and judge the result. There were several knocks on my door by officers and NCOs claiming that their troop had no one with talent and therefore could not compete. But I refused to give in and the appointed night for our squadron concert duly arrived. Everyone including the participants seemed to enjoy it immensely and there was one outstanding act which won the competition and was, as hoped, invited to perform in the next band concert, where it was well received, making us all very proud of our squadron.

Surprisingly Colonel John Willis did not interfere with my handling of B Squadron and this increased my confidence enormously. Most working days started in the tank park with a brief parade followed by scheduled vehicle maintenance. Normally I inspected just one of the troops and then for half an hour or more watched, questioned and listened to the men as they worked before withdrawing to my office to face the paper work. This gave me a chance to measure morale, attitude and standards being aimed for. From this and conversations in the corridor of the squadron block I found that the NCOs and men were enthusing me about the future plans for training in and outside the barracks more than the other way round. I felt very lucky that conscription had recently finished which meant that all men were now professionals with ambition to soldier seriously.

Meanwhile my weekends in Düsseldorf were being fruitful and enjoyable. I always stayed with Axel Joens, who was a bachelor living with his mother, and drove me around at high speed in his Porsche. In a delightful way I could feel them laughing at my Anglo behaviour while often I nearly died of amusement at the way they pronounced some English words and their German mannerisms. I ran a polo programme that included riding, hitting and tactics and could see a rapid improvement taking place from week to week. Later in life I appreciated that this had been a crucial period of the development of my system of instruction which I would take all around the world of polo.

The time came for my squadron camp, which was allotted two weeks and was mainly consigned to troop tests. I had seen my predecessors burning midnight oil and exhausting themselves preparing for and administering these tests and had promised myself that I would avoid a similar fate without knowing how. Polo team tactics, which I was trying to impart to the Germans, suddenly gave me the inspiration that each armoured car troop could be a team for running a test. So I simply studied the book on armoured car tactics and selected five subjects, one for each troop, and told the troop leaders to plan, organise and examine the other four troops in a test on their subject. I told them to ensure that every man had a constructive part to play.

The area which I had chosen for the training was in the hills near a place called Detmold which was conveniently close to the polo fields at Bad Lippspringe, where my ponies spent the two weeks. At the base camp my tent with a carpet was very comfortable and the SSM insisted on giving me breakfast in bed each day.

The first day in the training area was used for the troops to prepare their tests and a demonstration, for the end of the day, showing how it should have been done. Then each troop had their day of glory testing the others while I sat on a shooting stick and learnt much about minor armoured car tactics. At the end I gave a summary of good and bad points that I had seen. The Brigade Commander visited us on one day and appeared to be impressed by my system of delegation and the enjoyment, which all the soldiers had from it. It was truly wonderful to see the humblest soldier thrilled to be part of a judging team while others extended their efforts to make their troop look good. By an arranged coincidence the squadron weekly maintenance day happened on a Bad Lippspringe polo day and I played chukkas there once each week. It was a pleasant change to play without having responsibility either for the organisation of the chukkas or the direction of any team and it was most enjoyable.

When I next went to Düsseldorf I was asked to help organise a polo tournament there. They wanted me to advise on which visiting teams should be invited and, most important of all, to select the Düsseldorf team for it. It was crystal clear to me that they were not yet ready to compete as a team against any British army visitors but they were good enough to play in a British team. So I suggested that all the British regiments should be asked to send three men teams to which I would add one German. Initially they were furious and continued to insist on having their own team. This forced me to say that I would not help in any way unless they took my advice.

'The British will not like it,' they said.

'That is true but most of them will still come,' I replied.

Eventually they agreed to accept my proposal and I returned to Munster wondering how the British would react. Two weeks later, one after the other, all the invited regiments telephoned me and the conversation was identical each time.

'Dawnay, are you involved with the Düsseldorf Polo Tournament?'

'Yes, I am helping to organise it.'

'Why is it only three-man teams?'

'I will add one German to each team.'

'We do not wish to play with a kraut.'

'Don't worry, we will have enough teams without you.'

'Wait a minute, if you insist I suppose we will have to consent.'

And thus all the invited regiments accepted under protest.

A syndicate of regimental officers once again had a group of thoroughbreds being trained for German racing. David Shaw, our smallest officer, held the training licence and my horse Lindesfahn, bred at home was the best potential steeplechaser. On some mornings I enjoyed riding with the others and participating in the gallops.

The first regimental exercise of the year took place. It was a real test of all the vehicles, the radios and my overall troop control. B squadron appeared to do well, there were no serious mistakes and we completed all our commitments. Then came the weekend for the Düsseldorf Polo Tournament. The week before I had attended the final committee meeting. The Germans told me that all the invited teams had accepted and I asked where they were staying. This produced some bombastic arguing and many amusing excuses when I pressed them to invite them to their houses. Eventually half the British players stayed in German houses and this was the beginning of a healthy interchange of hospitality between our two nations for the first time since the Second World War.

The tournament seemed to be a great success with all the British expressing surprise at how well the Germans played and fitted in to their teams. The Germans were delighted with the way in which they were accepted by the British teams and they much enjoyed their participation. My team included two Germans and Martin Scott a strong army player. We won two matches to reach the final. Then on the Saturday night at a party I was cornered by players from Hamburg including a great character called Albert Darboven. They questioned me about many polo dimensions and finally Albert said, 'When are you coming to Hamburg to teach us?'

'Next weekend if you like,' I replied.

'Why not,' said Albert and we started celebrating the agreement. This turned out to be highly detrimental for my condition in the polo final the next day. My hangover caused me to miss a couple of goal chances and the game ended in a draw. We did not have enough ponies to play extra time. Nevertheless everyone appeared to be happy with the result and an excellent weekend concluded.

The following weekend, as arranged, I went to Hamburg. I stayed with Albert Darboven and his San Salvadorian wife Ines. After giving some polo coaching I was introduced to a wealthy and high living group of people who drank champagne like water and never stopped laughing. Amongst them was a wartime German army officer, called Prince Bentheim, whom everybody spoke well of, but he was not prepared to talk about any of his war exploits. This was the beginning of a relationship which was to develop in to a great friendship with several Germans and another challenge to coach and teach polo, which I willingly accepted.

Amongst all the sport there was of course some serious military work to do. As important as any was the week on the ranges at Hohne. The armoured cars had to fire their main armament and machine guns and the scout cars their machine guns at many different targets. The finale was then the individual troop battle runs during which I had to give them targets. Luckily I had some very good gunnery NCOs, who had organised the vital preparations excellently, but it was a big ordeal to be in charge of a gunnery range, while being watched by so many experts and senior officers. I faced the first day with trepidation, but to my pleasant surprise all the practices went smoothly and the squadron report was well above satisfactory.

The next big sporting event was the 1966 inter-regimental polo tournament at Bad Lippspringe. We, the 10th Hussars reached the final fairly easily but there we met the favourites, the 17/21 Lancers who had two strong players. Fortunately our team had a good day and I surprised the opposition from No. 2 so that we won by two goals. I have never felt so thrilled and delighted and it was extra wonderful because my father was there to watch. He had set me up with good ponies and helped me in so many ways and so his presence was really special. That evening at the polo ball my girl friend for the weekend had to put up with much celebration and drinking.

The following weekend we went to Hannover races where Lindesfahn, ridden by David Shaw, won the annual Military Steeplechase. It was another big thrill for me and I could not believe that at the same time so many things were going so well. Then at the Dalbaum I organised our own polo tournament which had to be completed in one day. So each match consisted of only one chukka but all the teams did play four chukkas on the day. The proceedings were rounded off with an excellent dance in our officers' mess. The next big excitement was the first post-war Berlin Polo Tournament. This was played in the ex-Olympic Stadium, the Maifeld, where in 1936 my father had played in the Olympic games to win a silver medal. Now thirty years later I played there in the next match! It was a magnificent stadium but the very small audience looked rather ridiculous inside it. We all immensely enjoyed playing there and the long weekend for me was extra fun because I stayed in style with General Nelson, the commander of Berlin garrison.

My team included two Germans from Düsseldorf and an American media man, Adam Snow, whom I had met at their club and had encouraged to play with us. Ronald Ferguson came from England to be the official umpire and even he, who had played all over the world, was clearly jealous of us playing in these surroundings. My team won the subsidiary cup and we received the prizes from the Mayor of Berlin, Willie Brandt, who later became Chancellor of West Germany. So I drove back to Munster, through the corridor between East and West Germany, very content with my first visit to this famous capital city.

We now had to prepare for the autumn exercises. For the big Brigade one B squadron was attached to the Scots Guards who had an eccentric Colonel who I suspected would be difficult to work with. We joined them in the field and I was quite worried about complying satisfactorily to his orders. Then much to my relief the rain came in such abundance that the whole exercise area was flooded. There was a long conference at the end of which the Brigadier reluctantly cancelled the manoeuvre. For the rest of the winter 66/67 I was occupied with administrative matters including report writing. The majority of my soldiers either qualified in a new trade or achieved an upgrade in another one. The administrative inspection took place and I was delighted that B squadron won the barrack block competition thereby defeating my old partner SSM Reddish, who was still with HQ squadron.

For Christmas I went for a week to a skiing resort called Saas Fe in Switzerland. I was the guest of my girl friend who was working there as a cook in a chalet. I had difficulty negotiating the hills and bends in my car during the approach to the resort. I had never skied before so I paid for a private instructor and experienced mixed results. I could not believe the instructor when he told me to lean left to turn right and once convinced I kept forgetting to do it. He credited me with making quick progress when I started travelling well down a short slope. So I took the ski lift and on a longer run could not believe how many times I fell over. By the evenings I felt exhilarated and exhausted and more than ready for the excellent meals prepared by my girl friend. I slowly improved and when the time came to return to Munster I felt reasonably satisfied with my first effort at skiing.

As 1967 began I wonder if I appreciated what now seems clear to me, while writing, that I had just finished an incredible year. I had commanded an armoured squadron with surprising results, my team had won the polo inter-regimental, my horse and I won the Hannover Cup and I had initiated a polo instructional system for the future with the Germans in Düsseldorf and Hamburg besides having my first ski.

Early in the New Year Bernard Greenwood took over from John Willis as Colonel commanding 10th Hussars. He immediately showed a good understanding of both the military and the horse situations and allowed me to accept a wonderful invitation to Hawaii. The Marquis of Waterford took a polo team there for two weeks. Ronald Ferguson, Ben Jellet, Waterford and myself completed the team. We were given a flight on Canadian Pacific which went via Toronto and Vancouver. Fred Daly, a wealthy hotel owner hosted our visit in spectacular fashion. We alternated between his hotel in the town on the beach and rooms in his polo club at the west corner of the island. Lunch parties, delicious dinners and glorious swimming happened every day. The climax to each week was the Sunday charity polo match. I played No. 4 and found I was a bit slower than I had expected. I realised that German polo has misled me to believe that I was quick when in fact the lack of good opposition had slowed me down. There were several amusing social incidents and I made a fool of myself more than once. At least I learnt the meaning of an 'American Brat'.

I returned to Germany for the start of my second training season with B squadron. I repeated my system of troop tests with them judging each other and again the results appeared to be very successful. But our hopes of winning the inter-regimental polo for a second year were destroyed in the semi-final although we led by two goals at half time. The 3rd Dragoon Guards took advantage of a stupid foul we committed when about to score another goal and then scored twice to take us in to an extra chukka where they got the winning goal.

My polo training of the Germans in Düsseldorf and Hamburg restarted with continued good results and my friendship with Albert Darboven deepened. I frequently stayed with him in Hamburg drinking an amount of good champagne. I probably improved his polo more than anyone else and while doing so always enjoyed his humour. He responded during a polo tournament by giving a magnificent lunch for all the players and we both gave little speeches which showed our mutual appreciation. Amongst Albert's friends there were two non polo players of interesting backgrounds and with distinctive characters. One an industrialist, called Horst Herbert Alsen, who had been ADC to a top German general in the war, had a large stud for racehorses, a yacht and loved champagne and pretty girls. The other, Prince Bentheim, had been an outstanding soldier under Rommel, carrying out many skirmishes behind the British lines, but in his latter years had allowed drink to interfere with his life, yet when sober was most interesting and entertaining.

My second year with B squadron on the Hohne ranges gave me another good learning experience. The scope for mistakes, accidents and disapproval from senior officers was considerable but little went wrong and we received an excellent report. I much enjoyed controlling each troop during their battle runs and seeing so many targets being obliterated.

A real surprise came my way from our regimental doctor. He told me that I had to meet a lovely Danish girl because she was looking for a typical British cavalry gentleman like me! He had been friends of her family for a long time and she would soon come to stay with him and his wife. For a whole year I had a most rewarding relationship with her. Several times she came to Munster for long weekends and I had a wonderful stay with her and her family in Copenhagen.

CHAPTER 10

Military and Polo Duties in Germany

THE SECOND ANNUAL POLO TOURNAMENT took place in Berlin. This time I represented Hamburg, playing with Albert Darboven, Baron Hans Albrecht Maltzahn and Peter Player from the Scots Greys. Maltzahn was potentially a good player but such a consistent fouler that I nicknamed him the 'Bad Baron'. Once again I stayed with General Nelson in the greatest comfort and experienced many amusing moments. There were some good polo games but I had an extraordinary disagreement with Herr Reinke, the pre-war German Olympic player. In the first round Hamburg played against a much stronger team with four British players in it. Therefore I kept the ball, as much as possible, on the side of the ground and slowed down the game in various other ways. We lost by only two goals (5-3) and I felt happy but Reinke attacked me saying that I had disgraced German polo by playing such a negative game. In the final Düsseldorf supported by another 3 goal army player were up against our conquerors and were beaten by eleven goals because they used no tactic variation. Afterwards I enjoyed saying to Reinke 'Is that what you wanted for Hamburg?' and seeing that he clearly had no reply.

That autumn the whole regiment took part in the biggest exercise that I had ever been in. To start with we had to set up a long armoured car screen south of the river Weser to watch the progress of an advancing American Corps. To get there we had to make a very long approach march during which many breakdowns caused several delays. When we finally arrived there was limited time for my five troops to find their correct positions in the screen and I had to believe them when they reported that they had arrived. But one of them was in the wrong location and it was there that an American tank crossed the river unseen and unknown to me. Luckily they had repeated the wartime mistake made by the armoured division commanded by the famous General Patton, of running out of petrol. Hence once we retreated, as planned, there were no Americans behind our lines and my reputation was saved.

For me there was a very amusing ending to the exercise. One of the umpires was an old friend of mine and he broke the rules by telling me that the ceasefire would be called in one hour. A little later my Colonel ordered over the radio that I should send one troop out on a special mission. Realising that it could not reach its destination before the ceasefire I did not dispatch that troop. But then the Colonel would not leave me alone by continually requesting a situation report about that troop. I invented the false progress of the troop and added a few problems that could have been encountered. When the ceasefire was announced, exactly as expected, all my troops centralised and then started cooking an enormous meal. Suddenly the Colonel ordered me to move the whole squadron immediately to a regimental regrouping area. I replied that we were still waiting for the troop on the special mission to return and would be slightly delayed. This was accepted and all the soldiers finished their meal in peace before we set off as instructed.

1968 had a slightly sad beginning because my two years commanding B squadron were over and I had to hand over to George Norrie. The time had flown by and I felt well rewarded by the experience of leading B squadron through mostly good times. My reward was a report which recommended me for command of the regiment. Once again I took over HQ squadron with SSM McKay as my sergeant major.

Any regrets quickly disappeared when I received two invitations, one to Kenya in February and the other to Hawaii in March. I had been appointed captain of the army team to go to Kenya for three weeks for what would be my third visit there. Roland Knotley, Peter Player and Beachy Blackett had been selected to join me in what appeared to be rather an unbalanced

team because we all preferred playing as Nos. 3 and 4. We played in four
locations, went on an exciting safari, had two days by the sea and were
entertained lavishly by our hosts in each place. After some experimenting
we settled down with Peter at No.1, Roland unselfishly at No. 2, myself
at No. 3 and Beachy at No. 4. Initially we played badly but it was mainly
because of our No. 4, who could hit prodigious big backhands, but liked
to gallop to take them on his own, giving opponents easy opportunities to
claim fouls against him. All kinds of pleading, ordering and threatening
had no effect. Finally I had to adjust my play, so that every time he had
a backhand, I accelerated to ride off the opposing No.1 or whoever came
looking for the foul. This was a good solution and we had some good
victories. Then came the last weekend when we played Kenya's second
team on the Saturday and their national team on the Sunday. The former
was a thriller which we lost by one goal after six fast chukkas. But they
were so delighted with the game that they gave us some extra ponies for
the Sunday match which was against a 17 goal team. This gave us a pony
advantage and with a 6 goal handicap start we scored first before they
started to catch us up. My special tactic was extra effective as Beachy hit
many long backhands all the way to Peter at No.1. At the end our pony
power really helped and to the surprise of many people we won by two
goals. We tried to be suitably humble because of the handicap and pony
advantage but nevertheless we had to be highly elated and I hope this did
not show too much in my farewell and thank you speech.

Back at Munster I had less than two weeks to catch up with my work
and reorganise myself before setting off for my second visit to Hawaii with
Lord Waterford. This time the route was via New York and San Francisco.
The team was completed by Waterford's brother, (Lord) Patrick Beresford
and Edmund (Lord) Fermoy. So as the only non Lord I had to step
carefully. The polo in Kenya really stood to me and I played faster and
better than the previous year which made the trip extra enjoyable. I had a
little romance with a divorcee and once more found the entertainment to
be wonderful. We won both Sunday charity matches during which we had
to make short speeches at half time. I said that the three Lords were trained
to speak in the House of Lords so I would leave them to say the important

words. Later in the middle of a wave in the sea I was rebuked and corrected by dear cousin Waterford, who said 'I am the only proper Lord with a seat in the house. My brother's title is honorary and Fermoy is an Irish title.' Who would have thought that Waterford was regarded as English?

Once more at Munster my life as HQ squadron leader was rather mundane but before long the polo season started. Our regimental team was now without John Willis and Peter Dwerryhouse and we failed to regain the standard of '66. Although George Norrie and Peter Schofield did their best to play my tactics we were unable to reach the inter-regimental final in '68. Nevertheless the season gave me many rewarding moments. These included winning the tournaments in Hamburg and Berlin and staging the first ever all German match between Düsseldorf and Hamburg.

A problem that goes with coaching and playing at the same time is that sooner or later you have to play against people you have coached. This happened many times in my post army career but the first time was at Hamburg. Here I made up a team called the 44s because we had two from the 10th Hussars and two players from the 15/19 Hussars. Richard Coxwell-Rogers who had survived Catterick with me way back in 1950/51 was a 15/19H major who was thrilled to be in the final with me but not so pleased when I requested that we allow our opponents, four Düsseldorf Players, coached by me, to give us a close match. The plan was that whenever we were two goals ahead we should ease up to let them score once. Richard made the obvious point that our plan could go wrong. In fact it worked smoothly until the last chukka when a stupid foul allowed the Germans to draw level. Pandemonium erupted from my team with all of them saying, 'We told you it would go wrong'. Luckily from the ensuing throw in I was able to pounce on a loose ball and score the winner just before the final bell rang.

In Berlin I played in a team drawn out of a hat and for the first time in this famous stadium I combined with three other soldiers. My tactics were accepted one hundred percent, my backhands worked better than ever and we won all three matches comfortably. As usual the entertainment at night was excellent.

The match between Düsseldorf and Hamburg gave me much pleasure. The rivalry was intense but both teams played relatively good polo in a close game narrowly won by Hamburg. Afterwards there were some healthy celebrations.

The polo season ended for me with a new coaching experience. In the Captains and Subalterns Tournament, the Irish Hussars, having already beaten my regiment, invited me to coach their team by visiting them at Wolfenbottle on the East German border. I was taken there by a helicopter from their regimental flight. They had a team of four players of equal ability and I proceeded to make them do several exercises aimed at making all four participate equally. The results were stunning and they easily reached the final where they met the red hot favourites the 3rd Dragoon Guards. To everyone's surprise they took a big lead in the final and then hung on for a glorious victory. I was delighted to have seen live proof that planned practical tactics could enable a weaker team to beat a stronger one. This gave me great confidence for the future and added extra depth to my system of coaching.

Suddenly our military life received a rude shock when we heard the worst possible news. The following year in autumn 1969 the 10th Hussars, as such, would be no more because we were to be amalgamated with the 11th Hussars. This was planned to happen at Tidworth where the new regiment, to be called the Royal Hussars, would be stationed for two years. With all our proud traditions, our record in war, our service abroad and our successes in horse racing and polo it was a bitter blow. To make it worse many officers and soldiers could not be secure that they had a place in the new regiment. Although I had a recommendation to command it closed the door to any possibility that I could ever be a colonel. Alone in my age group in 10H I found that 11H had six officers of similar seniority to me and three of them were had much higher qualifications than I did. The only good news was that my father was to become the honorary colonel of the new regiment and indirectly this must have helped me to be given a place in it.

Winter '68/'69, under the cloud of the amalgamation announcement, went by without there being much to record. SSM McKay, my sergeant major, controlled the affairs of HQ squadron for me in his usual way which was known to me through many years of working together in various dimensions. As if wanting to be a rebel his special humour criticised almost everybody and everything yet all missions were always completed on time. I played for the regimental squash team several times as number four or fifth string. I was grateful to be kept away from the strong opponents and thereby always having a close match.

In March '69 I went on my third trip to Hawaii. In the team were Lord Waterford, his brother Lord Patrick plus Michael Hare, who was the nephew of Lord Cowdray and at the time was captain of the Cowdray high goal team. We won the two Sunday matches and this time I kept out of trouble with the entourage of ladies. Our host Fred Daly had organised an extra special social programme which included a visit to the memorial in the middle of Pearl Harbour. Ten days later I was in Berlin with the squash team and crossed the border (the wall) to visit the Russian memorial to their dead in the Second World War. It was the size of a polo field with many sculptures depicting a story and at the end a sea of plastic flowers. It was uncanny that in such a short time I had been present at two amazing memorials.

My final summer in Germany was short but memorable. Because we in 10H were going home we could not compete as a team in the polo leaving me free to help another regiment the 13th/18th Hussars. I spent several afternoons with them at Bad Lippspringe and thereby improved their team play and general skills considerably. As well as this Albert Darboven invited me to go to Hungary. He often visited that country on coffee business and had enormous respect for their prowess at coach driving at which they were the world champions. One day he was watching a competition and made the comment that the horses from one carriage would be sufficient to mount two players in a polo team. 'Filthy capitalist sport' was the reply given in a mixture of humour and what was the obvious expected communist answer. However it started a conversation that had continued for the rest of that day and well in to the night in which Albert told them about the training he and others had received from me.

He then suggested that I should be hosted in Hungary to train people in order that there could be a polo exhibition. Apparently the carriage horses all originally came from the big herds which were born and lived on the extensive Hungarian plains called the Pusta. There they were looked after by horse shepherds known as gauchos. These men would each have at least one special horse which they used to control the herd that they were in charge of and actually slept with. A sheepskin saddle had the secondary use as pillow and when there was an emergency could be rapidly put on the special horse without girths. The halter already on the horse converted into a bridle after one quick adjustment and the herd could then be moved under control to safety. Hence these men were incredibly good riders and they and their horses had the potential to be trained quickly to play polo and the plan was to investigate how this could be arranged.

First a reconnaissance trip took place in which Albert and I went to Budapest to meet a committee of people who would be involved in the organisation. The difficult part was going through immigration because I had entered my employment as an Irish Farmer even though I had a British passport. It seemed like hours while a communist official examined my documents and looked at me without ever saying a word. We stayed in a smart hotel but the passages were full of prostitutes. After many discussions it was agreed that the exhibition would take place at an international horse show at Hortobágy, a place near the Czechoslovakian border, in early July. I was invited to go there for two weeks beforehand to train the gauchos and their horses to play polo.

I returned to Munster to ask permission which was granted without difficulty. Then a few weeks later I set off on this adventure by myself because Albert, the bad baron and two other Germans were to join me for the exhibition two weeks later. I flew via Vienna to Budapest where I was met and taken to a train for the long journey to Hortobágy. When I arrived there I stayed in a guest house and slept in a large Queen Anne four-poster bed. Then I heard the bad news in that the gauchos were all in prison and not available to be trained with their horses. They had become drunk and been involved in some trouble with girls. In their place I was given eight large horses and seven teenage boys, the eldest of whom was 18, and was

149

called Bachi. So I managed to organise a daily routine in which the morning was devoted to schooling the horses as a group ridden by myself and the seven lads with Bachi translating my German into Hungarian. Then in the afternoon I attempted to introduce the horses to the polo mallet and ball by riding one after another. In the second week I tried to teach the lads how to hit the ball but only made any significant progress with Bachi.

The weekend for the horse show arrived and with it enormous crowds in hundreds of buses. The Germans came in their Mercedes and we decided to play three aside with Albert, Bachi and myself against the bad baron with the two other Germans. The first day was a great success as we attempted to negotiate a water jump and a bank while trying to score goals. The Hungarian commentator screamed the name of Bachi who was so excited that he missed the ball at every attempt coming faster and faster in alternative directions. We played two chukkas with a short interval in between and received a tremendous ovation from a crowd of thirty thousand people. The second day was less successful because the horses were not so cooperative and it was difficult to get near the ball on them. It was as if they were telling us 'you caught us the first day but not the second, thank you'. However we completed the two chukkas and received quite a good reception if not the ovation of the day before. We left the stadium a little ashamed but were able to laugh at the ridiculousness of the situation. When I returned to Germany I had a great feeling of satisfaction that the exhibition had taken place, despite the problems, and all those involved had been trained by me at some stage.

During my last days in Munster my main work involved talking to all the soldiers in my squadron about their future in the army when amalgamation happened in England. We also had to prepare for the handover of the barracks, vehicles and equipment. My only polo connection was some final training for the 13th/18th Hussars whose team was preparing for the Captains and Subalterns Tournament. One afternoon at the officers' mess I had a surprise visit from Albert Darboven, Horst Herbert Alsen and Prince Bentheim. With pride I showed them the gold plate, the silver and all the pictures. When we came to the painting which showed the capture of General Von Toma by a 10th Hussar officer in the African desert I could not resist saying 'Look we captured one of your top Generals'. The Prince replied 'What only one, I captured five British Generals at the same time'. I thought he was joking but then recalled the story about General Combs and four other generals losing their way in a sandstorm and being taken prisoner by a daring German patrol that was working behind the Allied lines. Suddenly it was clear why the Prince was a famous soldier, the respect of the Hamburg polo players was finally explained and I was struck by the coincidence that he had visited our officers' mess.

My finale with German polo was to take a team to play in the Dublin Horse Show Tournament in August. The team consisted of Albert Darboven and Bad Baron Maltzahn from Hamburg and Stefan Glassmacher from Düsseldorf. We stayed together in the Gresham Hotel and had a smart chauffeur driven car to take us round Dublin during a hectic week. We went to the horse show everyday, to the races twice and played in three polo matches. Also we attended two hunt balls at night time. The polo was fun but a bit disappointing because our team committed too many fouls and we failed to win a match. But by chance there was a visitor, from Argentina, who came to watch the polo and was called Gordon Whitney. He was a business man who played polo, as a hobby, in Argentina and he volunteered to substitute, when a member of another team was injured. After playing, Gordon was in great form, drinking in the club bar, with all the club members, and suddenly he issued an invitation to anyone, who might visit Buenos Aires in the future. Knowing that my ambition was to go to Argentina, I took his card, warning him that I would probably accept his offer one day. Little did I know how useful this would be and what a big effect it would have on my life one year later. The rest of the week was hilarious and I appreciated living in the lap of luxury in the hotel.

After the Dublin Horse Show I spent a short time in Waterford checking that my old ponies were safely put into retirement. Then I went to England for the rest of my leave to look for new ponies for the following year 1970. Edmund, Lord Fermoy, had asked me to play in the Cirencester Autumn Tournament in his team and I combined doing this with trying a group of Jack William's ponies. The result was better than expected because although we did not win the tournament I bought four ponies and received an invitation to play for the Kirtlington medium goal team in 1970.

Then came the drama of meeting the new regiment, the Royal Hussars. We first assembled in Perham Down, a camp close to Tidworth. The days of armoured cars were over and we were to be equipped with the latest British battle tank. I was commanding what was now called the Administration squadron and the main priority was the preparation for the amalgamation parade after which we were to be stationed in Tidworth yet again. The next few weeks were memorable as we tried to settle down as a new formation and I found myself back on the drill square similar to when I had first joined the army twenty years before. This time I was giving many of the orders from a conspicuous position, out on my own, in front of the squadron, well aware that a mistake by me could cause chaos.

I received good news from Germany in that the 13th /18th Hussars had won the Captains and Subalterns polo as a direct result of my coaching. But in England the merging of two regiments, both with great tradition and character, could not happen without problems. Funnily enough the mixing of uniforms was appreciated by 10H members more than 11H. We put on their cherry trousers and cap with pride but they were not happy to wear our cap badge of three feathers. In the officers' mess I was the only bachelor major and my situation alternated between feeling old and smelly and being useful as a mediator between the young officers who clashed over traditions. Differences of custom, behaviour, discipline and attitudes had to be ironed out through patient discussion.

The dress rehearsal and the amalgamation parade itself were, for me, both daunting and exhilarating. Exposed where a mistake would be seen by all spectators I marched, with sword drawn, ahead of my squadron to give the salute to my father, recently knighted (Sir David Dawnay) in slow and quick time. After the parade in the new Tidworth officers' mess we had a big rich lunch. I watched my father tuck into it unaware that it was probably another notch in the destruction of his health which was soon to fail completely.

The stables of the new regiment were full of hunters including two bred by my father at Ascot. One was the daughter of Flying Rosette, who had given me that wonderful victory at Sandown. We had taken a regimental subscription with Vale of the White Horse hunt in Gloucestershire and I had some enjoyable hunts with them. In December I returned to Germany for a weekend in Hamburg with Albert Darboven. As usual champagne flowed as we rushed from place to place. On a impulse we telephoned Ireland to make contact and received the terrible news that my father had had a stroke. He had only been home for one month, after retiring from Ascot, at the end of twelve years of dedicated work. He had hoped for several uninterrupted seasons of fox-hunting and now clearly he would never ride again. He had also done so much to preserve and maintain our beautiful home, but had never lived in it properly. Now he would be there as an invalid.

Travelling by train and boat I visited Ireland, just before Christmas, to find a sad household. My sister Rachel was helping to rejuvenate my poor father, who was still recovering in bed and looking ghastly. Making things worse, he was worrying over a customs bill for a quantity of alcoholic drink, which he had brought from England, having collected it at Ascot, after some of the obliged entertaining he gave there. I jumped at the opportunity to return to England, by offering to take the drink back there in order to clear up the matter with customs, in the port of Fishguard. Then two days later I duly caught the boat to Fishguard, before continuing to Gloucestershire to accept an invitation, previously received, for Christmas in a private house of a Mrs Courage. She had a bevy of beautiful daughters and one of them, together with her female friend, provided wonderful company, both while I was in the hunting field, with one of my two horses, and during entertaining evenings. Despite feeling guilty I had a glorious holiday and I had succeeded in the cancellation of that large customs bill.

Before leaving Germany I had met a Pakistan Brigadier, called Gul Mawas Khan, who had extended to me an invitation, in January 1970, to play in his team in the Pakistan Polo Open in Lahore. Once again I obtained extra leave to be a representative of my regiment abroad in a sporting event. By coincidence a British team was also there, captained by Ronald Ferguson and including the two Hipwood brothers and Peter Gifford. Besides playing in the Open they were to play in a series of international matches with Pakistan. I stayed in a place, which I can only describe as being both primitive and luxurious. My bath water was brought into my bedroom and poured into a small bath on the floor. Yet servants were at my beck and call at any time and my clothes were beautifully looked after.

In our polo team Gul and I were joined by Heskey Baig and his brother. Heskey who had been my inspiration in Italy was still the same resilient character. He insisted in playing in his favourite No. 1 position, making me fill the responsibilities of the pivot at No.3. We won only one of the three matches but I gained much from the experience. Then I found myself in the difficult situation of umpiring the international matches. My fellow umpire and the referee were a touch biased towards the Pakistanis and I was in a minority for many of the decisions, although I was genuinely trying to be honest. Naturally Ron and the boys blamed me!

One night I found myself at the end of my bed with my hands above my head and hearing a loud grinding noise. The next day I was told there had been an earthquake in the mountains. Before leaving Pakistan I played polo in a low goal tournament, with three very novice players, against four up and coming young players. On paper we had no chance, but I told my team that I would acutely angle backhands to the sideline, and that we would never play down the middle of the field. These tactics were even more successful than expected, as our opponents were totally confused and we easily won. Sadly I had to leave before the next match but it had given me a good finish to my trip. In spring 1970 I made a short return to racing at a Larkhill point-to-point on the daughter of Flying Rosette. I rode overweight and considering that finished fairly close to the first three. It was hard to believe that I was racing again and I relived much of the old excitement and pleasure. Reluctantly I allowed a brother officer, who was lighter and quite a successful young jockey, to ride her in her next two races and then sold her before the polo season started.

The 1970 polo season gave me the opportunity to play in many tournaments all over England. Sometimes I played in two places on one day. I was given a supervisory appointment over Tidworth polo and with a good committee revamped the tournament organisation. Already committed to 14 goal polo with Kirtlington I was also coaxed into joining an 8 goal team from Tidworth, which we called the Tidworth Hussars. The Kirtlington team started the season by playing an exhibition against a team that included Princes Philip and Charles with my cousins Lord Waterford and his brother Lord Patrick Beresford. To everyone's surprise we won and this caused us to became excited about our prospects in proper tournaments. But first I went with the Tidworth Hussars to Cirencester where we won the 8 goal Gerald Balding Championship Cup, by defeating my Kirtlington mates in the final after an extra chukka. This made us the envy of many teams, because Gerald Balding was the only British 10 goal player, since the end of the First World War. Next at Tidworth, in the new Royal Hussars team, we won the inter-regimental cup beating the Queen's Own Hussars, with more than a little luck. When a goal behind, I saved in the goal mouth with what must have been a foul, but the whistle did not blow and we went on to score twice and win. It was a proud moment when I received the trophy from the Army supremo General Mogg.

Now came the Windsor tournament to which I took the Royal Hussars team in the 8 goal Archie David besides being with the Kirtlington team in the 14 goal Royal Windsor Cup. But in the first round of the 8 goal I mistimed a ride off and had a bad fall which gave me concussion. I ended up in the house of General Pert, the polo manager. In a haze I telephoned Germany and arranged for Antonio Herrera, a Mexican 6 goal player, whom I had met with Albert Darboven, to take my place on my ponies in the Kirtlington team. He played brilliantly, my ponies did ballet-type stops and turns, never seen before and they won the whole tournament. After this Antonio became established as a top professional player worldwide.

Later at Windsor the big event of the Centenary Polo Match took place. This celebrated the first game, ever played in England, which happened to be between the 9th Lancers and 10th Hussars a hundred years previously. Like them we played with eight in each team, made up by four pre-war veterans and four of our current officers. Prince Philip and Earl Mountbatten, dressed in tails and top hats were the umpires. The polo was chaotic with so many players and General Prior Palmer, whom I had helped to practice at Tidworth, led the 9th Lancers to victory in revenge for our win a century beforehand. After this epic I played in a 14 goal Cup with Paul Withers against Prince Philip's team. We were winning until I knocked down the Prince, who left in an ambulance saying 'Dawnay was in my way' and an ex-American international substitute took his place, to steal the game from us, by scoring three quick goals.

The annual big Tidworth tournament took place at the beginning of July. With parties organised for every night it was a successful week. My team the Tidworth Hussars won the principal event, the 9th Lancer Cup. The following week we went to Cowdray to continue at 8 goal level in the Holden White Cup, while my Kirtlington team played in the 14 goal Harrison Cup without success. However the Tidworth Hussars had a busy time losing the first round by a half goal, having led many times throughout the match, but then had a wonderful run of wins to reach the final of the Ruins Cup, in the consolation event. There we met Prince Charles' team and won the Cup after a hard fought battle, which included an amusing incident. In the third chukka I rode Dora, a little mare, which I had recently bought from Jack Williams. After trying to score a goal and missing the ball, I saw the Prince in possession, going at full gallop down the sideline. I pursued him by heading down the middle of the field. Thereby I cut a big corner and easily arrived in time to cut off the Prince before he shot at goal at the far end. After this the chukka ended and when I returned to the pony lines I saw Jack running from the grandstand shouting 'Hugh, you bastard, I sold you that pony too cheap'. Clearly he had not realised that I had cut such a big corner and Dora, to him, had looked like a Ferrari. The victory was extra sweet because I had brought a glorious blonde lady to watch us. Her name now escapes me, but when I went on leave to Ireland, taking the lovely blonde with me, I became very close to being madly in love. My father had made a good recovery from his stroke and we had a happy week.

CHAPTER 11

My Fifth Lottery –
I Meet my Future Spouse

PRINCESS ALEXANDRA WAS GOING TO open the British Exhibition in Buenos Aires in November 1970 and was taking an army band with her in a RAF plane. A group of generals were drinking coffee together, when one joked by saying 'Is there any difference between a piccolo player and a polo player?' Another jested 'There is absolutely no difference' and a third exclaimed 'Well now we have the solution for how to send the first ever army polo team to Argentina'. Quickly a call was made to Buenos Aires, a ten-day programme was agreed, the team was chosen and then included as part of the band to travel on the plane! Soon after returning to Tidworth I heard the exciting announcement that an army team would go to Argentina and I had, once more, been selected to be in it. Little did I know how this trip would change my whole life dramatically. Yet when the time came to go, although thrilled about the trip, I was saddened that my love for the blonde was definitely not reciprocated by her.

From the moment we landed in Argentina we were entertained with great hospitality and every day was packed with action. We practised on the ponies provided for us, we were taken to see the Argentine Open polo, the best tournament in the world, and every evening there was some entertainment with young lovely ladies in attendance. But I paid little attention to the female company because I was still thinking about my blonde in England.

Not surprisingly we lost the matches against the Argentine Army, but I felt that we played quite well and we much enjoyed some good polo. Before the last match there was a lunch, attended by a new group of young ladies, organised at the last moment by a General in the Argentine Army, who told his daughter to bring her friends, by force if necessary. One of them made me forget my blonde with a very unexpected action. We had each received some gifts including a polo whip and to my amazement Maria Ines Cermesoni picked up one of the whips, reached across the lunch table, and hit me on the head. We still discuss why she did it and reasons have included 'You only looked at the blonde next to you—you looked so bored and needed waking up—I never saw a bald man before'. Whatever the reason the result was that we were married one year later. The generals in England and Argentina had unwittingly collaborated to bring us together and alter our lives completely.

I had already arranged to stay an extra week by calling Gordon Whitney, whom I had met in Dublin fifteen months beforehand. With Gordon's help I met Maria Ines on every day. One evening we had dinner with the Bad Baron Maltzahn and I have remembered three things that happened. First on the table in the restaurant the Bad Baron built a house with knives and forks, second he boasted about bringing dry cleaning business to Argentina and beef to Germany while playing polo and thirdly he told me to marry Maria Ines because we were so similar. He explained that he and his wife Inge were both sneaky and that made their marriage a success!

I flew back to England in a RAF plane that had been to the South Pole. We stayed one night in Recife in Brazil and also touched down on an island in the Atlantic to refuel. When I arrived in England I had forgotten the blonde and only had thoughts for Maria Ines, whom I felt sure would become a big part of my future.

I enjoyed Christmas at home in Ireland enormously because of Maria Ines and seeing that my father's health and morale had improved so much. Also I had decided to leave the army in autumn 1971 and the farm was handed over to me with a consultant and manager in place. Through an amazing coincidence the neighbouring farm, Powersknock, of one hundred and eighty acres came on the market. An auctioneer from

Carlow, a distance away, had been given the sale, because the owner did not want his many jealous relations to know. He telephoned my Mother who informed me, which gave me the opportunity to make the best purchase of my life. Hence the farm land was increased to five hundred acres and we made a plan to build the milk herd from thirty to over one hundred. I started to have a feeling of destiny, linked to this wonderful estate, now handed over to me, with the possibilities of a productive farm, on which I could create a polo establishment.

What an incredible year 1970 had been for me. Looking back now it is hard to believe that so many wonderful things had happened for me, in that one year: Pakistan, a brilliant summer in England, followed by Argentina and winning my 5th lottery in that I met my amazing future spouse. I returned to Tidworth to start 1971 and started to encounter some short term memory problems although my long term memory remained normal. It was clearly the result of my bad fall at Windsor the previous year. If I was told to attend an event tomorrow I would forget and fail to go. But I could not forget a wonderful invitation from Albert Darboven to go to Salvador and Costa Rica in his polo team, which also included Simon and Claire Tomlinson, in February. In the back of my mind, without knowing how, I hoped to be able to continue on to Argentina to see Maria Ines. Albert's wife, Ines, came from Salvador and hence while Albert stayed with her family the Tomlinsons and I were put in a smart hotel. We were royally entertained but my principal memory is of water skiing on an enormous lake in beautiful weather. This was enormous fun but our legs stiffened up making it difficult to play well in the polo match on the following day.

Several times I tried to call Maria Ines in Argentina and only when about to give up I suddenly found myself talking to her. She agreed to meet me in Buenos Aires and to arrange a bed for me for a few days. For only a hundred dollars I changed my air ticket to take me to Buenos Aires and on to London. We flew on to Costa Rica where for the first time I met the trickery of polo hosts over the allocation of ponies. Very simply we had two matches against A and B teams and when playing one team we could play the ponies of the other. What could be fairer? we thought but we ended up on horrible ponies each time and were given all kind of excuses why the good ones were not available. Nevertheless it was a useful experience and we were very well entertained in the evenings.

Full of excitement I flew to Argentina. I will always remember my arrival at Ezeiza, the international airport outside Buenos Aires. I was overwhelmed by seeing and feeling the emotion expressed by the Latins as they arrived home. First the thunderous applause as we touched down safely, then the pure joy as they saw relatives waving followed by scenes of dramatic embraces with tears and laughter flowing. Then my own impossible dream came true when Maria Ines was there to meet me. This was followed by three glorious days during which my visit was so successful that I proposed before leaving and when this was accepted I arranged for Maria Ines to come to Tidworth for June and July that summer. My initial plan was not to announce our engagement until a month after MI's arrival in Europe in the belief that everyone would love her and immediately accept her. In the end I got cold feet and decided to make the situation a *fait accompli* by publishing it in the paper a week before she arrived.

For the 1971 polo season I had agreed to play medium goal for a Cirencester team which was organised by Jack Williams and included a 5 goal Argentine called Gaston Courreges. He did not arrive until May and during April I played three of the ponies allotted to him. This meant that in April every week I played twice at Cirencester besides three times at Tidworth and sometimes a sixth day at another club. Piers Bengough had taken over as Colonel commanding Royal Hussars and seemed to accept that in my last year in the Army I could enjoy this freedom as long as I attended to Administration Squadron business in the mornings.

I became very worried about the plans for MI's visit because there was a post strike in Argentina and in her mother's flat, where she was staying at that time, there was no telephone. Then one morning while having a rushed breakfast after an early ride I casually read a page of a newspaper, which was lying open next to me. This included my horoscope which said 'today you will be contacted by someone you love whom you thought was out of reach'. I threw the paper on the floor in disgust and disbelief and hurried to the barracks to start work. I spent most of the morning

Berlin Polo Tournament 1966 (Hugh Dawnay far right)

*Hugh Dawnay at Maifeld Olympic Stadium, where his
father had played in the Olympic Games in 1936*

Hawaii 1967 (RIGHT–LEFT): *Ronald Ferguson, Ben Jellett,
Hugh Dawnay and the Marquis of Waterford*

Amalgamation Parade, Tidworth 1969,
David Dawnay next to Princess Alice, Hugh Dawnay in front, sword up

Amalgamation Parade, Tidworth 1969

After winning the 9th Lancer Cup at Tidworth 1970

Salvador and Costa Rica tour 1971 (LEFT–RIGHT): *Mark Tomlinson,
Hugh Dawnay, Claire Tomlinson and Albert Darboven*

Hugh and Maria-Ines Dawnay's wedding day, 18 November 1971

Salvador and Costa Rica tour 1971

Michael Butler with Hugh Dawnay, Phoenix Park 1973

(LEFT–RIGHT) *Paul Ronan, Sebastian Dawnay, David Dawnay and Denise Power playing polo at Whitfield Court.*

Whitfield Court Polo School

Cyprus Polo Association

Whitfield Court Polo Club Tournament in August

Rotary Club Strauss Ball

in the vehicle park and only went to my office just before lunch. There I found a small parcel on my desk and inside it a present and a letter from MI! Later events revealed that her sister Marcela, who unknown to me was on an European tour, had taken a train from Andover to London and a bus to Tidworth in order to leave this parcel for me. Ever since I have taken my horoscope more seriously.

After MI's arrival in England had been planned I was offered, on the same day, an opportunity to play in a high goal match for the first time ever. The clash was infuriating but I was determined not to miss the chance and arranged for a friend to meet her at Heathrow. Of course this was heavily criticised by some but she at least appeared to understand. The match was at Windsor and she duly arrived there in the middle of the match after which I found her surrounded by my cousins Lord Waterford and Lord Patrick Beresford who were inquisitive to see what she was like. The first two nights we spent with Ronald and Susie Ferguson at Dummer before moving to Tidworth. Everyone, including Ronald's mother were enchanted and an encouraging telephone call was made to my parents in Ireland.

The next few months provided a real test for our future marriage. My brother officers, who were married, behaved magnificently by having MI to stay, one after the other. This meant she had to change houses every week and once she swore that she would never move again. This turned out to be the first of many extreme threats, which she would use against me without really meaning them but it took me a long time to learn the significance of them.

I continued to play much polo and had mixed fortunes. In my last inter-regimental we failed to reach the final which was very sad. At Cirencester in the coveted County Cup of 14 goals we had two good victories which took us to the semi-finals. There we lost with only ten seconds left after Gaston Courreges had done a brilliant run but then missed an easy tap in which would have secured a place in the final. But I was enjoying my polo and learning much from the experience. At Tidworth MI agreed to be timekeeper for one match and amused everyone immensely when her comments were added and mixed with those of the commentator. She must have been enjoying her stay because she extended her visit to a third month during which I took her to Ireland to meet my parents. They were enchanted by her besides being relieved that one of their children was to be married at last. She clearly appreciated my father's sense of humour and made herself completely at home at Whitfield Court. Finally it was time for Maria Ines to return to Argentina and when she left our wedding was confirmed and most of the arrangements made for November. The ceremony was to be in Buenos Aires but we would also celebrate with a party in Ireland at Whitfield in December and one at the Cavalry Club in London during January. After MI departed I only had a month left in the Army.

Suddenly twenty one years of soldiering was over and it was time for me to leave the Army. I had had wonderful experiences with the 10th Hussars and an enjoyable final two years with the Royal Hussars. But because the amalgamation had clearly blocked any access to promotion, I decided to concentrate on the possibilities at Whitfield Court in Ireland. Having bought the extra land, there was great scope to improve the farm and I was determined to develop my polo instructing and coaching to a much higher level. Deep down inside me there continued to be a thrilling joyful anticipation, that coaching would give me a second career, guiding me to wonderful opportunities, which would involve leadership on my part, required to remove the scales of blindness from the Polo Establishment in Britain. Sadly on the same day that I drove out of Tidworth en route for Ireland my father had his second stroke and never again recovered consciousness. I arrived home just before he died on 3 October 1971 and immediately set about organising the funeral. We decided to have a service in Waterford Cathedral and the burial at the local Kilmeaden Church. People came from all over the British Isles and included a large group from the North Irish Horse, who came from Ulster. He deservedly received some wonderful obituaries. He had had a very successful life in sport, in the war, as a post-war General and at Ascot racecourse. He left me a magnificent home at Whitfield Court and had given me a valuable background, although I knew he had overprotected me in too many dimensions, leaving somewhat unprepared for life outside the military surroundings.

One of the best obituaries mentioned was the winning of the Silver Medal at the Olympic Games in 1936, at Berlin, where he captained the British Army polo team. An account of this was written at the time, and I now feel that I should share that with my readers.

At the games Argentina won the Gold Medal, Britain the Silver Medal, and Mexico the Bronze Medal. The British team were four army officers, who had played more against each other than in a team together. The British team were, Captain Frizz Fowler (5), Major Luny Hinde (5), Captain David Dawnay (7) Team Captain, and Captain Humphrey Guinness (9).

Argentina arrived at the Games with 40 ponies and a large group of assistants for every dimension. The British had half that number, which belonged to the selected players, and had been regularly playing at home or in India with a rest. The handicaps of their two teams were similar, but the superiority and freshness of the Argentine ponies was overwhelming. At least three of the Argentine players went on to become 10 goals, during the period of the Second World War, when their polo seasons continued uninterrupted.

The Olympic Polo Medal Ceremony produced some surprises. Before receiving the valued Medals, all twelve players from Argentina, Britain and Mexico had a crown of laurels placed on their heads. Then it was thought that Hitler had arrived with an exotic award for the Argentine team Captain. This was a tiny sprig from an oak tree. That very same oak tree can today be found in Buenos Aires, at the palace of polo, the Palermo Stadium, where the historical Argentine Open is played every year. Outside and fairly close to the Chandon Bar, the flat bottomed oak tree has for years been incredibly useful, as a meeting place for Argentines and visitors from all over the world. Apparently on the way home by boat, to Buenos Aires, the emotional Olympic victors kept the strip alive by applying to it the water for their customary maté drink.

Descriptions of the British Army Players:
Frizz Fowler was an officer in the Royal Horse Artillery, who had strong connections with Ireland, where he retired to after the Second World War, and married the war widow of the famous British polo player Chicken Walford (9). Frizz was the father of the current leading lady

Irish racehorse trainer, Jessica Harrington. He was a very distinguished horseman, and three-day event rider.

Luny Hinde was a pre-war cavalry officer in the 15/19 Hussars. He finished the Second World War as a successful British General. His nickname of Luny was earned by the wild behaviour of his fun-loving wife, who regularly swung off chandeliers at dances.

David Dawnay was a pre-war Cavalry Officer, in the 10th Royal Hussars (PWO) who were famous for playing the first ever polo match in Britain in 1869. David added to this regimental fame and tradition by being in the 10th Hussars team, which won the Indian Inter-regimental Tournament in 1937, a back-to-back feat never achieved before or since, and he played in the Olympics in between these two victories. He became a General soon after the Second World War, and was knighted after completing twelve years in charge of the Royal Ascot Racecourse. His son Hugh and second grandson Sebastian have both played international polo and are proud to bear the name of the only surviving family that represented Britain in the last polo Olympics.

Humphrey Guinness was another pre-war cavalry officer in the Royal Scots Greys, who rode these magnificent grey chargers in famous cavalry charges. Humphrey was the outstanding British Army player for several years, before the war. He was a Colonel after having a distinguished war. He returned to polo for a few years after the war, to give great encouragement to many of the new British players. These four British soldiers and Olympic polo players, who won a silver medal at Berlin, were thrilled to have played for their country to earn a Silver Medal. They never mentioned the score in the final, and the popular answer to that question is, 'Do not talk about the score, only the glorious and treasured Silver Medal'.

The most unforgettable match at those Olympics was played between the Hungarians and the Germans. In this game the Hungarians were initially very quick, on their own breed of fast ponies, scoring all the early goals, while leaving the Germans a distance behind them. Then the success began to make the Hungarians overexcited, with the result that the competition for the ball was between themselves, causing more than a few collisions. In the existing chaos, the Germans on their slow big ponies started to catch up on the Hungarian lead. However, the Hungarians were literally saved by the bell.

Throughout the 1936 Olympics the Germans Organisers imposed very strict disciplinary measures on the competitors and spectators. All were rigorously searched when entering the stadiums, because they had been forbidden to carry walking sticks or umbrellas. On a day when rain was expected, David Dawnay refused to accept the risk of himself or his polo equipment being soaked. Hence he placed the umbrella inside one of his trouser legs and was seen by a group of anxious British supporters, moving in a manner that might have been the goose step or a pony badly lame behind. The result was mad rumours circling the British contingent, one suggesting that he had joined the enemy, and another that he was badly injured. Nothing happened about it, to everyone's relief.

There was a lot of speculation about the non appearance of the United States Polo Team at the Olympics. They were in England then, preparing for the Westchester Cup against England, the speculation was rife, but answers were not given, and life went on.

I was immensely proud of my father, I missed him very much, I was facing in to a new life, I was engaged to a woman I loved, I then faced a big dilemma. Six weeks later I was due to be married and should I go ahead or postpone it. The invitations had gone out for the three parties, already mentioned, and Buenos Aires was so far away that it was extra difficult to change plans. Rightly or wrongly, I decided to go ahead, although my mother was not prepared to travel, but my sister Rachel agreed to come. Hence in mid-October I set off for Buenos Aires. After a few days there with Maria Ines and her mother, the two of us went together by train and bus to Salta, a province in the North West of Argentina. MI's father, Danton, lived there as a doctor and MI's relations, all of Italian descent, came from there. As the bus arrived in Salta my tummy started reacting to the food, eaten earlier, and I had to rush past my future father-in-law to find a bathroom. Afterwards he gave me some very effective pills and I soon learnt that he had a wonderful sense of humour besides being a brilliant doctor.

In the following days I met many cousins, relations and friends and much appreciated the love and affection displayed between them all. I discovered that MI was a comedienne as she made everybody laugh all the time, although I could not understand what she was saying to them. It appeared to me that Salta time operated three hours behind, because it seemed that we had lunch at 4 p.m., tea at 8 p.m. and dinner at 11 p.m. even though they were planned for 1, 5 and 8 p.m. We returned to Buenos Aires to see two weekends of spectacular Argentine Open polo. In between I accepted an invitation from Eduardo Moore to go to his home in Carlos Casares, where he gave me ponies to play and try. We had much fun and I bought six ponies and arranged for them to be shipped to Ireland three months later. The big day, 18 November, the wedding day was approaching fast. A few days before Rachel had arrived and gone to stay with Gordon Whitney, who had agreed to be my best man as, through a misunderstanding, Albert Darboven had changed his plans at the last moment. Danton arrived on the 16th to a mixed reception because he had been separated for several years from MI's mother. On the 17th we went to the brief civil ceremony and a big car plan was made for the 18th.

Three cars appeared on the wedding day. One for MI and Danton her father, one for her sister Marcela and Great Aunt Emma and the third for her mother Mercedes and me. My drive to the church was filled with drama, because the traffic lights were all red and Mercedes kept worrying that we would be late. Then she let out a scream when the driver took a wrong turn that caused us to begin again the one way system, so that we had to repeat all the same lights, which once more were all red. However we still arrived before the bride and all the worrying had been unnecessary. When MI entered the church the organ played 'Land of hope and glory' much to my surprise and delight, because I had loved that tune for a long time. My morale was also helped by seeing in the Church, from the British polo fraternity, Julian Hipwood, Paul Withers and Ronnie Driver. At the reception I met many more relations and friends of MI's family and received an amount of advice about married life. Then came the dramatic drive to the airport hotel, where we were to stay for a night, before our flight to our honeymoon in Barbados. At halfway the car faltered with engine trouble and then the driver lost the way. I could not believe what was happening as the expected one hour drive became more than three hours.

In Barbados our room was a little cottage in the hotel garden and it was lovely, except that MI was distracted by the harmless lizards which frequently ran across the ceiling. We sunbathed and swum every day and during the honeymoon looked at much of the Island. We then came home to Ireland through New York, where we went to the top of the Empire State Building. The weather was incredibly cold and MI complained that she had lost her nose.

In December 1971 we took up residence in Rose Cottage, Annestown, on the Waterford coast. It felt very comfortable, especially as new carpets had been laid and my sister Rachel had helped with the decorations. However there was a problem of damp in the walls, caused by the proximity of the sea. Every day I went to Whitfield to ride horses and watch the progress on the farm. On Tuesdays and Saturdays I hunted with the Waterford hounds. It was wonderful to be able to hunt regularly in Ireland for the first time in my life. I met the new American Master, Harry Meckling, who had been recruited by Robin Hunt, to replace my Dad, and was renting Robin's second house for the winter. I watched Harry have a difficult time, trying to be Field Master, while learning how to survive crossing our countryside on horseback. Needless to say the results were chaotic, especially when he was frequently upside down in a ditch, on the far side of a bank, with his horse running loose after the hounds, taking time to be caught.

My mother came once a week to have dinner with us at Rose Cottage, behaving a little like royalty, but showing much appreciation of MI's cooking. Just before Christmas our second wedding party took place at Whitfield. Many of our local friends came to inspect MI and the house seemed to enjoy being filled with so many people. Then in January '72 I took up the Army's offer of a retirement course. I picked the subject of business and went to London for six weeks, back to school. MI came with me and we rented a flat near the Thames. While there we had our third wedding party at the Cavalry Club, and most of my army friends came. MI started being sick in the mornings and a doctor duly pronounced that she was expecting a baby. This was earlier than we had planned and it rather damped our social programme for the rest of our time in London. However I completed my course and felt that I had learnt some useful information, although not as much as I had hoped.

I returned to Ireland and noticed that a neighbour in Annestown had lost a big amount of weight. He proudly told me about his success with the Canadian Airforce exercises and told me where I could buy the booklet. I quickly purchased it and started the exercises, which I continued doing for thirty years. I found them to be a wonderful way to stay healthy and fit, while keeping thin. The 1972 polo season provided me with much exciting action and an amount of travelling. I had been telling people that I had a coaching background and wished to extend it with further experience. Many friends and acquaintances commented that it was a good idea but not one person offered me any work. However my visit to the Phoenix Park, the previous summer, had been fortuitous, because a wild Dublin character, John Mulhern, offered me an arrangement, whereby I could coach him and play in his team, if he kept two ponies for me in Dublin, besides allowing MI and myself to stay with him, whenever we wanted. Michael Hannah joined the team and a fourth player had to be invited for every match and tournament, as suited the conditions. The driving at weekends was boring and difficult for MI, but we much enjoyed the humour, jokes and stories told by John Mulhern. Being a player coach is harder than doing the job on its own as a non player. It is difficult to divide, both praise and blame, between oneself and the other three team members. However my team mates started to show appreciation about my example on the field and to obey much of teaching, including tactics. We then surprised everyone by winning the 8 goal Derby Tournament in June, which delighted them and gave me enormous pleasure plus a welcome boost to my coaching ambitions.

I accepted an invitation to return to Germany to judge the polo pony class and umpire the final of the inter-regimental. MI and I drove out via Luxembourg, where we stayed a night and enjoyed the sightseeing. In Germany we stayed in Paderborn with Richard and Martha Coxwell-Rogers. He was commanding the 15th/19th Hussars and I felt strange, as a civilian, in the army polo ambience, although they were charming. Next

Jack Williams invited me to England to play in a medium goal team at Windsor. The team included an exciting Argentine called Tayo Astrada, but we had to play without practising together and no coaching, except negative abuse on the field, and did not win a match. However I received a one-off invite to play in Tidworth, which resulted in an invitation to play for Dougie Brown, in a good low goal team, including the Indian Kishen Singh, at Cowdray in July. In fact I had only just returned to Ireland, when I received a summons back to England, for the Cowdray medium goal by Jack Williams. I quickly called Dougie for permission to play in both low and medium. This was agreed to but with a warning that it must not affect my pony power, when playing for him. There followed, for me, the most amazing week of polo, when I played five matches in five days. These included a practice 8 goal, two qualifying matches for two different Cowdray tournaments, one for medium goal and one for low, and then a first round for each of those tournaments, played at Cowdray Park. For the medium Tayo had moved me to play No.1 and I practised my own preaching, in trying to be the link to goal, for his lovely long backhand and forehand passes. This was rewarding and fun. We were victorious in all matches except the last, the low goal, but at least we could continue in the subsidiary of this.

The following week I had one of the best games of my life in the quarter final of the medium. Continuing to enjoy playing No. 1, I effectively marked a 7 goal player and scored two goals from awkward angles. Near the end, with scores level, the 7 goal opponent, in frustration, hit my pony with his mallet. He was penalised, that gave my team a free shot at goal from 60 yards. Up came Tayo and hit it over the top of the goal and we were in the semi-finals. Sadly there was a national newspaper strike and the match was never reported. Then in the first round of the subsidiary of the low, called the Ruins, I had quite an adventure. I had arranged for Jack Williams to deliver to me a particularly good new pony, which I had just purchased, direct to the polo ground, where we were playing; but he was late. We were losing the game by two goals and my patron was cursing loudly about me not having enough ponies, when suddenly, as if from heaven, the pony arrived in time for the last chukka.

The pony played absolutely brilliantly for me, we scored three goals and won the match, in the last minute. The new pony turned out to be one of the best low goal ponies I ever played and helped me in many succeeding tournaments, before being sold to an insisting enthusiastic polo pupil.

In the semi-final of the medium, I tried to repeat the marking, this time on Howard Hipwood, 8 goals, but failed to contain him sufficiently, and we lost by two goals. Once again a good sideline coach could have helped us, especially when Tayo stopped trusting me, by trying to do too much himself. But in the Ruins we had an easy win, in the semi-final, and were then faced, in the final, with playing against two Princes, Charles and Edward. Knowing that we needed umpires that were not biased in favour of royalty, I did what I now call 'playmaking off the field' by going to the polo office, where I suggested in a loud voice, in the presence of the famous American, Billy Linfoot, that he should be one of the officials. Taken by surprise, in front of a crowded office, the polo manager and the great Billy Linfoot agreed. The result was that the Princes were shocked, when they were frequently blown for fouls, giving us a comfortable victory. However we were not exactly popular at the prize giving, because many ladies had arrived, wearing their best hats, in the hope of being seen, when the Princes should have received the Cup.

I returned to Ireland for the Dublin Horse Show and the August medium goal tournament. I played with my cousins, Lord Waterford and Lord Patrick without much success. Once again the lack of a coach to coordinate us clearly affected our tactics negatively. However the week was highly enjoyable, in many ways, with the horse show and polo parties adding much entertainment.

I found that my dairy farm development had made great progress when my farm manager, Joe Daniels, proudly showed me round the new dairy yard and all the fields which had been improved beyond recognition to provide better grazing. In conversation Joe suggested that in the upper parkland there was a place for a polo field. I jumped at his offer and, there and then, we took the most significant decision of my post-army life. The suggested location was to be ploughed in September, in preparation for sowing corn there, for harvesting in 1973, 74 and 75, when it would be also under sown, with the most ideal grass seed, for a polo field. This process was intended to prepare and clean the area thoroughly, besides binding the earth sods strongly together in order that it would be able to withstand the battering by horses and people in the future.

The birth of our first child was rapidly approaching. Our doctor, Eddy Hill, proposed that it should take place in a bedroom at Whitfield. Many discussions followed, but in the end MI insisted on going to hospital, to come under a specialist, Dr Gallagher. The wonderful Tia Emma, great aunt of Maria Ines, arrived from Argentina to assist with the baby and on 15 September David came into this world. I will never forget the thrill of seeing him for the first time and being surprised how well formed his face was, instead of the expected baby features.

The winter 1972/3 went by in a flash. MI and I took David to be inspected by in-laws and relations in Argentina. We set off for a long trip including Christmas. My mother-in-law made us very welcome in Arenales 3745. Also Manolo Torino, David's godfather, insisted on lending me a station wagon for all my time in Buenos Aires. The first day I took to the streets, in this quite large vehicle, I was frightened by the intimidating manner, in which most of the Argentines drove. Suddenly it occurred to me that my only chance of survival was to behave in a similar way to the local people. Soon after that I was driving with great confidence and enjoying it. Actually this changed my style of driving, for the rest of my life, with a mixture of consequences. Some passengers appreciated and complimented me but others, I suspect those with poor hand-eye coordination, often became upset and alarmed, making complaints about my aggressive driving manner. I returned to Carlos Casares and bought two more ponies, for a very reasonable price, from Eduardo Moore. One was a very ugly grey, called Feo Chichon, who seemed to be unbelievably fast and strong. As before I immensely appreciated watching some of the thrilling polo matches, that were part of the triple crown of the Argentinian Open tournaments. Then we headed for Christmas in Salta with MI's father, Danton. Having twice been the Health Minister for the Province of Salta, Danton had humbly returned to the mundane important work of being a family doctor. His surgery was at his home in the village of Carrill, which is fifteen miles from the city of Salta. There were wonderful stories about his caring work with very poor families, whom he allowed to pay him with eggs and vegetables.

I was surprised to find their Christmas customs quite different to Ireland and England. The main party is held after midnight Mass and on in to the early morning. The next day, St Stephen's Day was for rest and recovery. Nevertheless I tried to show them how we do a Christmas lunch, by inviting twenty people to eat a turkey. To my horror everyone brought a guest, their boy or girl friend, with them, and we were nearly forty. Somehow the poor turkey was stretched to feed everybody and they appeared to enjoy themselves.

I returned to Ireland by myself to be met by Joe Daniels at Dublin Airport. I enjoyed my second season hunting with the Waterford hounds. One of the reasons for this was that Harry Meckling had miraculously become a competent Field Master, which not only helped the hunting, but was also a useful example for me in the future, when I took the job. Robin Hunt was having his last season as Huntsman and finished his esteemed career by continuing to show some great sport. After each day hunting I would have to describe, in detail, to my mother the story of what had happened. She was very appreciative and I enjoyed sharing my experiences with her. Throughout the winter I was planning my polo season for '73 and becoming frustrated that the sport of polo, appeared not to be interested in my coaching skills. In the back of my mind, the fact that my own polo ground was now a reality, was telling me to examine the possibilities of using my home as a coaching base in the future.

Harold Bamberg invited me to join his team at Windsor, covering my expenses, and we found a house to rent. Old polo friends of my parents, Claud and Emma Pert had located one near Slough, called Tiger House, which we took for three months, May to July. We moved there from Ireland with baby David and Tia Emma. It was exciting to be back in England, meeting old friends, making new ones and being involved in the great Guards Polo Club. MI's first cousin, Mercedes, and best friend, Nellida Maria, came from Argentina to spend a month with us, adding much comfort to the young mother and amusing company for Tia Emma and myself. I played No. 2 in our polo team, in many tournaments, including one high goal, with no success. My new ponies were sick on arrival and caused many problems, but I always had enough ponies for every match. The Argentine Pro was friendly but neither a leader nor a coach. Yet again I was surprised that that patrons like Harold Bamberg could spend so much money on us, as a team, without employing a coach for team coordination and strategy planning. However there were positives, in that I learnt many lessons, from the mistakes and by experiencing more fast quality polo. Also a resolve started to build within me, that I had to do something untoward and novel that would change the outlook of others and bring to me people that wanted to be coached constructively. We made some good new contacts and we had many enjoyable times in England, especially with our young son David.

We returned to Whitfield in mid-August to find that the first year's plan for a polo field had been completed. Effective levelling had taken place and the first crop of corn, on the field, was ready to be harvested. An eager Granny welcomed us with all the local news, including a pleasant surprise for me. The American, Michael Butler, famous for producing the musical play *Hair*, was in Ireland with his ponies and two powerful New Zealand professionals, looking for opposition. Hence the Marquis of Waterford had invited his brother Patrick and me, to form a three aside team, to play them at Curraghmore, on a small field in the old gardens, the following Saturday. Remembering how much I had enjoyed being No. 1 in Cowdray the previous year, I volunteered to play that position, much to the relief of my bold cousins. To my delight all my ponies were now in excellent form, especially Feo Chichon, the ugly grey I had purchased from Eduardo Moore. Whenever a pass reached me he pounced to escape the strong opposition, allowing me time to hit accurately and score goals. We were thrilled to have a close win against two such eminent players. Miraculously I had a close escape from injury, when I was hit by a ball, that caught the back of my helmet.

The next day, Sunday, our opponents of the previous day plus the Marquis and his wife Lady Caroline came to a large dinner party with us at Whitfield Court. I think we were 16 and the New Zealanders were more than impressed with our beautiful Palladian home. This made me believe that the house could be used as an international polo venue, if our plan to create a polo field continued successfully and sufficient stables were added to those already in the yard. The following Wednesday I drove to Wicklow to play with and coach Robert Morton, after which he persuaded me to stay to dinner. Then I had an adventure driving home when I tried the short cut in order to miss out the Wexford town called Enniscorthy. In the dark I did not see a left turn to the south and then rounded a bend to head north unwittingly for several miles before I realised my mistake. I arrived home at 1.30 a.m., extremely tired but relieved.

We had a return match against Michael Butler, two weeks later, on Sunday 19th, on an improvised polo field near Wellington Bridge in Wexford. This time we played four aside, with the Hawaiian, Michael Daly, joining the Kiwis and the Maltese Darmiani, added to our team. We were unable to produce the same teamwork with our newcomer and were well beaten, but enjoyed the outing.

Unexpectedly my polo season was extended to Sunday, 16 September with several visits to both Wicklow and Phoenix Park, Dublin, for chukkas and matches. When the polo season ended the ponies, after so much travelling and playing, gratefully went for a long rest out to grass. It appeared that Robert Morton wanted me to be involved with him and his polo the following year 1974, by coaching him and managing a team for him, throughout the summer season. Back in Waterford I was delighted to see that Rachel's new house was ready for roofing and we enjoyed some tennis with the de Bromhead family. Wednesday, 19 September was a significant day at Whitfield Court when the cooks were separated, proving the old saying 'there is no room for two cooks in one kitchen'. What had been the study, next door to the drawing room, had been fitted up as a handy little kitchen for Maria Ines, assisted by Tia Emma, to operate in with their inventive recipes, including lovely Argentine delicacies. Nellie, a bastion for dear Mum for many years, was thereby left supreme in the main house kitchen and a peaceful atmosphere was established.

CHAPTER 12

Fox-hunting in Waterford and Polo Abroad

AUTUMN '73 WAS FILLED WITH excitement as my mother, 73 years old, planned a two-month trip to Australia, via a short time in England. She was going to stay with my Dad's old friend Charles Gardner, who had been Governor of Western Australia, before retiring to live in the state capital Perth. He had also played polo with my Dad in the 10th Hussars team, which had won the two inter-regimentals in India and England in 1936, a feat never done before. Mum made detailed arrangements, which I am now reading in her diary for that year. Our wonderful family friend, Boda Griffin, who had been housekeeper for my Granny Sue and kept us enthralled with stories of the past, kindly gave my mother valuable help with preparations and packing. On Tuesday, 25 September I drove my mother to Dublin Airport for her flight to England. There she stayed a night with another old 10th Hussar, Colin Davy, also a well known author of horse racing stories. It appears she went to a doctor for a cholera injection and tried to persuade him to backdate the entry, without success, thereby risking being sent home on arrival in Australia. Nevertheless she safely reached Perth on Saturday, 29 September to receive a wonderful welcome.

I started my third season of Irish fox-hunting, since leaving the army, by buying a fine new horse from my distant cousin, Charlie Blacque. I planned to treat myself to some extra days' hunting with the Kilkenny Hunt that winter. There was big excitement in the hunt with our new Master and Huntsman, John Rohan, taking over from Robin Hunt.

John had bought my uncle's estate, Woodhouse near Stradbally village, where he now kept the hounds. When out with the Waterford hounds, I was disappointed to notice that, our American Master of Hounds, Harry Meckling, had once again changed character, as Field Master. Now he appeared to be overconfident and was too quick to become angry with some hunt followers over unimportant small matters. Hence it was even more clear to me that his second year, in charge of the hunt followers, was the example for me to follow, if I ever took over this difficult task.

On my farm the dairy herd was growing rapidly according to plan. Inevitably disease took its toll and the first cow death was from 'Red Water'. Later brucellosis and tuberculosis appeared from nowhere, from time to time, to inflict unpleasant losses. On the positive side I was delighted to see that my farm manager, Joe Daniels, had made great progress with all the farmland by clearing brambles, thistles, gorse, nettles and stones in order to maximise the pasture area. Most of the stones were from the remains of the original Whitfield house, knocked down by Mr Christmas, after he built our lovely home, calling it Whitfield Court.

Bulletins about my mother in Perth Australia came frequently by letter and picture postcard. She was clearly having a marvellous time including many social engagements, race meetings, a sightseeing coach tour and a visit to Perth's Parliament House. Maria Ines received exciting news from Argentina that her only sibling and sister, Marcela, was going to be married in Buenos Aires in March. This finalised our winter plans in that we decided to wait until then for our next visit to Argentina to see her parents and relations.

The Opening Meet of the Waterford Hounds took place at Woodhouse, Stradbally, John Rohan's new residence. John had invited the local priest to bless the hounds and, in the middle of his prayers, a dog hound went over to him and lifted a leg to pee on his surplus! Not a word was said or complaint made and the day was enjoyed by those mounted on horses and the foot followers. My Uncle Billy (Lord William Beresford) who had moved from Woodhouse to live in Thomastown, in County Kilkenny, died while my mother, his sister, was still in Australia. His funeral was held in the village of Stradbally. There was an emotional service because of his recent ownership locally and his association with the hunt over the years as both Secretary and Chairman. On the Saturday of that week the meet for the hounds was cancelled because of several days of heavy rain. So John Rohan decided to take the hounds out in his estate below Stradbally. To his amazement there was a screaming scent and the hounds hunted a fox up the hill and down the main street of Stradbally before going into the graveyard to stop by Uncle Billy's grave. Hounds had often been in this area previously, but never had they come near Stradbally village let alone the graveyard.

On Saturday, 8 December my mother returned from Australia and I met her in Dublin. She was full of stories including the surprise reunion she had had with distant Beresford cousins. On arrival at Whitfield she was thrilled to see the big 'Welcome Home' board above the front door and the wreaths round the pillars. On my next day's hunting Harry Meckling was not present and, to my shock, I was appointed Field Master by Robin Hunt. I reluctantly took on the role and tried to copy Harry Meckling's second year. There was a long slow hunt which probably was lucky because control was easier than during a fast run.

My brother Peter arrived for Christmas bringing our house party to seven including Rachel, Tia Emma and our little son David. There were some good parties and festivities, but our enjoyment was spoilt on New Year's Eve, when news crossed the Atlantic that my mother-in-law's apartment in Arenales, Buenos Aires, had been robbed with an amount of jewellery taken.

We were now in 1974 and unexpected events rained down upon us. At the first weekend we were surprised by a visit from my noble cousin the Marquis and his wife Lady Caroline, being accompanied by Atty Darboven, his new wife, a Princess, and Susie Ferguson, who told us she had left husband Ronald. The latter had had one affair too many and Susie was now enamoured with the big Argentine polo player Hector Barrantes. This was to lead to several interesting situations. The second weekend produced a violent storm, leaving us with no electricity for many hours. Despite this we got to Woodhouse to lunch with the Rohans and enjoyed meeting John's cousin, a renowned horsewoman and character,

Pegg Watt. Then when returning to Whitfield I received a telephone call, which changed completely our plans for the next two months. Jack Williams was inviting me, in ten days time, to fly out on a polo tour to Jamaica, Costa Rica and Nicaragua. Immediately we decided that Maria Ines and David would now go earlier to Argentina and wait for me there for her sister's wedding. This precipitated me into a hectic ten days of social events, meetings about the hunt ball, clothes distribution to poor families and farm business, together with the preparations for our different journeys, that would rejoin us as a family in Argentina. Somehow Maria Ines fitted in a day's shopping in Dublin with Tia Emma, while Rachel, now resident in her new house Coolbaun, looked after David and I had two more hunting days enjoying much good sport.

I was away from 23 January to 8 March. First I went to Heathrow London, to meet up with Jack and Marjorie Williams and David Gemmell, before taking off for Jamaica. We enjoyed a cheerful flight out, celebrating with champagne the prospects of visiting Jamaica, Costa Rica and Nicaragua. On arrival in Jamaica, at Montego Bay Airport, we were met by our hosts, the Mastersons. John and Paddy with daughter, Sheila, had prepared a superb programme for us. This included several polo matches, enjoyable spells on the beach, with a lovely warm sea to swim in, and many good parties. Most of the evening entertainment happened quietly in private homes. We were very happy with the ponies they gave us and our team worked well together, winning every game. The owner of a grey pony, which I played, generously told me that I had improved him.

John Masterson was the greatest exponent, that I have ever met, at being low key about everything, when in reality he was a big time business man, a high class athlete in more than one sport and an amusing strong character. His wife Paddy was a charming hostess, who attended to all our requirements. Hence we left Jamaica in fine spirits and headed with equal expectations for Costa Rica. In this Central American country we encountered people with a totally different outlook to our Jamaican hosts. Their polo ambitions were solely geared to beating their visitors and even humiliating them, while their hospitality was quite good, but it all took place at the polo club and we never saw the inside of any player's house.

Our introduction to the Costa Rica players gave us false hope. They told us that they had the fairest system of allotting ponies to visitors, in the world. We would play two matches against teams A and B and, when against A, we would ride B's ponies and then change to A's ponies to play B, on the second day. Therefore when we were well beaten by A, whose ponies completely outpaced ours, we consoled ourselves with the belief, that we were going to greatly enjoy the second match, on A's ponies! However in the next game we recognised very few of the ponies, which we had both played against and those that we had ridden ourselves! The result was another sound defeat. So we went to drown our sorrow at the evening festivities and were partly rejuvenated by the repeated cry of the club's President 'This is just the beginning of a wonderful party'.

In Nicaragua we were treated well, being given reasonable ponies and quiet pleasant hospitality. We won the first match, narrowly lost the second. The night was fairly entertaining, but not enough fun to placate us, and we enjoyed being guided round some interesting sightseeing. It had been a great experience, visiting these three countries, and I had much enjoyed playing in a team with Jack Williams and David Gemmell. Now I had to set out for Buenos Aires, to join up with Maria Ines, to attend the wedding of her sister Marcela.

The best route available for me, by air, was through Lima, the Capital of Peru, where I had to change planes before continuing to Buenos Aires. So I boarded a multicoloured Branniff airliner, to find a luxurious interior and the most beautiful, smartest dressed air hostesses, that I had ever seen. But when the time came for take off many seats were still empty, the doors remained open and the smell of fish, from the harbour, was pervasive. Suddenly a stream of smartly dressed athletes, in blue blazers and ties, entered the plane, as if they owned it. They chatted and laughed, without sitting down, for at least half an hour. We finally took off an hour late and, looking across to the other side of the isle, I recognised a famous face, but initially could not remember who he was. When a hostess served my food, with silver cutlery, I asked her the name of this team to be told 'Boca Juniors Club soccer team, from Buenos Aires'. Immediately the name 'Rattin' came to me, as I recalled the 1966

World Cup in England, when in the semi-final, in which England beat Argentina narrowly, Rattin had been sent off. After the match finished he had tried to re-enter the field, with the intention of attacking the Referee, and the next day his picture was plastered across every newspaper. I was just recovering from the shock of being so close to such an infamous man, when two of the Boca Juniors team jumped out of their seats, each carrying a bag, which they proceeded to fill with the silver from all the passengers' trays. Then the hostesses collected the trays without saying a word, as if nothing had happened. On arrival in Buenos Aires I looked for an official, to whom I could report the theft, but failed to find one.

I found Maria Ines and David in good form. The marriage of Marcela to Carlos Palacio, in Buenos Aires, was attended by a small congregation and the wedding reception was low key, but it was a happy occasion and a good opportunity for me to reunite with some of Maria Ines' relations, whom I had only met, once before, at our own wedding. It was rewarding to see the love and closeness, between the sisters, and the genuine affection, shown by their cousins, to us and my parents-in-law. While in Buenos Aires I had a meeting with Juan Lalor and Negro Hauregui, two 7 goal players, with whom I discussed a crazy idea of forming a high goal team with them in England. The truth is I really do not know whether I was serious or not, but I definitely wanted to discover what was involved with costs and planning. There must have been a ridiculous optimism inside me that a golden egg could miraculously appear from nowhere, before the coming European summer, because I told them that I would investigate and let them know from Ireland.

Before returning home to Whitfield, by myself, the three of us flew to Salta, where Danton's cheerful character and exuberant behaviour was entertaining. He was thrilled with his grandson and delighted that we had christened him David Danton. I had the opportunity to get to know my father-in-law and found him to be a fascinating character, with a great depth of knowledge, and a lovely sense of humour, which explained where my wife's vitality and charisma came from. Danton had studied to be a doctor secretly, to avoid the interference of his father, who had disapproved of his medical ambitions. He had been rewarded with a celebrated career as a much loved GP, before he was appointed the Minister of Health for the Province of Salta.

My journey home was without incident, arriving in Ireland on 8 March. Once settled in to the comforts of Whitfield, I took time to get up to date with world events, including happenings in Argentina, which had escaped me during my travels. Floods in the Province of Buenos Aires had made 100,000 people homeless. There had been a bomb in London and a general election in Britain, won by Labour, reinstating Harold Wilson as Prime Minister and causing the resignation of Ted Heath. A VC 10 aircraft had crashed in France, killing 347 and Red Rum, the double grand national winner, had dislodged his jockey at Haydock racecourse. Locally my sister Rachel had settled happily in her new house, having had valuable assistance from the skills of Tia Emma, with the completion of all her curtains. The foals of my two faithful polo mares, Cyriaka and Lujosa, had grown healthily with some good photographs to prove it.

I was quickly back in the hunting field and managed 4 days, including one in Wexford, before the season ended. The enjoyment of good hunting in Ireland is hard to describe, because it is multidimensional, while not requiring a fox to be killed. The beautiful Irish countryside gives him more chance to escape than elsewhere, and the jumps encountered are extra entertaining, because of their variety. Pat Stevenson had to take over from my groom Michael, who sadly returned to hospital for cancer treatment. One day I went to Galway to buy a lorry and arrange that it could be adapted to be a horsebox. I returned to receive unwelcome news, to end the month of March, that my excellent farm manager, Joe Daniels, was giving three weeks' notice to leave for a job on a much bigger farm.

March ended gloriously with the daffodils looking their best and our local heron was seen with three chicks. Maria Ines called from Argentina to confirm that she and David would be home on 3 April. I came to my senses, when I checked our finances, to find that no golden egg had materialised, and I cancelled all plans for a high goal team in England that year. April opened gloriously for me. On the first of the month Stella Annesley, who had been the Dame (Eton language for Matron) in my house at school, came to stay for three weeks with my mother. She was one of those people, who transmitted tranquillity and charm, with a beautiful smile and kind word to everybody. On the 3rd I drove to Dublin to meet and collect Maria Ines and David. Now one and a half years old David was the centre of attention. He loved to have short rides in front of me, on the neck of my horse, between the stable yard and the front door of the house. It was hard to keep him entertained, so we built an extra large playpen on the lawn and put a net over it, as a roof, to prevent him getting out. He made great efforts to climb out without success. My mother and I were fascinated by a surprise visit of three members of the Christmas family, the original owners of our beautiful home. They in turn were delighted, when unexpectedly we showed them my cousin Mark Girouard's book, in which he describes many of Ireland's outstanding houses, including Whitfield.

To support the Waterford Hunt I made a brief return to racing, by entering my grey horse Danny in the members' race, at the annual point-to-point. I enjoyed the preparation, which involved several gallops with others, in different places. Then in the race itself he jumped well, but lacked the pace to keep up with the leaders, after the first circuit. So I pulled up before the second last, quite happy with the experience. Our Master and Huntsman, John Rohan, won and celebrated in style afterwards. Another excitement was taking Louisa, the 3 year old filly daughter of Lujosa, who had served me so well in Germany, to be broken by Mickle Power, in Stradbally. She had grown to be exceptionally good looking and strong. She would become one of the best ponies I ever owned. Then I heard that our new horsebox was ready for collection from Galway, and set off with all the family in our Volkswagen to drive it back to Whitfield. I had been driving on an English licence, and now used the lorry as a way to obtain an Irish driving licence, at the same time qualifying me for larger vehicles in Ireland. On Sunday 28th I took 4 ponies, in the lorry, for the opening of the polo season in the Phoenix Park, Dublin. I was expecting that polo that summer would mostly be with the team of Robert Morton, both at Wicklow and Dublin. He had told me that he was the most patient man in the world, who could never be upset by the behaviour of others. However when, later that month, after two trips to Wicklow to play, we turned up for the first May tournament in Dublin, Robert was told, not too tactfully, that he had to make way for an outsider for two of his chukkas in the match. Without a word to anyone else, he instructed his groom to load all his ponies, in his lorry, and take them back to his farm. He never played again, anywhere and since that day, I have stopped believing anyone, who tells me that they are patient.

Our feeling of security in Ireland was shaken by two events, in mid-May. First there were bombs which exploded in Dublin and Monaghan and second my mother, late at night received an unpleasant telephone call, telling her that we had 4 hours to get out! The latter was probably a drunk or a nut, because we had always enjoyed amazing good will, in the local area, despite our part English origin. This we attributed to my wonderful Granny Sue, who was known to have helped all the neighbours with great kindness on many occasions. Nevertheless none of us slept much that night, while poor Maria Ines became extremely anxious. I am happy to report that there was never a repeat of that nasty call or nothing like it ever happened again.

In England Jack Williams had come to my rescue by inviting me to play for his team, Beachanger, in the Windsor medium goal tournaments, during Ascot Week races. He had recruited the 7 goal player Hector Barrantes to pivot the 14 goal team and I was to be the No. 2. My ponies left for Cirencester on 4 June, while Maria Ines and I followed three days later. There followed a most entertaining two weeks, during which we had a successful practice at Cirencester, before moving to Windsor. There we won three matches to reach the semi-finals, where we were robbed of a place, in the final, by a bizarre decision of an umpire. We were leading by a half goal, with the big clock, at the end of the field, showing less than a minute left. An opponent committed a blatant right angled foul, to prevent us scoring, which would have sealed our victory. To our amazement there was no whistle blown, to give us an easy penalty, while that same opponent flew down the field with the ball to score the winner for his side as the final bell sounded. After the game the umpire came to us to apologise very sincerely, saying 'I saw the foul but thought the bell would ring immediately, making it unnecessary for me to give you a penalty, with the game already won!'

Maria Ines and I returned to Whitfield to catch up on the many events that had happened while we were in England. Lord and Lady Donoughmore had been kidnapped by the IRA and held for 4 days, Prince Henry, Duke of Gloucester, who had been Colonel in Chief of my regiment, had died and a bomb had been discovered in Westminster. Also our new farm manager, Eugene Morgan, had started work, while poor Michael O'Sullivan, my groom, had lost his battle against cancer and was in hospital with only a short time left to live.

Our hectic lifestyle continued through the following two weeks. My famous cousin, Mark Girouard, author of renowned books about great houses, including Whitfield, arrived to stay with his wife Dorothy. The soccer world cup had started giving us some exciting matches to watch on television. The Derby Polo Tournament, in which I played, without success, took place between Thursday and Sunday. Then on the Monday Maria Ines and I left, once again, for England, to stay with our old friends George and Celia Norrie, while I played in a Cirencester Polo Tournament.

We only had a few days to relax before setting off in the Volkswagen to Germany, via a ferry to Le Havre in France. My old regiment wanted me to work a quick miracle with their Captains and Subalterns Polo Team, before their annual tournament. I did the same training, that I had previously applied to army teams, especially emphasising the drill behind the goalposts, for the forwards, when attacking close to goal. I enjoyed seeing them improve impressively and was able to stay long enough to watch them win the semi-finals. I then departed for Dublin, where I was committed to play in the annual August Horse Show Polo Tournament, with Renata Coleman's team. Imagine my thrill when I received a telegram from Germany saying that the Regiment had won the Polo Cup, finishing with the words 'Winning goal from goal post drill'. This further success, with my coaching, in helping an inexperienced team to beat stronger opponents, added to my growing determination to create an international establishment, where I could offer my expertise to those, who wished to benefit from it, badly enough to bring them to Ireland.

Our team in Dublin played superbly to reach the semi-final, while I had my best game of the season. This gave us such confidence, that I persuaded my reluctant mother, to come all the way from Waterford to watch our next match, expecting that she would see us win again. Sadly we all played badly in the semi-final and were easily beaten, making my poor Mum regret that she had travelled so far to watch. The rest of August was filled with visits to Whitfield from family relations. My late father's brother Uncle Peter, the Admiral, arrived first with his wife, Angela. Then my cousin Hugo, with his Italian wife, Anina, who had sheltered him from being captured during the war, appeared. Lastly Uncle Ronny and wife Sibi, who lived the other side of Waterford City, came to meet the above four for a delicious dinner, prepared by Maria Ines, after which we had amusing games of carpet bowls. In between the entertainment at Whitfield, I returned twice to Dublin for polo, including giving one session of coaching to a few players, who had been converted to seeking assistance from me, as a result of my growing reputation, I presumed.

September provided both Maria Ines and I with our first opportunity to visit Scotland. Renata Coleman had accepted an invitation to bring a team to the Perth Polo Tournament. We flew from Dublin to Edinburgh and were then driven on to Perth, where we stayed with the Drummond-Murrays. The experience of getting to know new people in a different part of Britain is more memorable to me than what happened in the polo matches, in which we had fun but did not excel. One opinion given, from around the dinner table, was a contradiction so relevant to the problem of Ireland being a divided country, that I will never forget it. The speaker said 'I have great sympathy with our brethren in Ulster, for their situation, although I know that most of them come from the area in Scotland, that breeds the dullest, dourest and most obstinate type of people that we have.'

When we arrived home at Whitfield we encountered a problem typical for a shared premises. My mother could not find the key to the oil tank which was almost empty, threatening us with no hot water or heating. After a short panic somebody remembered where the key had been put and our little crisis was over. During the remainder of the month I met the Colemans on several occasions, to discuss plans for the 1975 summer polo and what was required to prepare for it during my upcoming visit to Argentina. I went to Dublin twice and they visited us once. Cecil was trying to limit the costs but finally agreed that I could buy two more ponies for Renata.

At Whitfield a vital step for future polo plans was taken, when Jimmy Keane started work as my head groom. He and I were set to spend 14 years together, during which we would survive many adventures, while taking part in a variety of equestrian sports and meeting polo people from many countries. On the farm the harvest was completed without rain interference, and this included the second corn crop, taken from our future polo field, as part of the three year preparation plan.

During a shopping visit to Waterford Tia Emma and little David had a narrow escape. Maria Ines left them in her car, while making a quick purchase from a store. The hand brake ratchet must have become weak, because the car started to roll forward, slowly down a hill, with a gradual descent, and then crossed a road, ending up against a wall, with a small bump. Who was the most frightened will never be told, because David does not remember the incident, Tia Emma could not articulate her fear in English and Maria Ines did not see the car rolling, but later could imagine what might have happened if another vehicle had been moving on the road that was crossed.

I went to Argentina with the mission to find a groom player for Renata Coleman and to buy some extra ponies for our planned polo team in summer 1975 and in preparation for the expected opening of my polo school the following year. This precipitated Maria Ines and I going to stay with Negro Goti, near Balcace, after which we spent a few days on the beach at Mar de Plata. At Goti's I rode many different ponies and met his head groom Diego, a 3 goal player, who agreed to come to Ireland for the 1975 season. This plan seemed to be excellent, because Diego was prepared to travel to Ireland with all the ponies, after which he would be able to play the ones he already knew. At Mar de Plata, for the only time in my life, I lay on a densely crowded beach. We enjoyed it because it was different, the variety of colour, a mix of people including beautiful ladies, the atmosphere and the carnival spirit, that was all around us on the extensive sands.

In Buenos Aires we were lucky to see some incredible polo between Colonel Suarez and Santa Anna in the Argentine Open polo. The

Harriot and the Heguy brothers were against three Doringnac brothers, in two teams that in the future would both become worth 40 goals Also the Mar de Plata team, of Tanoira and Goti brothers, made the above two fight them hard, before they conceded defeat. The pleasure and excitement from watching the long hitting and accurate ball passing, the pony control that allowed their speed to change from full gallop to canter and back to fast velocity in a few seconds, while making some 180 degree turns without halting, together with brilliant anticipation, connected to daring clever tactics, was huge and emotional for me. My friend, Heriberto Schoeffer, had qualified as an agriculture engineer and had developed a business with a group of farmers, whom he visited regularly by bus. Because of this we could only see him a few times. He showed me one farm plan, which was impressive, and I imagined that he also cheered them up, with his wit and jokes, when staying with them.

We returned to Ireland for Christmas and some good fox-hunting. The first day out I was told that I was appointed Field Master, without being asked if I was prepared to do this difficult task. As previously explained I had watched my predecessor, Harry Meckling, after a weak start in his first year, develop in his second, an effective manner, which became angrily overconfident in his third. Hence I immediately tried to copy his second year, grateful that I had had an opportunity to witness and learn. Jimmy Keane suggested lunging my hunters over banks and this especially helped my grey horse, Danny, have more courage in the hunting field, when we met the big fences. In fact it worked even better than expected, surprising the hunt members, following behind me, the Field Master, when he fearlessly tackled the highest and largest banks.

John Rohan, who was the Master and Huntsman of the Waterford hounds, was living in Woodhouse, Stradbally, the old home of my uncle Lord Billy Beresford. He was showing good sport, which encouraged me to start negotiations with him, about becoming a joint Master for the 1975/76 hunting season. In hindsight I have wondered why I considered taking on such responsibility, that would add to my hunting costs and make me a target for the complaints brigade. Chairman of the hunt, Robin Hunt, (a name coincidence, especially as he had been a brilliant

Huntsman for the Waterford Hunt) had been hinting strongly that it would be appropriate if I followed in the footsteps of both sides of my family. I believe I had several different instincts, which, when combined together, persuaded me to become involved. These included respect to my late father, being in search of a challenge, looking for the excitement from the very front of the hunt and giving myself visibility, which could bring me openings in other dimensions.

Big excitement was injected to our lives when it was confirmed that Maria Ines was expecting our second child. She was dreaming of a daughter and we agreed, if that happened, to call her Mercedes. For the summer polo season Renata and Cecil Coleman lent us their cottage, in the garden of their house, near Dublin. I gave many hours of polo training to Renata and some to Cecil, besides playing polo regularly with both of them. Diego, after a few games, started to fit in well with us and we won some matches. The Derby 8 goal Tournament in Dublin was to be the big test for our team. We did some extra practices together, including sessions of tactics on foot with Renata and Cecil. Diego and I agreed to share No. 2 and 3 positions. So that Renata would stay at No. 1 and Cecil in No. 4. I succeeded in changing Cecil from being the worst fouler in the club, to becoming the one who made no infringements at all, in this tournament. Before lunch, on the day of each match, I made him run across his lawn to simulate riding me off, in different situations. To my surprise it worked perfectly, because not only did he never commit a foul but he also stayed in the No. 4 position throughout the three matches, while taking several opportunities to hit the ball constructively. Renata also remained in her position, at No. 1, so that Diego and I were able to give her many passes, which sadly she seldom hit, but when trying to she often neutralised her opponent, thereby allowing Diego and me to back her up and score goals. Unbelievably we won the tournament and in retrospect this provided a superb example of involving all four players, with the ball, within their abilities in simple team tactics, which worked effectively.

Next we took a team, without Cecil, to England to play in a tournament at Tidworth, my old army home. There we competed, at the same time, in an 8 goal and a 4 goal tournament. Freddy Damiani, from Malta, came with us for the 8 goal and we conscripted, from the Army, a young officer for the 4 goal. I arranged for Renata to rent a house for us near Newbury, Berkshire, from George and Celia Norrie, old friends from my regiment, and from there we drove to Tidworth daily. Renata had many adventures, including a car accident, which made her late for one polo match. We had to play the first chukka without her, but luckily she arrived just in time for the second, as otherwise she would not been allowed to take part. Our tactics continued to work well and we won four matches to reach the final of both tournaments, while also enjoying good evening parties.

Therefore Sunday became a very big day, the only day in my life, in which I played in two finals. First in the 8 goal we came up against a 6 goal Argentine, called Daniel Devrient Kidd, who could hit the ball the length of half the field. We had a tremendous battle throughout, with our ½ goal handicap advantage swinging for us and then against us, on many occasions. Diego played very well but Freddy Damiani appeared a little confused by the speed generated by the big hitting of a 6 goal player. Only in the closing seconds did our opponents score the winning goal. However the 4 goal final ran in our favour all the way. We were considerably helped by having superior pony power, because our opponents were playing ponies, whose only food was basic grass in the field. They were a wonderful fully amateur team and I was unhappy winning so easily against them, but of course we enjoyed the triumph and the extra fun of two finals in one day.

We returned to Ireland and prepared for the Dublin Horse Show Tournament in August. I suggested to Renata that we should invite John Masterton, from Jamaica, to join our team. Renata agreed and all the arrangements were made on the telephone. Previously I had only played against John in Jamaica, where he was the Head of Polo besides being a renowned player. I much looked forward to being in the same team with him, but sadly I believe that jetlag took its toll, because John was never able to show that extra speed and skill that I encountered, when I had played against him. We failed to win any of the matches, but nevertheless much enjoyed John's company, the Horse Show and several good parties, which we were invited to. Also there was a thrilling final to the polo tournament, which was highly entertaining

On 3 October 1975 Sebastian was born in Waterford. It was a long birth and for this reason his face was not so pretty, for the first few days. When he was produced in the hospital we even thought there had been a mistake and queried that he was ours! However he soon turned into a beautiful baby and when MI returned to Whitfield with him, we were all very proud of him. Then we much enjoyed the christening of Sebastian at Kilmeaden Church when Declan Collins and Heriberto Schoeffer agreed to be his godfathers. Soon after the festivities I planned a trip to Argentina, which had to be short, because I was required to be back in Waterford, for the opening meet of the fox-hunting season. This was important because I would be, for the first time, one of the masters of foxhounds.

In Argentina Heriberto Schoeffer paid me back handsomely, for my previous friendship, by driving me around the city of Buenos Aires. Quite often this contained an exciting dimension, because Heriberto's car would run out of petrol and we would jointly have to push his vehicle, to the nearest garage. Heriberto also took me to a private polo ground, belonging to the Perussi family, to play some practice chukkas and participate in a polo tournament. My team was too weak to have any chance of winning, but I enjoyed this opportunity to experience my first tournament, played in the leading polo country of the world. While there I made an agreement with the Perussis to have one of the grooms, known as Rubio, in Ireland during the following summer, 1976, to help me to open the polo school. Also I was once more thrilled to be a spectator for some of the big Argentine Open polo matches, at the Clubs Indios and Hurlingham, before returning to Ireland.

On return to Whitfield, before the hunt opening meet took place, I attended some of the cub hunting, when I learned much more about the skills and technicalities about hunting the fox. For the first time I had to take on the task of meeting the farmers, in order to get their agreement and hopefully their blessing that the hunt would be allowed to cross their land. John Rohan and I visited some of the farms together and I went alone to meet many others. Nearly all of them were very welcoming and interesting to talk to. I had offered Whitfield Court to be the venue for the Opening Lawn Meet. As I drank a wine cup I felt great pleasure that I was following in the full steps of my parents and other ancestors by being a Master of Hounds. In the full regalia, of red coat and hunting cap, I lead the field to the first covert, which was the wood beyond and below our house. 'Pride comes before a fall' because on the path, above the wood, a small man on a little pony, out of order, pushed past me and preceded to kick at my horse, catching me on the knee. The pain will never be forgotten by me, yet I had to stay with the hunt followers, trying not to show my discomfort. Suddenly a fox was found and we had a quick first hunt, across some good jumps, enabling me to forget the pain for a while. Later there were some other enjoyable short hunts and then we finished the day with a welcome drink in the Sweep pub close to home.

That season of hunting was memorable for two reasons. First the fun we had following John Rohan, together with his whipper-in, Joe Flynn, who came from Cork every day, as they seemed to be able to achieve a hunt, out of every situation. Secondly the last covert, a pub, where we drank and sang many songs, normally lead by the mercurial voice of Joe Flynn. Nevertheless being Field Master gave me problems, in that often I had to prevent the rest of the field from following the route taken by John and Joe. If they had escaped my control, the farmers would probably have banned us from hunting, in the future. To offset this pressure I sometimes had one drink too many and returned home, in the evening, mildly inebriated.

The other big excitement of that winter 1975/76, came from opening the daily post, in expectation of people replying to my advertisement, about the opening of the Whitfield Court Polo School, in May 1976. Enquiries from several different countries arrived and slowly these were followed by some confirmed bookings. Finally I was happy to know that five groups had confirmed for five different weeks. I hoped this would be a sufficient start, optimistically believing that the effects of word of mouth would generate many more bookings, which would then follow on.

CHAPTER 13

My Sixth Lottery –
Whitfield Court Polo School

IN THE PLANNING OF A DAILY programme for the polo school, I was determined to create for my visitors the maximum scope for learning, connected to an enjoyable experience. This was to be done by allotting two ponies to every client in order that they could be on horseback twice in the morning before playing four chukkas in the afternoon. Later after my experience in other countries, I developed a system with one pony per client, that worked sufficiently well with an improved schedule. I clearly made a mistake by charging too little, while not working out an accurate budget, which would have quickly shown my miscalculation. However many years later a good friend said to me 'How lucky that you did not make a business plan, because if you had, there would never have been a polo school at Whitfield.' Nevertheless that summer, 1976, I started a phase of my life, which turned out to be incredibly fulfilling in so many ways.

The weeks prior to the opening of my first venture, other than farming, in Ireland, were filled with preparatory hard work, excitement and emotion. Paddy Fitzgerald, the original odd job man, was putting the finishing touches to the polo field, besides his work in the garden and the many demands from the house. Jimmy Keane, with a small team of grooms, was preparing the ponies, approximately twenty, for their task, plus looking after mares and foals. I personally took on the manual work of preparing an outdoor riding school, in part of our kitchen garden, by removing many

Hugh Dawnay with his newly born son, David, in September 1972

Hugh Dawnay with his son David

Hugh Dawnay with his son Sebastian

Hugh Dawnay with his son David

Hugh Dawnay and his mother Lady Katherine and son David

One of the first teams in the Whitfield Court Polo Club. (LEFT–RIGHT):
*Sebastian Dawnay, Edward Grant, Eduardo Albarracin, Polo Client,
David Dawnay, Polo Client, Hugh Dawnay, Tommy McGrath*

Waterford Pony Club (LEFT–RIGHT): *David Dawnay,
Sebastian Dawnay, Roos Tierney, Shawn Ormond*

Opening Lawn Meet at Whitfield Court 1975

Hugh and Maria Ines Dawnay at the Masters' Reunion Dinner, New York

Whitfield Court Polo Club (LEFT–RIGHT): *Raul Ramirez, Polo Client, Tom Driver, Hugh Dawnay, Polo Client, Polo Client, Polo Client, David Dawnay*

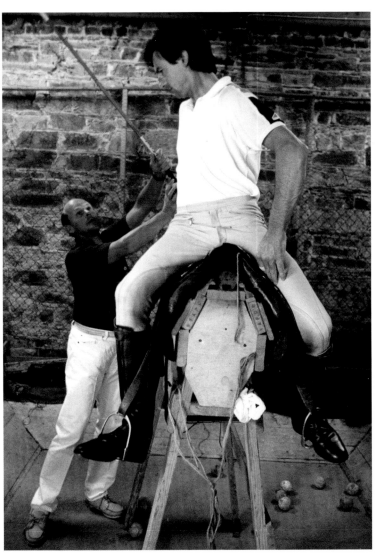

Hugh Dawnay teaching with the use of the wooden horse

Rope exercise to cure ball chasing

Whitfield Court Polo School

Whitfield Court (©COLM HENRY)

Hugh Dawnay's own breed of polo ponies at Whitfield Court

Hugh and Maria Ines Dawnay (©COLM HENRY)

Hugh Dawnay with David and Sebastian at Disney World, Florida

stones, of all sizes, from the ground to the surrounding hedge. The Hon. Georgiana Crofton, who was destined to enter our lives in a surprise fashion thirty-five years later, was staying with us in the house as an assistant, in various dimensions. Working with the ponies during the day, she was also ready to help us host the visiting clients inside our home at night.

Before my first polo school clients arrived we had, for me an emotional day, when in the morning we christened the polo field, and in the afternoon went to Stradbally, for the wedding of my cousin Nicola Beresford. The first chukkas on my brand new field was naturally a special occasion. The bold Marquis of Waterford, brought his sons Lord Henry and Lord Charles Beresford, plus his groom, brother of Jimmy Keane, to join Jimmy and I in a 3 aside game. An extra thrill was the proof that the 3 years preparation plan had worked so well. The field played like a lawn, the ponies seemed to enjoy the surface and we found that the ball travelled fast and straight across the grass. Hence there was good reason, at the end, to open a bottle of champagne to celebrate this memorable day.

The wedding, with the reception at John Rohan's Woodhouse, Nicola's and my Uncle Billy's old home, was an enjoyable follow on. The speeches were greatly improved by the wit of my Uncle Ronny, my late father's brother and the garden looked really beautiful.

The first group for my polo school came from France and there followed a week that will never be forgotten by our family. The leader of the group introduced himself as a Cuban lawyer, who had escaped from the Bay of Pigs, before becoming a leading advocate for Pepsi Cola in Paris. With him came an American in Paris, a French dentist and two French businessmen. The first day was unbelievable as everything went so well and everyone was delighted with the programme, the amount that they had learnt and the delicious food. The cooking was being done by a family friend, Jenny Hunt, who had agreed to help us make the food first class. She had international experience and a great cooking reputation. Maria Ines had prepared the house with her lovely touch and eye for detail, so that the bedrooms duly received worthy compliments from our first polo guests. Alfredo, from Argentina, fitted in extremely well with everyone and Jimmy Keane had all the ponies looking and going well. When all had retired safely to their bedrooms, I celebrated by drinking a glass of my favourite liquor, while saying a short prayer of thanks. The knowledge that the process I had started with the Germans, in Düsseldorf ten years earlier, was now sufficiently developed to share it, from my beautiful home, at the first ever residential international polo school, was at that moment really pleasing and exciting. Furthermore inside me there was a good thrill feeling, that I would learn much more, from teaching my visitors and, as a result, I should probably be able to build an effective, complete and constructive system of polo instruction, for individuals and teams. All the above looked set to give me the second career that I was looking for.

The second and third days were equally successful and I was surprised how much they all appeared to learn, as proved by their actions. At lunch everybody laughed when the dentist used the cutlery, together with the salt and pepper, to demonstrate, on the dining room table, how France should have won the battle of Waterloo. On the fourth day disaster struck, while we were playing the chukkas. The Cuban had, what appeared to be, a harmless light fall from his pony, after a collision with a Frenchman, who was in his own team. To our horror, he did not move for a few minutes, then tried to speak some words, before becoming completely unconscious. An ambulance took him to Waterford, where it was decided that he had a serious injury and should be sent, immediately all the way to Dublin, for an important operation. Apparently the ambulance reached the street in Dublin, where the hospital was, but the Cuban died before he could enter into the theatre. Incredibly the magnitude of this terrible disaster was considerably reduced by the wonderful attitude of the Cuban's widow. She, a French lady, much younger than him, told me by telephone, that he had died in one of the happiest weeks of his life, because she had received a letter from him, describing how much he was enjoying being at Whitfield. She also said that she was now expecting their third child and this news had given him extra joy. Many years later I heard that, only a month before that drastic accident, the Cuban had fallen on his head, in Spain, where he had been warned that he could never again risk hitting his head. Maria Ines and I went to Paris for the funeral and that was when I really felt that I was experiencing a terrible nightmare. In hindsight I believe that, if fate decreed that we should have one death, at my polo school, then the very first week was really the best time to have it happen, so that it could quickly be put in the past. Luckily this was to be the only one.

The next three groups were successfully completed without any disasters and all the participants seemed to be delighted with the results. I recall that in each there was one person, who would become significantly helpful to the future of polo and to me. In the first Michael Seckington, a well known vet and great character from Rutland, England, later assisted me and many others, when purchasing ponies, so that we were less likely to make basic mistakes. In the second Edwin de Lisle, a great enthusiast, helped to develop the Rutland Polo Club, in several dimensions, including organised coaching and became their Chairman before retiring. In the third David Stone, a successful show jumper, went on to become the kingpin of Phoenix Park polo, in Dublin, for many years. We appreciated the extra comradeship of so many people and my mother, then 76, enjoyed having dinner with them in the evenings and told of some of her experiences.

After this I took the opportunity to invite some local people to learn to play. Also I went to Dublin to play in some tournaments and invited four of their players to visit Whitfield to take on my best four beginners. Everyone was very surprised how well the Waterford beginners played and a local support group were thrilled when the match ended in a draw. At the end of my first year of polo at Whitfield, I made a plan to go to the World Cup of Polo, which was being staged in Chicago, USA. I booked flights to Argentina, via Chicago, so that I could buy more ponies for my polo school, after the World Cup finished. I stayed in the Drake Hotel in Chicago and found my way to the Oakbrook Polo Club, where the matches were to be played. The hot favourites were the 38 goal team, which included three 10 goal players Alberto Heguy, Gonzalo Tanoira and Alfredo Harriott. They duly easily reached the final, where they were expected to have a simple task against four Americans. Prior to the final Alfredo Harriott had succeeded with all his sixty yard penalties. However in the final he started to miss them and for a while it appeared that the Americans might have a chance. But the

Argentines finished with a flourish and in the end won comfortably. Billy Ylvisaker, chairman of Gould, was the entrepreneur behind the tournament. I met him and felt that he viewed me rather sceptically. Little did either of us realise how much we would connect a few years later. I achieved some publicity by handing out my brochures and attending a meeting of the United States Polo Association, when I was given a few minutes to talk about my polo school.

One day I found myself cornered by Adam Winthrop, my host at Myopia in 1966. He insisted that I must delay my flight to Argentina, in order to go to Myopia, to umpire the two matches between the alumni of Harvard and Oxford. Somehow he made the offer too attractive to refuse. Hence a few days later I was in the lap of luxury at the Winthrop mansion. During the alumni matches the commentator gave me good publicity, by talking about my polo school. We had some hilarious moments with Adam and his house party and they gave me a wonderful send off to Argentina. In Buenos Aires I stayed with my mother-in-law and again met up with Heriberto, who helped me to find my way around. We went together by bus to visit the Avendano family, at 25 de Augusto, to buy ponies. While waiting for Enrique to collect us at the bus stop, we played chess on the side of the road. This was a wonderful way to pass the time and gave much amusement to the passing traffic. For the next three days I played in many chukkas and tried a big number of ponies. The conditions were hot, dry and dusty and each evening I was exhausted. I was then revived by a swim followed by good steaks and whisky. Then I had a pleasant surprise, when the prices of the ponies were not too expensive and I was able to buy a group of five. As a bonus I was offered a 2 goal player, Paul Espain, to assist me at Whitfield the following summer. We returned to Buenos Aires, where I watched some wonderful matches of the Argentine Open Polo, before returning to Ireland for the hunting.

The 1976/77 hunting season had a spell of very wet weather which led to several cancellations. However when we did hunt John Rohan showed that his confidence had further increased and we enjoyed some excellent fast hunts. The whipper-in Joe Flynn, on his horse Bolackey, jumped some incredible places including a bank with three strands of wire on it. The last covert (the pub) started to last longer with more drink consumed and extra songs sung. Joe Flynn continued to entertain with wonderful songs especially 'Man with a coloured coat'. The negative side meant that too many horses were left in their trailers for too long, waiting to be driven home. I was grateful to have Jimmy Keane, who took my horse straight to Whitfield after hunting finished.

The 1977 polo season started well with visits by several German groups. Paul arrived with the Avendano ponies and the number of local players increased. The Ballyduff Soccer Club wanted to have a soccer pitch, while they were developing their own. So I allowed them to use the parkland, next to the polo field. Suddenly I realised that this could be a second polo field, which could be used in wet weather, thereby saving the first field from damage and maintaining its smooth surface. With its gradual lateral slope, it would also be safer in wet conditions. Over the years this second field allowed us to play much more polo and in nearly all conditions, which made a big difference to the polo school and club. At the end of June I took a club team with Paul and two locals to play in the Derby tournament in Dublin. We won three matches and the Cup, but only after a big battle in the final, when I had to change positions with Paul. He became unhinged by the superiority of the strongest opponent, which pulled him out of position on top of me, the number 3. Thus I now adjusted to Paul, instead of vice versa, allowing our team to regain the initiative and score twice in the final chukka.

Then I was delighted to meet Jim Haigh, who came to my polo school. He is a man of great substance and charm, who from humble beginnings had, in Yorkshire, used his many talents to invent industrial procedures and develop a very successful textile business. He came twice for a polo course, before inviting me with Paul to play in his team in England. We went to Tidworth and reached the final, where we only lost because Paul had goals disallowed, for hitting his pony with the butt of his polo stick. However we enjoyed the experience and the company of Jim Haigh, who was so well informed in many dimensions of life.

In July and August, together with the continued German invasion, we were thrilled to greet people from many other countries in search of polo knowledge and skills. These included English, French, Americans, Austrians and one Israeli. Suddenly it appeared that many parts of the world now knew about my polo school and that there clearly was a demand for our services, indicating that no other similar establishment was in existence at that time. These experiences with my own polo school continued every summer until 2002, a total of 27 years. People from 31 different countries came to be coached and taught the skills of polo, with emphasis on team play. These polo clients included polo players from 11 European countries, 7 from the Americas, 4 from the Middle East lands, including a group from Oman, 5 from countries in the Far East, plus Australia, Zambia, Kenya and Zimbabwe. Some of these countries produced only a single representative, who were extra welcome, and the three main contributors were Britain, USA and Germany. The latter made a mini invasion in 1977, 1978 and 1979 and then having noted how I employed a player from Argentina, to lift the level of play, decided to copy and replace me, by inviting one to each of their polo clubs. I believe they mistakenly thought that this one guy would serve three purposes, a knowledgeable groom, a strong player for tournaments and a polo coach. In fact the Argentine groom/players were not coaches, but in due course, Michael Keuper and Alexander Schwarz, who had been to Whitfield Court, themselves became good and effective coaches. Another German, Wolfgang Kailing, delighted me by writing to explain how he had inspired his team to use my general tactics, to beat stronger opposition and thereby had won one German polo tournament.

The British came to Whitfield as individuals and groups from clubs, fairly consistently. However there were many more, who failed to carry out their good intentions to visit me, several of whom openly confessed that they had planned to attend my polo school, but had never got round to organising the trip across the Irish Sea. The Americans proliferated after I started work at Palm Beach, Florida, which is described in a later chapter, but also many were separately attracted from reading my book *Polo Vision*. Coming all that distance across the Atlantic, seemed to make them extra appreciative of the polo instruction and, what they called, the luxury of my home and our delicious food. The main credit for the latter clearly went to Maria Ines, who lived up to her award of being my 5th lottery, by making Whitfield Court so comfortable in every dimension.

Each subsequent winter I travelled to do a mixture of coaching and pony purchasing, as and when required. The bonus of giving almost continual instruction, throughout each year, was an inevitable broadening and improvement of my knowledge and teaching technique. Hence I was continually experiencing the thrill of making big and small constructive changes to my daily and weekly programmes. This included a gradual reduction in the length of my polo courses. Having started with a plan covering 5 days, I ended up feeling confident of being able to impart the same quantity of skills and knowledge in 3 days. Other benefits were gained from this satisfactory evolution, in that my ponies faced an easier summer polo school routine, often cut down to every second week. This in turn allowed my staff more time to train the home breed, which was increasing alarmingly every year.

One winter I arranged for Jimmy Keane to spend a few weeks in Argentina, in order to add to his knowledge of polo pony management. This paid me serious dividends, because Jimmy returned with two major suitable changes for our summer routine with the ponies, besides implementing many small effective and valuable details to the daily stable life. The first alteration was to empty the stables at night by putting all the ponies, except invalids, out to grass, followed by corralling them, in a bare paddock during the day. The stables were still useful for tacking up, prior to polo school training, chukkas and polo matches. The second significant change was that we ceased riding on the local roads, during the pre-season preparation, which now took place on the many hills within the farm and estate. This had multi benefits, but primarily prevented the frightening possibility of accidents to ponies and riders, on the hard roads, or that we might be the cause of vehicle crashes, resulting in injuries to people inside them. It had been a miracle, that in previous years, when riding and leading up to 20 ponies, round a road circuit, we had never experienced any such disasters. Occasionally a led pony had suddenly pulled back to become loose, for a short period, but luckily they had always been caught before anything horrific occurred. The new system also assisted by reducing costs, because the labour requirement was less and the horse food bill was smaller, when good grass, eaten at night, became the major part of the ponies' diet. Added to the above the wear on horse shoes was much less, hence the blacksmith's bill became smaller.

All my instructional training in the Army had made me aware of two key dimensions that were required to be a good and effective teacher and coach. These were the right questioning technique and the art of giving encouragement. Questions may have a little humour, but should not deliberately ridicule anybody, although, ideally, everyone should be made to think for a few moments, before an answer is given by one surprised, named, individual. Hence there is the expression 'thinker question'. Besides increasing the will to learn, encouragement to produce answers can be used as a subtle way of confirming the application of some of the many basics. However it took me more than a year or two of running my polo school and travelling to coach abroad, to discover that praise that is justified should be given far more than criticism, which can be negative.

The replaying of chukkas by video, provided a wonderful way for my clients to criticise themselves. The words 'What is wrong here?' followed by several replays, can produce very successful results, without having to lower their morale. Otherwise I think and hope I learnt to precede criticism with praise. My ambition at Whitfield was to prove to myself and others that tactical positioning, derived from a 'thought process', designed to increase early anticipation, is always the highest priority. However accurate pony control and a good hitting technique is then needed, to allow all players and teams to take full advantage of having achieved this anticipation. Also I continued preaching to all, that team play, through passing the ball regularly, was always more important than using the pace of the ponies to make individual runs.

Earlier I have described my system of changing venues frequently, to cover all the above and up to 1995, the major theme that was relevant, wherever I met my clients, was my philosophy of *Polo Vision*, the name of my first book. This is applicable to all polo players' behaviour, both while participating at the sport and in planning their future development of playing abilities. For the former the achievement of 'all round vision' from on top of a pony, at all times, could be life changing and concerning the latter I wished to establish the vital vision of ongoing coaching, being a necessity for all players, at every level, but especially for the less skilled. In search of providing full understanding of the benefits and how to implement 'all round vision' I employed exercises for pairs and teams, related to tactics, together with formation riding, connected to detailed pony control. For both I never ceased to emphasise being 'outside the pony'. Then to these were added 'thought processes' and techniques for striking shots, from both sides of a pony, and at different angles.

The publication of *Polo Vision* by J.A. Allen in 1984 gave me a big red letter day. I proudly held up a copy of my book, while looking in a mirror and saying to myself 'You are now an Author!' My coaching ideas were in print and being read, giving the hope that this would increase the desire for ongoing coaching. Every winter, between 1983 and 1994, I went to Florida to give polo clinics. This greatly added to my coaching experience and, more importantly, to my knowledge, gained from watching so many of the world's best players in action in Palm Beach tournaments. By 1990 the first edition of *Polo Vision* had been sold out, giving me the opportunity to include the benefits of the above, in an extra five chapters, that were added to the second edition, published in 1991.

Then when I was invited to Mexico (my other experiences there will be told later), the significance of their facilities fortuitously forced me to experiment further with my new found awareness of the 'playmaking' theme. Despite beautiful sunshine on scenic smooth polo fields, there was no corral or enclosed area, in which to do my riding drills. Hence I began doing them on the side of a polo field and suddenly saw the scope for combining riding drills with team positioning and playmaking, all at the same time, without using a polo ball. Furthermore the lack of any enclosure inspired my clients to achieve full pony control, in order to remain accurately attached to a team. With delight I saw weak riders quickly gain confidence which suppressed any fear. Necessity is the mother of invention and, from then on, in Ireland and wherever I went to coach, I started with playmaking riding drills and kept finding new ways to make the playmaking dimension relevant to all parts of my daily coaching programme. In 2000 I started work on the playmaker polo book, so that the combination of writing and ongoing coaching showed me how to extend my new book title, to everything a polo player has to do, on and off the polo field. At the same time it gave me further proof that universal coaching is required, if we want to fill our polo teams with playmakers, thereby improving the general standard of polo out of all recognition.

My previous experience in Germany and with military teams, added to what I had learnt in Dublin, with the Mulhern and Coleman teams, had given me my own clear structured system of how to explain the basics, followed by methods of putting them into practice, before repeating them in controlled constructive chukkas. Hence my initial success with the polo school, in which everyone felt involved sufficiently to learn much more than they had expected. This gave me a sustained feeling of excitement, to which continual thrills were added, by further new ideas occurring to me and being immediately implemented. When some of them worked surprisingly effectively I had the extra pleasure of regarding them as my inventions. Now, thirty-five years later, I cannot begin to record the order in which these ideas and inventions sprung to my mind. Hence the following list is not in any order of happening or consequence, but the content might interest my readers and prepare them for explanations and stories that follow below.

Being Outside the Pony
Rope Exercises
Hand positions for Looking Behind to Stop
Diamond Attack
Starting Each Shot
Making Pony Follow You
Box Defence
Sweet Spot
Playmaking Riding Drills
Making Ball Follow You
Ball & Pony Clocks
Eyeballing Opponents
Barrier in Middle of Team

Aiming Hand at Ball
Turn Behind Tail of Opps
Rules for Each Team Position
Five Hitting Circles
Mnemonics SLOSH LATET PASSF

LATET is surely a profound though simple recipe for tackling every situation at Play or Work. The letters stand for words as follows in capitals: LOOK first then ADJUST within your TEAM followed by ENGAGING any opposition while ready to TURN (change course) before the next significant event happens.

There was a big bonus to my entrepreneurship in 1976, which now could be called playmaking, of bringing polo to my home in County Waterford, Ireland, in the dual form of a polo school and club. This gave me the unbelievable privilege of being able to play polo 300 hundred yards from my own front door, regularly during spring and summer. And because I had already earned and held a 3 goal handicap, for 10 years, through my ability to pass the ball regularly to all my team, I found extra enjoyment in directing my home chukkas, in a manner that shared the ball, between the members of both teams on the field. I achieved this by playing No. 3 and seldom trying to score goals myself, while setting up others to shoot at goal or pass to another player. I also instructed the No. 3 of the opposite team, normally an experienced player, invited to be my assistant in this dimension, to play a similar role. There is no doubt that polo skills, the ability to contribute to team play and confidence of every player is quickly improved, by this method of conducting chukkas, which in turn increases the enjoyment of all involved. I wanted the players to experience equal satisfaction, from giving good passes, as they did from scoring goals. If only there were more players, who could take pleasure from participating in this effective manner, even if they do not always win. The result should see the overall enjoyment being quadrupled. Also frequent post-match assessments, that recognise positive statistics before negatives, given by coaches, could add another creative step to progress and fun.

A comical side of polo can be seen by spectators if they watch with sufficient concentration to identify the ball-chasing behaviour by many of the young and new players. These include people who are highly intelligent and even eminent in other spheres of life. Quite simply, for them, the ball's attraction seems to overrule any logical consideration to where the ball is going in relation to the positions of other players. Hence it is hilarious to see them charging in the direction of the ball, only to find, when they arrive, that the ball is no longer there. There are different methods for coaches to employ as a cure for what could be called the disease of ball chasing. One is to invite them to reverse the process, by making the ball chase them, by going to positions, where the ball is anticipated to arrive. But if this suggestion is met with a stupefied look, an extremely basic explanation has to be reverted to. This was the case when a German dentist, who had been trained by me at Düsseldorf between 1966 and 69, but had not been playing polo for a few years, arrived at Whitfield Court in 1978, intent on making a new beginning. Wolfgang, who had booked in for two weeks, explained that he wanted to relearn all the important tactics and believed that he needed to do two courses to achieve this fully. After a long break from polo, the excitement of hitting the ball again must have temporarily unbalanced Wolfgang, because he started chasing the ball with incredible vigour. Then when we played chukkas, he even fought his own team for possession of the ball, switching from No. 1 in every attack to being No. 4 for the next defence! I had never before witnessed such a serious case of frantic ball chasing.

Every explanation that I could think of failed to change his attitude and actions, making me desperate to find a new system that he would understand. I was dreaming of this one night, and I woke up the next morning with the memory and clear picture of a ROPE. I could not wait for the period after lunch, when we would walk through tactics on the mini pitch, next to the house, on the lawn. When it came I produced a rope and experimented as follows. Client A held one end of the rope with his left hand, and Client B held the other end, representing Nos. 1 and 4 of a team. I then, with left hand on the rope, placed myself at No. 3, in front of 'B' while inviting Wolfgang to be No. 2, between 'A' and me. Then the four of us walked up and down the mini pitch, throwing a tennis ball with our right hands to each other. The moustache of Wolfgang went up and down, his face went purple and his eyes turned red, but he never dropped the rope and could not leave his position as No. 2, because 'A' and I held the rope taut throughout.

Immediately after this training we went to the polo field to play chukkas and my team consisted of the same four players, who had been on the rope, with Wolfgang at No. 2 in front of me at No. 3, with 'A' and 'B' at Nos. 1 and 4. To my great delight Wolfgang stayed in No. 2, throughout the four chukkas, and finished his second week as an extremely happy player totally cured of his disease of being a bad ball chaser.

Delighted by my invention, I experimented further with other clients and came up with what I named 'the rope exercise on ponies' for teams, on a polo field. I had briefly flirted with the idea of connecting the ponies by using wool, to replace the rope. But I soon found that it was unnecessary, because once I had established a solid universal thought process, of consistently staying, a similar distance apart, when on the mini lawn, with a rope, players showed that they could apply the same mind set, when on ponies, without artificial help. The start positions for the exercise were as follows. No. 3 stood next and to the left of the ball, on the back line, No. 4 prepared to hit the ball by starting from at least 10 yards behind it, with No. 2 ahead of the ball by 15 yards and No. 1 on the 30 yard line. The call of Play signalled all to move at the same moment, being prepared to receive a pass from No. 4, depending on the length of shot. Hence a long hit would be for No. 1, a medium length shot for No. 2 and a weak pass for No. 3. The aim was to score a team goal at the far end, with no one ever taking two successive hits, while ensuring that all players did have a strike, so that the ball was shared.

Many teams took 3 or 4 attempts before they scored a goal, but they clearly enjoyed and profited from the experience. Even more important they were now prepared and ready to attempt the more sophisticated exercises, described later, which all teams should be proficient at when playing in matches. However although many were surprised, by the simplicity of the rope and appreciative of how helpful it was, inevitably, it did produce problems. A Californian arrived, after a long flight from the west coast of USA, and stated that he had not travelled such a great distance, to be made to hold a rope. As a result, when we moved on to the polo field, he was the only one, continually in the wrong position, trying to chase the ball. Also I had a feed back that some jesters, seeking to mislead others, at my expense, were telling tales that I tied people together.

The first of the more advanced tactics, I called the Diamond, which could be used for hitting from the backline or penalties taken far away from the goal. The concept was that the hitter could choose which point of the diamond to hit to, making opponents spread out to cover all of them. Yet all the team, moving at the same moment, hoped to be quickly in the rope formation after two passes had been given, heading towards the goal. It required accurate lateral movement to re-establish the players the correct distances apart. The second, named the Box, was the defensive answer to opponents hitting from their backline or penalty. This square formation momentarily allowed two players to take on one opponent, while the others formed a defensive rope either side of them. The aim was to turn defence in to attack either immediately or during a defensive run down the field. The third, known as the reverse rope, provided opportunities for No. 4 to enter attacks, from a defensive rope, through a surprise switch with No. 3, who created the move by hitting an accurate angled backhand. Naturally the No. 4 had to start very early, before No. 3 hit and the other two in the team needed to adjust laterally to be the right distance apart on the new attacking rope.

Once my clients were applying the correct style of hitting and were successively scoring goals in practice, I enjoyed surprising them, by introducing races in order to deliberately put them under more pressure. It tickled my sense of humour to see the most confident suddenly start hitting badly and sometimes completely missing the ball. Yet after several races on different days, they were able to participate in chukkas much more effectively than before. Ideally I started with stick and ball short races for individuals, then moved on to half field contests for pairs of players, taking alternative shots and finished with teams of either three or four players from end to end of the field, sharing the ball. I have always been convinced that the way to learn to take pressure is to be frequently exposed to it, in this way.

To implement tactics effectively necessitates good accurate riding from all team members. Watching the top Argentine players so often, in the knowledge that they have acquired their riding skills over a long period of time, starting as children, inspired me to search for short cuts for adults, who start polo and riding at the same time. This produced my brightest revelation that the best polo players permanently had 'all round vision' which they achieved, probably without knowing it, by being, what I called 'outside their horse'. From then on I consistently used these two terms and backed them up by saying, repeating and revising the following, 'Never look at your pony, instead maintain your eyes in the direction you are going, turning or even circling, while also watching the other seven players on the field'. I further explained that this was made easier to do by turning the lower body including feet and toes, like the Argentines do. Although it required me to instil extra discipline, the simplicity of the above produced fast progress.

A chance conversation one day about predators, like humans, having eyes in the front of their heads, and non predators on the side of their faces, in order to see a predator stalking them, placed everything in perspective. From then on, by using this explanation, I found it easier to convince people that the pony wanted to follow the rider, but would be prevented from doing so, by them looking at the pony, instead of the complete scene around them, including the point or person that they wished to reach at any one moment.

Analogies to other sports and dimensions are interesting and effective, when told to enthusiasts trying to grasp exact meanings and explanations. The driver of any vehicle on a road, in heavy traffic, has to be outside that vehicle (i.e. eyes only looking outside and at mirrors) in order to survive, similar to a good polo player.

Looking back, to stop a pony, and looking where you are going, before turning are both natural extensions of 'being outside a pony'. I discovered the effectiveness of these, while playing in a tournament and was quick to add them to my coaching. Naturally the basic application of strong legs and gentle hands could not be forgotten, to back up the action of the rider's turning body. Clients who learnt this skill from me were ecstatic about the double benefit of a quick stop, while observing all around and behind them.

I have described my fortuitous experience in Costa Careyes, Mexico, which gave birth to my design of playmaking riding drills and exercises. These improved the results of my coaching, because they advanced the reaction time of participants, who copied the actions of others, rather than waiting to hear verbal instructions. To achieve this I initially placed them in one horizontal line, with the first playmaker, whom they had to copy, in their middle. After a series of turns, circles and halts had been completed successfully, I would nominate a new playmaker, forcing them to look in other directions. Ideally this change of playmaker would be repeated until everyone had taken the role. Then at a suitable stage, depending on the standard of participants, I would change the formation in to a vertical line, while continuing the playmaker exercises. This pushed the players to achieve 'all round vision' in exactly the same situation as required in a chukka of polo. I always felt a satisfied thrill from observing the instant enjoyment, experienced by those complying effectively to a playmaker, for the first time. It also gave them comprehension of the importance of relating to players more than a ball, which was, of course, not being used for these drills. Furthermore the sight of even the weakest performers giving leadership, as the appointed playmaker, was very satisfying.

For any group, who were showing confidence, I normally added, on the last day, what I called the Cavalry Charge. In one long line abreast, we slowly increased speed, going uphill, in order to simplify control, to reach an enjoyable velocity before I called out ' look back and halt'. Just as LATET had helped me to connect 5 crucial tactical thoughts in to one process, I came up with SLOSH to do the same for riding. This should continually remind polo players to be SEATED on the front of the saddle, while always applying LEG grip and being OUTSIDE their pony. STEERING is done indirectly, by neck reining, to make the pony follow you, while being quiet and sympathetic with their HANDS, when making contact on a pony's mouth.

The dreaded ball chaser has already been described as a demon, intent on hitting the ball, without regard to how the pony is ridden, or to any tactical dimension, involving other players. My aim in the school was to convert this demon in to a playmaker, who finds a thrill, when discovering that sharing the ball gives more time to execute the required detailed technique, including application of the pony and ball clocks, listed among my so called inventions, for achieving both accuracy and extra length of shot.

At the school the participants experienced three different mediums for learning all round shot making, in order to build confidence for giving good passes and scoring goals. These were sessions on the wooden horse, stick and ball exercises on the polo field, including races, and chukkas played daily. The latter were structured to allow all players to have a fair share of striking the ball. Our garage, which was situated in the stable yard, was big enough to have two wooden horses, in separate wire mesh cages. Experience taught me to develop a system, that occupied six people at one time, around the two horses. Inside each there was a hitter and a ball boy, and outside each a critical observer to praise correctly applied basics and spot reasons for errors. This allowed me to alternate between the two cages, while a planned sequence of half shots, forehands and angled backhands was completed. On the last day of a course I normally judged a competition to find the wooden horse champion of the week.

The stick and ball exercises, on the polo field, gave me a satisfying opportunity to be creative. After individual drills were satisfactory, I was continually seeking new ways to combine mobile striking with tactical movements, involving forehand and backhand passes. Starting with pairs working together the exercises, which always ended with a shot at goal, were expanded to include three and/or a complete team of four. Constructively there was great scope for praised confirmation of good shot technique and reasons for mistakes. As mentioned previously races were introduced to add the dimension of pressure and prevent any overconfidence, besides giving much enjoyment.

The use of the video camera to film the chukkas gave me a final method of critiquing the many details of the striking skills. Replays in slow motion, watched in the comfort of my home prevented me missing chances to congratulate the better shots and be helpful over any faults. The latter normally came under one of the headings taught by my mnemonic PASSF which covers PREPARE—APPROACH—SLOW SWING—SWEET SPOT—FOLLOW THRU.

Every day of polo tuition for a visiting group would always include one period of tactical theory, while sitting in comfort imbibing coffee or tea and eating biscuits. I believed these sessions were vital for creating a clear understanding of the factors that coordinate good team play, by distinguishing the different jobs of all four positions. These must be skilfully combined and interchanged, in search of controlling the polo field more efficiently and effectively than your opponents. I found that by employing 8 miniature model ponies on a table, laid out as a polo field, for explaining the above and set piece tactics was better than using a blackboard and paper diagrams. They were also ideal, at the end of a course, for examining all the alternatives for taking and defending every kind of penalty plus the rules that must be obeyed.

Everything discussed around the model table was then put in to practice, as described previously, firstly on the mini lawn, secondly during the stick and ball exercises and thirdly in the daily chukkas. Finally the video review confirmed to the players and myself, how well the tactical, riding and striking lessons had been implemented. When necessary multiple replays of any situation were used to convince those, who misunderstood or argued about the good and bad points, that I highlighted. The final day of each course produced mixed and varied feelings, beginning with satisfaction, that a large amount of polo basics had been covered, and ending with excitement, before the final chukkas, which were staged as a match. Then suddenly everyone was leaving, causing an element of sadness and anti-climax, in the realisation that new friendships would be interrupted or cease. Depending on weather, numbers of clients and variable factors, this last day programme could be flexible. Normally I judged a wooden horse competition, followed by a ride around the estate and a last tactical theory session, for revising all the strategy concepts. Then I concluded with a summary, of all subjects, before announcing the teams for the match. As we said farewell, I often sensed a healthy expectation, that they would return home, to showcase the results of their experience.

In 1991 my dear mother, Lady Katherine, died aged 92. She was lucid until her death, she had driven her car until she was 89, and I think that the Gardai in Waterford, breathed a sigh of relief when she handed in her driving licence. She was the second child of Sir Henry de la Poer Beresford, 6th Marquis of Waterford. She grew up in the halcyon days of Curraghmore, which then comprised 45,000 acres in Tipperary and Waterford, and 20,000 acres in County Wicklow. The 1911 Census of Ireland showed that there were 40 indoor servants, 9 grooms, and 10 gardeners. The Marquis hunted his own pack of hounds, and there were 40 horses stabled there. She cherished rosy memoirs of an Edwardian childhood at Curraghmore, fostered by the presence of an English nanny, butler, and coachman, and a Scottish housekeeper. She would be taken to the drawing room at 6 p.m., dressed in a white frock with a blue sash to demurely play with a music box, while being admired by the constant guests of her mother Lady Beatrix (Granny Bertie). After an hour she would return with her nanny to the nursery floor.

She encountered an awful tragedy in December 1911, when her father was accidently drowned. He had returned after a day hunting, and as he did every evening he walked along the bank of the Clodagh river to visit the kennels. The river was in flood, dusk was coming, and he fell in. His body was found the following morning. His heir, Lord Charles was 10 years old, and he was in Eton. The estate was then managed by trustees, until he came of age. Life continued as normal and she came as a bride to Whitfield Court in 1926. She was a noted horse woman, and she regularly hunted with the Waterford Hunt until the mid-1960s. She took a great interest in the Whitfield Polo School, and she delighted in meeting the clients, presiding at the dinner table very graciously. She was buried in Kilmeaden Church cemetery, beside her beloved husband Major General Sir David Dawnay. Her death was the end of an era, she was the last of the 6th Marquis's family. I was heart-broken, as was Maria Ines, and her grand children David and Sebastian.

CHAPTER 14

Pony Sales at Whitfield Polo School

You would think it should be a no brainer. A polo school, well attended by international clients and Irish polo players, should become a perfect set up to have a flourishing trade in polo pony sales. Nevertheless I discovered that it was not that simple, for a variety of reasons, including the fact that players completely rely on their ponies in order to give a good performance themselves. Players therefore become seriously upset, when any of their ponies have the slightest problem, for which they will normally blame the vendor. Also it was hard enough to keep together a good group of school ponies, without having to find replacements for any that might be sold. Hence initially I desisted from the temptation to look for this extra dimension of income. However when I was on my travels in Argentina, buying a few replacement ponies for my own multi purposes, I saw that there were such a vast number of ponies for sale, giving me the temptation to procure a few extra to have for others to buy from me at Whitfield. Furthermore it gave me the excuse to enjoy many extra chukkas, trying out more ponies while visiting estancias in Argentina.

During another winter mission to obtain ponies in Argentina, I arrived in one estancia still looking for 6 ponies. From a group of 15 ponies, shown to me and tried by me, I only selected three that I liked enough to buy and asked to be shown more. The owner tried to insist that I should have liked more from those already played by me. When I refused I watched him have a long discussion with his manager and head groom. After a further short delay 3 good looking mares appeared, with some story about being kept for another buyer, and 3 more chukkas were played. To my delight all 3 mares were almost sensationally good, having considerable speed and light mouths. I duly added them to the first 3 to complete my required purchase of 6 to take home with me. Later on I reluctantly sold one of these last 3 to an army friend and waited with excitement to play the other 2 in the coming summer season. At home my 2 new, thought to be sensational mares, early on in the new season lived up to my hopes, going very well in our early chukkas, making my expectations for them in the coming tournaments even higher than before. But then the shock in the very first match was severe when both of them, started brilliantly only to lose their mouths, a technical term for becoming uncontrollable, after 4 minutes of fast play. In hindsight it is clear that these mares had, in Argentina, been played too fast, too soon, in their first polo season. Then when I played them my hosts must have deliberately controlled me and the flow of the chukkas, in a particularly skilled manner, that prevented any long galloping happening which in turn avoided the exposure of their nasty problem, while showing off their best points. My old army friend reported exactly the same situation with the mare I had sent to him. My only way of cutting my losses was to add these two mares to my breeding enterprise, using my own stallion. One of mares had 7 foals and the other had 6. Then all 13 turned out to be excellent polo ponies, and were either retained for my two sons and myself to play, or sold for good prices. Ten years went by, before I happily concluded that an ill wind had truly blown good, long after I had purchased these 2 difficult mares in Argentina.

I liked to believe that I became clever, from experience, at making nearly all my clients happy by my selection of ponies for them. I was aware that our school had a good reputation for ponies, but always realised that many different factors had to be considered to keep all comers content. These included riding knowledge and ability, smooth and rough characteristics of people, size and weight of riders. Once all members of any new group had arrived and told me about themselves and their previous experiences, in all dimensions, I would enjoy the next moment of privacy, in which I applied myself to this important task. Inevitably adjustments, at times, were necessary, as the week progressed, caused by surprise factors, especially injury or poor health of ponies, and unexpected habits or problems of some clients. Over and over again I was saved by the amazing Don Felipe, a Spanish older pony I had bought from the famous Dr Billy Linfoot, an ex 9 goal American international with little confidence and even those clients, not blessed with good anticipation, were all helped to participate more effectively by my wonder horse. When retired in his late twenties Don Felipe, one day, broke out of his field, to come and join in the chukkas. Tragically and so unfair for such a gentleman, he was killed by lightning, which was only discovered after a post mortem.

A male visiting client was unhappy that I was playing against him on a pony that was faster than his. He was referring to Doubty, one of my own breed, whom I loved to play, although I had to ride him differently from the other ponies by stopping or slowing him by pulling the martingale strap instead of the reins. I explained the problem to him and then offered to allow him to play on Doubty for one chukka. Arrogantly and stupidly he accepted, but halfway through the chukka I heard him yelling 'Get me off this horse'. I duly stopped the play and I exchanged ponies once more with a very chagrined man.

A very rewarding side to the polo school was the exposure to people from so many different countries. This often provided unexpected non polo original experiences, mostly pleasant with only occasional unwelcome consequences. Stan Yassikovitch was an extremely charming, most interesting and amusing gentleman, who came for five consecutive years to do a polo course at Whitfield Court. Stan had a Russian father, a French mother, was married to a Rhodesian white lady, had been educated in the USA and was enjoying a highly successful career in the banking industry. Amongst others, he was Managing Director of Merrill Lynch, Great Britain, and the European Bank. When Stan was in my house I seated him at the top of the dining room table, where he quickly became the centre of attention, enthralling us all with multi topical stories, opinions and information. This changed the normal situation during polo school weeks, when I struggled to keep away from the subject of polo, during meals and rest periods, because nearly everyone wanted to hear about my experiences and opinions about the game. I genuinely wanted a change of subject, but felt obliged to answer properly any polo questions, that were put to me. Then I had to turn the other cheek to all, including my wife and family, who accused me of talking nothing else except polo. A story told by Stan, during one visit, is so ridiculous, yet possibly true, and because it touched a nerve in my relationship with Maria Ines and her family in Argentina, I will never forget it. Stan claimed that a soufflé was the trigger which started the Falklands (Malvinas) War! Apparently Lord Carrington, the British Foreign Minister, had been having regular meetings with his Argentine counterpart, with a view to solving the dispute between the two countries. Hopes were raised that only one more reunion was necessary, to bring about a progressive step, that could achieve a mutual understanding, from which an agreement should evolve. However Lord Carrington was not only late for that meeting, but when apologising for his delayed arrival, added that he had to proceed immediately to the British Embassy, for a dinner, for which he had to be on time. The reason, incredibly, was that there was on the menu a soufflé, which would go flat if he was late. The Argentine Foreign Minister was so infuriated and incensed to have to wait another month for the next meeting for this trivial reason that he returned to Buenos Aires and recommended war! Stan was adamant that all the above had happened, making it no coincidence that the only British politician, who resigned, after the war was over, was Lord Carrington.

A Californian, who has become a very close friend of mine, came twice to Whitfield as a client to join others on a polo course. Charles Betz had come to England working for Citibank, was married to a lovely Swedish lady Birgitta, before settling to live in Buckinghamshire. Like many of our visitors he enjoyed a game of tennis after a busy polo school day. This was played on our hard court, which as the result of an accumulation of rain had a bed of moss underneath it that caused a few minor undulations on parts of the surface and an amount of crooked bounces. When playing I had a local knowledge advantage making Charles and I laugh continually, thereby discovering that we had a similar sense of humour. Looking back I am extremely happy to have developed a long term enjoyable friendship with Charles and his charming family. He has since become the supremo of the Schools and University Polo Association (SUPA), which he has developed to be a great example for all to admire, even achieving an entry in the *Guinness Book of Records*, for the most teams ever to play in one tournament.

The event, which probably gave the most joyful surprise to polo visitors, was the only time that some of the cattle, from my dairy herd, broke out of a field, in the late evening. With excitement my polo visitors collected and tacked up enough ponies, for all of us to go out, like a posse, across fields and woods, in search of the missing beasts. We found them, when the light was failing, and by the time we had returned to the stable yard, it was pitch black. We then celebrated the successful mission, with a very cheerful drink or two, while the details of such an unexpected experience were told and recounted from one to another.

You seldom meet an elder man, who adds significant dimension to your life. Tom Harris, a Californian vet, who specialised in dogs, brought his quiet charm and gentle behaviour to Whitfield, when attending a polo course. He was knowledgeable and constructive in many subjects and gave us all food for thought throughout his visit. He was so appreciative of my system of coaching, that he invited me to stay in San Francisco, so that I could give a clinic to a group in Menlo Polo Club. This is covered later under my American trips.

He had been a Master of Hounds and he extolled to me the enjoyment of attending the annual Masters' Reunion weekend, which took place annually in New York. Then out of the blue, one year, he invited Maria Ines and I to join him and his wife, in New York, for this event, which began with the Masters' Dinner on Friday night and a Hunt Ball on the Saturday. He encouraged me to accept, by pointing out that his journey from California would be an equal distance of our flight from Ireland. We procured reasonably priced return flights from Shannon to JFK Airport and set off on the journey, thinking that we were mad to make such a venture in the confines of a long weekend. Friday's Masters' Dinner had been boosted, by a guest speaker, in the form of the recent Aintree Grand National winner, who was himself an American Master of Hounds. Even better the film of his triumph, as one of the few amateurs, ever to win this tough contest, was shown at the end of the dinner, with a commentary by the heroic jockey himself.

I have never seen so many pink tail coats as there were, on the Saturday night, at the grand Hunt Ball. We met many famous American hunting people and heard some fascinating stories, about their experiences following their fox hounds across the countryside. The dinner was magnificent and was followed by dancing to an enormous band, with an enjoyable atmosphere. On the Sunday we joined another American polo client, George Davison Ackley, for a delicious lunch at his New York club, before going again to JFK to board our return flight. We arrived back a Shannon in time for breakfast on Monday, having had a truly memorable long weekend.

One of my visiting polo clients, on his arrival at Whitfield, knowing about my military past, gave me a present of an interesting book, the autobiography of General Auchinleck. In the Second World War, he had commanded the 8th Army in North Africa before Montgomery, amongst many other of his war exploits. The main theme of the book was to explain how unfair Winston Churchill had been, when he had replaced the author with Montgomery. Auchinleck claimed that he had selected Alamein, himself, as the ideal location, for the 8th Army to defeat General Rommel and the might of the Germans, because there the enemy's line of communications would be further stretched than ever before. At the same time Alamein provided a long narrow piece of terrain, that would prevent the Germans from employing a wider front, in order to avoid the concentrated strength of the Allied Armies. When I had finished reading the interesting life of Auchinleck including all the fascinating details of his argument that explained his preparation for Alamein before he had been unhappily replaced, I was determined to learn the counter argument of the great prime minister and brilliant leader, Winston Churchill. My Granny Susan had left us a lovely large library of books, at Whitfield Court, that included many historical descriptions of wars. Among these are the 5 volumes about the Second World War, by Winston. Previously I had stupidly avoided these books, in the mistaken belief that they might be heavy reading. The answer, which I was searching for, was eventually found in Volume 4, but luckily, in hindsight, I had commenced this marathon read at the beginning, because I enjoyed every chapter immensely. The contents was incredibly clearly written and easy to follow, giving me a much appreciated learning experience of history, together with many surprising and deeply interesting dimensions of war, which I had been unaware of. My understanding of Churchill's answer to Auchinleck's claim, was that the Allies were exhausted and low in morale, after several hundred miles of retreat. Therefore Winston and other commanders believed strongly that inspiration from new leadership was a prerogative.

My experience at the polo school was that mixing well known, experienced polo players with novices, can only work and be beneficial, when the intention is genuinely to help the improvement of others. The problem was that although they promised to conform, many of the better players, having never or seldom coached others, found it difficult not to revert to showing off their individual skills, in a way that prevented the novices from participating. The father of Adolfo Cambiaso, now the world's most famous player, also called Adolfo, looked for a week of relaxation for himself, by coming to Whitfield, bringing a young client for me to train and coach. As often happens with Argentines, soon after their arrival, the telephone rang and a friend of Adolfo senior was imposed upon us the next day. Alex Mihanovich, an ex 7 handicapped player, who had competed successfully in England for many seasons, both on the polo field during daylight and with the girls at night, arrived with boots and helmets. As there were only four polo clients that week, I invited these two polo gladiators to play in my school chukkas, on condition that they complied with my plans for sharing the ball continually with the novices. From the beginning Alex and Adolfo completely disobeyed my wishes, by trying to do clever shots and then, like naughty boys, giggling about it. My response, as I carried the all powerful whistle, was to trump up fouls against them and then ask my novice clients to take the penalty hits. They were surprised to find that I also had a sense of humour, but were still totally unable to adjust to the demands of helping others to improve.

Lord Oaksey, the son of the famous judge at the Nazi War Crimes Trials after the Second World War, who had inherited his title, arrived at Whitfield to report on my polo school for the *Daily Telegraph*. He was called John and was famous in his own right for having been one of the most successful amateur steeplechase jockeys in Britain and for being a highly esteemed racing correspondent for the *Daily Telegraph*. Obviously I was extremely happy that John had been chosen for this mission and we much enjoyed having him as our guest. He was enormously enthusiastic and very easy to teach and coach. In the evenings he treated us to some great stories. We were thrilled when his article was published in the *Telegraph* and then confident that it would provide good publicity for our polo school. Nevertheless I was surprised, after all his lordship's eagerness to play with us, that he did not attempt to continue his polo career in England, although it was clear that his work must have been time consuming.

Stowe, a well known English international boarding school, was the first academy to send me a group of boys for polo training. These pupils were refreshing with their enthusiasm to learn and the master in charge of them was so pleased with the results of their stay that he returned to Whitfield with a new group during another year. This time we had a rewarding experience when discovering a creative and significant solution for assisting anticipation. Previously I had had success with other clients by encouraging them to verbalise their tactical thinking. One example of this was to call out 'turning' before or even while changing direction. The Stowe boys were inhibited and hesitant about complying with the use of this word, forcing me to search for an alternative, until I suddenly remembered having been impressed, when hearing the concept of 'playmaking' being discussed, while watching a different sport. Without hesitation these young men immediately applied our new word with vigour and determination with surprisingly good results. I was then inspired to develop the concept of 'playmaking' as being relative to most dimensions of polo coaching. A few years later *Playmaker Polo* became the title of my second book, published in 2004. Rugby was the second school to bring boys to Whitfield Court. Besides being famous for inventing the game of 'Rugby', the grounds of this famous school had been utilised for the introduction of polo before the Second World War. Hence for me it was very pleasing that our polo school played a part, however small, in the re-establishment of polo there fifty years later.

After our unforgettable shocking experience in 1976 during the initial week of the polo school, I was well aware of the danger dimension that always existed, but I never expected that someone would fall off a wooden horse, in a cage. Then a rather excitable Italian appeared on one of our group of clients and proved me wrong. He lost his balance when reaching for a ball too far away from him, fell on his head and broke his wrist. Needless to say he was unable to continue playing, but remained with us, listening avidly to the rest of the instruction, while keeping everyone amused with his many comments.

Our dairy herd on the farm provided us with fresh milk, but the cows and milking operation caused very little interference to the pony routine, the polo and ourselves. Furthermore, the dairy yard where the milking took place, was of sufficient distance from our house to be considered out of harms way for our visitors. A nasty and smelly part of having cattle on a farm is the slurry pit where the liquid manure is stored, before being spread on the land, thereby reducing fertiliser costs.

Unknown to me, one of our clients was going for a run each morning before breakfast. On his last day with us he tried a new route, which took him through the dairy yard, where he ran straight into the slurry pit. History does not relate how he escaped drowning or asphyxiation, or how he was able to reach safety. Maria-Ines found him in a sorry state in the stable yard and brought him back to the house for a much-needed bath.

A gentleman, who worked in publishing in London, took the trouble to discuss in detail, with me, the possibilities of a polo book, about my coaching concepts and systems, being published. I had always thought that the potential market, for an instructional polo book, was far too small to be viable. However he was convinced that, one way or another, my structured inventive programme should be put in to writing. Luckily, perhaps a mini lottery for me, this client personally knew Mr Allen, the leading British equestrian publisher, who liked to support worthwhile books, with small sales prospects, by subsidising them from the profits of his best sellers. I feel indebted and most grateful that this valuable introduction, which I was then given to Mr Allen, created the opportunity for my first book, *Polo Vision*, to be published in 1984.

CHAPTER 15

Palm Beach Polo and Country Club

FOR SOME CONSIDERABLE TIME I HAD heard about Palm Beach Polo and Country Club (PBPCC), when I became aware that their management had sent a delegation to visit the Royal Dublin Horse Show in August 1982. John Oxley and his two sons had during the 1960s and 70s been the kings of Florida, USA, winter polo, at Boca Raton. Then Billy Ylvisaker, whom I had met in 1976 in Chicago, where he produced and organised the first ever Polo World Cup, for teams up to 40 goals, bought a large acreage at Wellington. This was in Palm Beach County and only a short distance west of the famous Palm Beach Island. Here he created PBPCC in which he developed 10 polo fields, 2 golf courses and a tennis centre with multi courts, plus several beautiful housing estates. The second Polo World Cup was played in 1978, at this magnificent new club, in Wellington, Palm Beach, thereby establishing a new winter headquarters for the polo world between January and April each year, when many other tournaments were also played. However initially there was no planned coaching of any level at this new club. I had wondered if this would be rectified and had enquired about this from a friend, who had suggested that I should contact the club directly. After much thought I decided it would be preferable if they came looking for me.

Hence when I received a surprise telephone call, telling me that Gary Stribling, the President of PBPCC, and his wife would like to visit me, I was naturally quick to suggest that they should stay a night with us at Whitfield Court. I will never forget the conversation, during and after dinner, swinging from one topic to another, without any mention of

221

any plan for coaching at PBPCC. I gave Gary Stribling a fairly detailed account about my polo school, which was then over halfway through our seventh summer season. Just before going to bed, Gary requested a lesson from me, on the wooden horse, after breakfast the following morning. The lesson must have gone extremely well, because as Gary jumped off the wooden horse he pointed at me and said 'You are coming to Palm Beach to run polo clinics for us next year'.

It was a heart stopping moment that changed the lives of my family and me. There and then I felt I had received total confirmation of winning my 6th lottery of finding the perfect second career for myself. I reflected that the lucky valuable experience of coaching in Germany had created this fortunate situation. In mid-January 1983 we set off, as a complete family, full of excitement for a dream trip to Florida. David and Sebastian had been taken out of school for a term and Whitfield Court had been handed over to Jack and Marjorie Williams, who had agreed to be caretakers. Pure luck had helped us to discover that it actually suited them to do this. I was feeling that a big weight had been lifted off my shoulders, in that I had delivered my first book *Polo Vision* to the London publisher J.A. Allen. However I had become accustomed to writing and editing, which made me feel wound up like a clock. To counter this problem I had started writing a novel with a polo story about a ball chaser, which had been in the back of my head for a long time. The many ball chasers, to whom I had applied the rope treatment, were wrapped up in one character, who chased the ball and girls, with equal zest, to ridiculous limits.

Little did we then know that I was destined to make this journey for twelve consecutive years, during which PBPCC would have four different owners, while I had to answer to three polo club managers, all with very distinctive characters. On arrival we received a great welcome, before we were taken to our allotted house, which was two miles from the club. Then I went to meet the staff and see the incredible facilities. I encountered an atmosphere of superiority that must inevitably breed egos, as anyone who lives in an aura of pure magnificence will surely agree. Billy Ylvisaker had made his dream come true, with manicured lawns, gorgeous colourful flowerbeds and twinkling water courses, free of weeds, spread attractively throughout the grounds. The many polo fields also looked like lawns, because they were cut and rolled after every match and practice game. There were several areas of stabling, each one designed by architects, to fit in to the environment of excellence. At the No. 1 polo field the grandstand, an attractive landmark, provided comfortable spacious seating, besides containing smart offices and tidy stores. The best polo players in the world were there to exhibit their skills, in some highly competitive and thrilling tournaments.

To all the above my ten weeks of polo clinics would now be added, offering instruction in the basics of the sport, coaching on team play and an opportunity to participate in constructively organised chukkas. To my obvious delight all ten clinics were fully booked. I quickly became aware that the secondary object of this handsome club was to sell houses. The development of these, in varying shape and sizes, was ongoing in several different areas of the club grounds. A large PR and sales team were in evidence, around the club. Some of them talked to us about the general price structure. The famous Palm Beach Island was a few miles to the east of Wellington Village, where PBPCC was situated. We drove around in the car, allotted to me, discovering one incredible supermarket after another and an array of amazing shops. While Maria Ines purchased all our house requirements, I remained in the car scribbling succeeding chapters of my ball chaser story. After a few days the serious part had to begin. I was shown the ponies that had been selected for my clinics. There was one for myself and each participant of a clinic, stabled inside the club. In reserve, in a local riding school, belonging to Walter Kuhn, there were a few that could be called on at short notice. I discussed the format of each week and I was invited to design my own programme. However I encountered great difficulty in explaining my concept for the chukkas, which would be played, on four of the days, as a finale to the lessons. This playing session was the only time I would require an assistant. Hence I insisted that 3 students would play with me and 3 with the appointed helper so that, as in Whitfield, we both could deliver passes for others to score goals. My boss obstinately continued talking about groups of 8, instead of 6 or 9 to fit my plans.

Throughout the clinics, I met an interesting mixture of people, from very distinguished backgrounds, high-powered employment situations and a cross-section of American society. That first year my clinic programme ran from Wednesday to Sunday lunch time, after which we watched the big Sunday match together. My riding school drills, wooden horse hour, stick and ball session, tactical lectures, walking through set piece plays, chukkas and watching a video of the play was augmented, once a week, by viewing a recording of a thrilling high goal match of the previous year. Thus I watched this same video ten times, but only near the end of that memorable first visit to Palm Beach, did I spot an extremely significant fact about the build up and scoring of one of the goals. After twice badly miss hitting the ball, a No. 4 unintentionally ended up by the corner flag, to the right of the goal, which he was attacking. Then he struck a perfect tail backhand, to land the ball very close to the goal, allowing his No. 2 to score with a simple tap in. Why, I then asked myself, could not a team tactic be to plan deliberately a similar approach to a goal via a corner of the field, as a surprise action. I even showed it to a team captain, who rejected the idea in an extremely negative manner.

To my joy the first clinic was deemed to be a great success by the participants and the club staff, which made me feel on top of the world. But little did I know that, round the corner, we would face the wettest February and March of the century in Florida. This meant that five out of the remaining nine clinics could not be completely finished, causing a mixture of delight and dismay for many of the participants. They experienced an enjoyable taste without covering the whole programme. They were only partly consoled by an offer to return free for the missed portions, in the knowledge that this would be complicated to arrange. When the weather allowed I felt that I continued to achieve good results with the visiting clients for the polo clinics, while appreciating meeting people from so many different states in the USA. Several of them generously, separately, invited me to dinners in local restaurants, when the conversation was often entertaining, although inevitably the topic about the stupidity of polo without coaching, was always raised. When possible, I went to see a few high goal polo matches, in order to watch constructively,

Hugh, Maria Ines, David and Sebastian Dawnay

Hugh Dawnay with the pony club in Northern Ireland

The four men in the Dawnay family – David, Nicolás, Hugh and Sebastian

 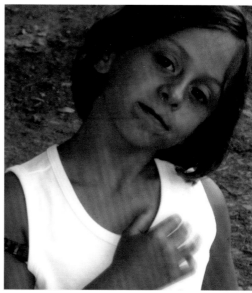

LEFT : *David and Aisha Dawnay.* RIGHT: *Lucia*

Louisa and Sebastian Dawnay's wedding

Whitfield Court Polo Club (LEFT–RIGHT):
Chris Hennessy, James Kennedy, Hugh Dawnay, Peter Reilly

Whitfield Court Polo Club (LEFT–RIGHT):
The Major, Pat Flahavan, John Flahavan, James Kennedy Jr

ABOVE: *Costa Careyes polo fields, Mexico*

FAR LEFT: *Costa Careyes team*

NEAR LEFT: *Hugh Dawnay*

BELOW: *Exercising polo ponies on the beach at Costa Careyes*

Dublin Horse Show, Phoenix Park. (LEFT–RIGHT) *Sebastian Dawnay, David Dawnay* (FAR RIGHT) *Major Hugh Dawnay*

PHOENIX PARK (LEFT–RIGHT): *The Major, Andrea Vianini, Sebastian Dawnay, Greg MacKinley, David Dawnay*

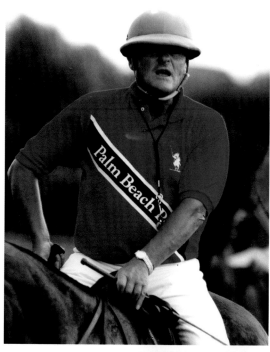

(LEFT AND BELOW)
*Hugh Dawnay at
Palm Beach Polo Club*
(©RICARDO MOTRAN AKA SNOOPY)

Hugh Dawnay

hoping to learn and advance my own knowledge, for the benefit of my polo clinics. Maria Ines made a few new friends, including Lorraine, who was to become a lifetime close associate. David and Sebastian took school lessons from a tutor and must have benefitted from this Florida experience. This involved some golf lessons and an introduction to American football, which was unwisely played, as an inter-family battle, leading to inevitable petty squabbles between the younger members. Yet this did help us to understand the matches on television.

Billy Ylvisaker had planned and supervised the development of a club that provided almost everything and anything, that gentlemen and their ladies could wish for. A fleet of white Cadillacs provided luxury transport for VIPs and sports heroes. Adding much to the lifestyle of this warm winter climate were restaurants in the polo and golf clubhouses, a cafeteria at the tennis, swimming pools in many locations, a croquet lawn and a vibrant bridge club. At the end of that first year at Palm Beach the club rewarded me by providing one of the white Cadillac cars for us to go, as a family, to the famous Florida Disney World at Orlando. We stayed one night in the Disney hotel, giving us time to visit and try all the wonderful facilities and stands. Mickey Mouse had given us a personal welcome, making David and Sebastian extra excited about the two days in front of them. We all enjoyed the experience and returned to Palm Beach, thrilled that we had been to a Disney World.

Despite the unexpected periods of wet weather, my first visit to PBPCC was clearly regarded as a success because, before departing, I had been booked to return in 1984. I was determined to improve the polo clinic routine for the benefit of my clients and myself. Hence from the second year onwards, the daily and weekly programme was modified as follows. The clinic opened at midday on Mondays and finished by lunch time on Saturdays. From Tuesdays to Fridays we started at 9 a.m. and, without anything more than a short break, we continued through to 2 p.m., with a positive finish on ponies at a polo field. Then I invited my clients to meet me again at 3 p.m., at the ground, allotted to the high goal match of the day, so that we could watch together the best players, to observe and critique their skills. This provided a welcome opportunity to those, who did not have other arrangements for their lunch, for buying a hot dog or hamburger and drinks.

This greatly improved system, allowed us to see 3 or 4 high goal matches, besides the Sunday game, giving us great scope to focus on and discuss the tactics and skills of many of the best players in the world. Furthermore we had the opportunity to confirm some of the riding and striking basics, which we had been covering earlier. Added to the above, I had the pleasure of watching plenty of good polo, from which my learning curve went sharply upwards, giving me an opportunity, to increase the contents of my coaching there, at Whitfield and wherever I travelled to work.

The arrangements for provision of ponies to the clinics was also much improved. It was all covered by Walt Kuhn, who had reinforced his riding school with extra ponies, making my life much easier, with only one person to deal with. Walt was a very cheerful special character and I was incredibly lucky to have his reliable service, guidance and assistance throughout my 12 years at Palm Beach. Not only did he always produce the right kind of ponies for the clinic but, when required, he often played himself to make up our numbers for chukkas. He tried hard to fit in to my system and generously provided ponies for David and Sebastian to play, whenever I asked to include them. They came to Palm Beach nearly every year, for varying lengths of time. Their participation in clinic chukkas, added so much pleasure in many dimensions. Firstly to me, secondly to them and thirdly to my clients, who were enthused by their enjoyment and other good qualities, that improved the play for them. David soon started to exhibit adult polo qualities, while Sebastian surprised and delighted many with his pony control and constructive hitting despite his small stature at that time.

The handsome white pony, which Walt provided as my personal steed, called Roger, can be seen on the cover of the second edition of my first book, *Polo Vision*. He was for me a really comfortable thoroughbred ride, although he loved to jump and bound, when I was approaching to hit a ball. However this did not prevent me, in chukkas, carrying out my normal ball distribution to my team, or from giving demonstrations on him, when required during practices. Casual observers wondered why I accepted riding a bounding horse, but he would not have suited any of my clients there and I became extremely fond of him.

Every year our family accommodation arrangements were changed. In 1984 Susanna Holt, the artist for my book *Polo Vision*, offered to rent us an apartment, which she owned, very close to PBPCC. Because it was nearer than the house, which the club gave me, for the first year, I quickly agreed. Then in 1985 Billy Ylvisaker appeared to confirm that I was required, for the long term, by offering us what is called a condominium, inside PBPCC itself. Each year, from then on, we were given a condo, in a different location within the club, but always one with 2 bedrooms, a sitting room and kitchen plus close access to a small swimming pool. I much appreciated living so close to my work and where the big polo matches were played, while living in contented luxury.

The extra pleasure I derived from my annual visits to Palm Beach was the valuable opportunity of meeting the eminent people who attended my polo clinics. They came from a variety of important professions and well known cities. In the very first clinic of all in 1983 Micky Tarnapol, the CEO of Revlon, participated and within two years he had returned as a high goal patron, which he continued to be until my last year in 1994. I was delighted when every year Mickey requested me to give him some private lessons, which I much enjoyed because we would successfully rehearse situations in which he, the No.4, could temporarily enter a team attack. However my health was not improved when I watched his team play in a tournament match and saw that his pros completely ignored Mickey, when he positioned exactly as we had practised.

I was extremely lucky throughout my 12 years at PBPCC that I always had a competent assistant to play as the other No. 3 opposite me in the clinic chukkas. Experience quickly taught me how to employ many alternative formats to produce 4 aside teams, that included the assistant and myself, for all the chukkas, regardless of numbers in a clinic.

Initially I started with Martin Glue, a 3 goal player from Cowdray in England, who had a good job at PBPCC, looking after the ponies of a wealthy American team patron, except that he was precluded from playing in matches or chukkas. Hence on most days my clinic chukkas at 1 p.m. were ideal for him to be available, and our gentle speed of play suited perfectly the novice ponies, which he was training for his boss. Martin could hit every angle shot in the book, enabling him to send passes in all required directions, that kept his three team members highly involved in a good learning experience. A small world connection was that Martin's wife had once been taught polo by me, when I was visiting Kenya, her home, to give courses to large groups of players.

One year Martin informed me that his boss was starting to object to him being permanently committed to my polo clinics. However he was rapidly replaced by another Martin, an Argentinian, called Martin Aguerre, who had heard about my requirement and volunteered to take on the task of being my assistant. I was at first suspicious that he, like many of his brethren, had ulterior reasons for helping and also, that as a 7 goal player, he would be too superior to fit in. To my relief and delight Martin was excellent in a low key manner, besides giving me extra confidence with his continual encouragement, by complimenting my chukka system and the results attained by the members of each clinic. Naturally he could deliver perfect passes to his team without any difficulty. Then for my last few years at Palm Beach Walter Kuhn came up with a very satisfactory solution for himself, me and the clinic. He offered his son, Steve Kuhn, an experienced 2 goal player, who had come home to help with the organisation of all Walter's ponies, to be my assistant. Steve competed with me to give more passes to his team than I did to mine, thereby strongly unifying our efforts to teach 100 % team polo.

I cannot remember the exact evolution of events that happened before I finally unearthed the perfect arrangement, which allowed my clinic chukkas to be always enjoyed, on one of the club's beautifully manicured polo fields, instead of an ugly practice area. Unbelievably I had to suffer all kinds of ridiculous opposition and invented problems, that initially denied me availability, from such a wealth of wonderful fields, spread over the vast club area. Ironically it was only a chance observation, which I made to a friend, that made me suddenly see that a solution existed, within the unique system employed at PBPCC, for maintaining their fields to such a high standard. I was at the time watching a team of gang mowers move in to action, on a field, immediately after a polo match finished, when I said 'That has to be unnecessary, wasting that machinery and man power, when that field is still in great condition, almost as if there has not been a game played on it!' Then I responded to myself, 'My Clients would be thrilled to play on that field just the way it is right now and our speed of play could not cause any unacceptable damage!' Hence I took a proposal to the head groundsman, that after an 11.30 morning match, we would always be happy to use the same field at 1 p.m., when no one else was playing and before the mowers cleaned it up. To my surprise this was not only agreed but also praised. Thereby we made the clinic members very content and highly pleased with our chukka locations, while causing no extra work for his excellent maintenance team.

We developed the use of the wooden horse in Palm Beach. These wooden beasts took a long time to be established satisfactorily in one location. This was because there was intense competition between all the departments of the club for any facility areas. Finally I arrived in Florida one year to find 6 wooden horses, all together in line abreast, with nets to hit in to, both in front and behind them. From then on it was easy, whatever the numbers in a clinic, to keep all of them occupied, either hitting balls or collecting them. Our maximum was 9 people, which was ideal because it gave me 6 hitters and 3 ball boys/girls, who could also learn by being asked to critique the shots of others by me. I was pleasantly surprised how well the line of 6 responded to military type drills, when they all took the same shots together. The competition dimension greatly improved the overall standard, as when mistakes took place, they stood out clearly for the ball collectors and me to see and comment constructively.

What often amused me was when I noticed that some players dressed for the wooden horse, similarly as for playing a polo match. Wearing breeches, boots, knee pads and even spurs they looked as if they were ready for battle, rather than a quiet little practice. Nevertheless the progress from the daily hour on the wooden horse, now became significant for large and small clinic groups. The competition, which I organised on the last day of each clinic, became extra exciting and the shots on the polo field were visibly more accurate.

The periods when we reviewed and critiqued the clinic chukkas are carved clearly in to my memory, because they brought Snoopy in to my life. Ricardo Mottron of Argentine/Lebanese extraction is a totally unique character, who is well known in the world of polo, for his outstanding photography. This was his main occupation, under the trade name of Snoopy, during the 3 months Palm Beach polo season, although to earn extra dollars he ventured in to videoing polo matches and my clinic chukkas.

Tall and corpulent, he has dangerous charm and is an impossible timekeeper, being frequently late for meetings and assignments. The polo club had booked him to film our chukkas and to deliver the resulting video to me on the following day. Often I thought he had failed to turn up for our chukkas, only to find that, on the next day, an excellent tape had arrived for showing. On other days the arrival of the video happened at erratic times, together with the most ridiculous excuses. Yet it was difficult to complain when his work was always high class. In later years I had an unforgettable experience with Snoopy when making an instructional video with him, which will be told in another chapter. However he rallied brilliantly to give many wonderful photographs for my second book *Playmaker Polo*, which enormously enhanced the publication, making it in to a coffee table book, besides being instructional covering a wide subject matter.

My previous experience at Whitfield Court Polo School was naturally useful in many dimensions. Especially use of my humour to insult the professions of my clients, as the Americans seemed to give me more scope and I heard friendly comments about my English dry humour. One interesting profession, which I had not encountered before, was a head-hunter. He worked in New York and openly talked to me about the absorbing challenge of his job. When he reached the end of his clinic, after the graduation chukkas he said 'Major this has been one of the outstanding weeks of my life, my gratitude is boundless so please let me know if there is anything that I can do for you.' Although I was surprised I bounced back with 'You are a head-hunter, please find me a brilliant agent.' He had not been expecting this and his face of surprise, shock and incredulity stayed in my memory for a few months.

PBPCC was a hive of activity, with tournaments at three levels, involving a large number of polo playing pros, with different handicaps, varying from 2 to 10 goals. The best of them were booked for the whole Palm Beach season and beyond in other places and countries. The less well known were always searching for extra work, there and in the future, in other parts of USA and the world of polo. No better target area for locating potential team patrons than the participants in my clinics, when they were together under my control. Initially I naïvely thought the pros, which I kept seeing around us, were giving me support, by showing an interest in what I was doing and by encouraging my clients. Later on I sadly realised that most of the smiling faces, belonged to Pros, who were imparting a sales pitch that my clinic was too novice for them and therefore suggesting that employing a playing Pro was the best alternative for them in the future.

Equally misleading was the attitude by the hierarchy of the United States Polo Association (USPA). I had expected them to be enthused to know about the format of my clinics, by coming to visit me in action here and there. Furthermore I was optimistic that they would then follow up, by exhorting many USPA clubs and their members to sign up for my clinics in future years. Yet although I was introduced to various Presidents, Chairmen and Secretaries of USPA, during all my years at Palm Beach, when I automatically invited them to come to watch and meet my clients, I was never made aware of any constructive action by USPA to support or show appreciation of my Palm Beach clinics. However I was thrilled and delighted to hear Billy Ylvisaker, being quoted as saying, that the polo clinics were excellent and also a success in the way they helped with the sales of houses, built inside the grounds of PBPCC.

I thought I had found the perfect practical way to improve my coaching and control, while playing chukkas, when I read an advertisement for an intercom system between players. So I took a risk by purchasing 8 sets of ear pieces and batteries etc, which I took with me to Palm Beach one year. With excitement I fitted out all my clients, my assistant and myself, to discover that communications were initially good. Although playing in one team as their No. 3, I found that I could give constructive advice to players, from both teams, thereby continually helping to create a near continual flow, up and down the polo field. After a couple of successful weeks with the ear phone system a surprise negative factor interfered. It just took one player to start complaining about a discomfort of wearing the equipment, to upset the whole system. For example one week it might be the weight of the battery, the next week it could be about a sensitivity of a ear leading to discomfort, and a third week there was a player, who kept dropping a part of the equipment on the ground. Hence I had to abandon the project and withdraw the equipment from all, because there was chaos unless all players could hear and react to the system at the same time. Also too much time was being wasted distributing and setting up each player with the system and then recollecting it when one of the problems occurred.

During my 12 years at Palm Beach approximately 600 clients participated in my polo clinics. I was only ever aware of one, who brought a strong complaint against me, called John. He was a large, overweight and unfit Englishman, who had booked for two weeks consecutively. John said that he was really only using the first week as a way to get fit for the second, in which he hoped to shine, having learnt an amount that would improve his game. Despite John's stated intentions, during his first clinic, I managed to keep him satisfactorily involved in most of the training and much of the chukkas, up to the end of the Friday. However this had made me worry that the others might be starting to resent, that their progress was being handicapped, and therefore on the final day, Saturday, I deliberately allowed the graduation chukkas to speed up beyond the abilities of John, in the belief that he would have been very content with his participation of the previous days and be understanding of the situation. At the end, when we congregated for the presentation of graduation certificates, John refused to attend and departed without saying a word to me.

On the Sunday I heard that John was complaining bitterly to everyone, he met, and was threatening to withdraw from his second clinic, starting on Monday. By chance I read my horoscope, Sagittarius, in a local magazine, which clearly said 'Someone will try making big problems for you, by complaining, but if you do not mention it and treat him, as if nothing has happened, all will go well for you.' Remembering my remarkable experience in 1971, when my horoscope forecast an impossible connection, I obeyed my stars to the letter, and on Monday I greeted John with the other members of the new clinic, without mentioning anything about the previous week. Later I heard that wonderful Walt Kuhn had taken much trouble, to explain my position to John. During the second week the problem was not spoken about and John kept up with the other participants, appearing to enjoy himself and be highly satisfied with his own performance.

I always insisted that all polo clinic participants carried a whip, when riding a pony, for two very clear reasons. Firstly because complete pony control, on the vast majority of ponies, is simply not possible, without the use or deterrent of a whip. Secondly the astute employment of a polo whip, is itself a skill, that should be learnt, in order to achieve the best results, as long as cruelty is avoided. One American, Bob, who owned a warehouse of equestrian tack and supplies, so that he dominated the market and sales of equine products in his home town, arrived in Palm Beach, for my clinic. Bob had all the necessary polo equipment with him except a whip. He surprised and shocked me when he blatantly refused to buy, beg for, borrow or steal a whip, from another person or from one of the many tack shops in the local town, Wellington. Bob, as a result, spent the whole time, when on top of a pony, struggling to conform to all the drills, exercises and tactics in which he was participating. I continued to explain the reasons for obtaining a whip and even suggested finding a tiny branch, from a tree, if not a proper whip. Despite all his self-imposed suffering, Bob battled on with a determined look on his face which gave the message, 'No one is going to make me buy something that I already have in abundance in my warehouse.'

The art of giving good compliments that satisfy the recipients is extremely skilful. At Palm Beach the Americans taught me the valuable lesson of how to accept praise graciously. 'Thank you Major' frequently rang out across polo fields, in reply to my briefest encouragements, such as 'Good shot Bill' or 'Clever adjustment John' or 'Well ridden Tom'. The best of the Polo Vice Presidents, at PBPCC, whom I had to answer to, consistently said to me, at the end of Clinics, 'They tell me you have the patience of Job'. Although he genuinely wished to raise my morale and I was grateful to hear this, my work in that unusual special atmosphere could never have been done by an impatient coach. Ironically I have often been criticised and pleaded guilty to lack of patience in other dimensions of my life, including family matters, when travelling and during volunteer work. Patience comes naturally when you completely know what you are doing. The most magnificent reward for me was receiving grateful letters from clients, who attended Palm Beach and Whitfield Court. I still have a file full of their kind words, together with a number of appreciative newspaper and magazine articles. Added to the above the commentator at the Sunday matches, often spoke highly of my work, which pleased me despite realising that he had been briefed to advertise the clinics for the club.

What became music to my ears was a comment, that was almost inevitably made, during every Palm Beach clinic: 'Major what you are teaching us is wonderful and practising it is enjoyable, BUT there is one big problem, when we return to our home club nobody else will be playing in this way.' Initially I wondered if this was a backhanded compliment and I must have exhibited a shocked reaction, until time established that my normal automatic retort derived magic results with the suggestion 'You have two alternative adjustments, either bring them to me or take me to them at your club'. By the end of my 12 years of visits to Florida, I had been invited to 16 other clubs in the USA, many other countries and several groups from the clubs of previous clients had attended my Palm Beach clinics, while many more American individuals had come for coaching at Whitfield Court.

Hence I have to admit that there were many worthwhile positives, from these extra trips to USA, although there were annoying negatives, which reflect the ongoing blindness that so sadly exists at club and association level. These bonuses and disappointments are fully described elsewhere. Nevertheless I personally benefitted enormously by seeing much more of USA, while adding invaluable knowledge and experience to my CV, besides being the recipient of a big amount of generous hospitality. I believe that my clients in each place improved their polo abilities considerably, yet sadly without receiving ongoing revision, of the many basics, which I imparted, they never had the full advantage that they deserved from participating in my structured lessons and clinics.

A patron from Boston, Massachusetts, with a 3 handicap, recruited 3 Argentinian professionals to play in his team at Palm Beach in two consecutive 26 goal tournaments, which had large entries. These players' handicaps were 9, 7 and 7, and without a coach to advise them, they decided to line up (play) in front of the patron, who being a big man, wished to be the No. 4, at the back.

The first tournament, sponsored by Rolex, was a knock out, in which they were comprehensively beaten by 6 goals and thus eliminated in the first round. Their conquerors, called Cartier, had two very famous players from Argentina. The second tournament had the different format of two leagues, each of seven teams, with the eventual winner of each league designated to meet in the final. The Boston team duly began their programme of 6 league matches and had lost the first 5, in my opinion without appearing to have any chance of winning, at any moment in the games. The day before their 6th and ultimate league match, which was to be again between Boston and Cartier, the Boston patron requested to meet me to ask some questions about Ireland, where he was planning to go to visit his relatives. I believe I was only able to help him, in a minor capacity, but before saying goodbye I could not resist asking him 'Are you enjoying playing at Palm Beach?' At first he replied 'Yes' but then he added, 'I would enjoy it much more if my team could win a match'. I quickly replied, unable to stop myself, 'How can you expect to win, when your team is wasting 7 goals?' I then went on to explain my opinion that the No.1 in their team, a 7 goal handicapped player, had remarkably little involvement with the ball, making it physically impossible for his team to beat other 26 goal teams, while wasting 7 goals.

The following day I went to watch Boston's final match, wondering if my words would be seen to have any effect. To my absolute delight, from the beginning the other players conspicuously passed the ball to their No. 1, whenever possible. The result was that the Boston team quickly took the lead, which they continued to increase in every chukka. The commentator was heard to say 'This is the biggest surprise of the whole season'. At the end Boston defeated, by 8 goals, the Cartier team, which had previously beaten them by 6 goals. The No.1 had only scored a few goals himself, but he had been fully involved throughout, receiving and giving passes, to set up most of the goals in different ways. Meanwhile behind him the 9 and the other 7 found themselves with more freedom than before and played brilliantly, scoring frequently.

My observation had clearly been listened to and acted on, making the gigantic difference of 14 goals, compared to the previous time these two teams met. I never actually met the No. 1 there, but I was genuinely thanked by the other three players. Sadly the Boston team departed from Palm Beach the next day, and never played together again. I have told this story to a number of people, who always gave me the impression that they thought I was exaggerating, or even inventing the tale.

Ten years later I went to Argentina to see the Open Polo tournaments and spend Christmas there. For the latter I went to the coast of the province of Buenos Aires, with my wife Maria Ines, our son David, his wife Aisha and their children Lucia and Nicolas. The house, which we rented, was a 15 minute walk from the sea that we enjoyed daily, because the route took us through a lovely wood and past some pretty cottages. One day a familiar looking man appeared, in front of us, as he left a cottage. I recognised him as an Argentine polo player and he saw my bald head and immediately knew it was me. He was in fact the Boston No. 1 and when later we met for a drink, he remembered his experience at Palm Beach, but had no idea why the fortune of his team had been so radically reversed in the second match against Cartier. Reference my argument about the vital importance of polo coaching at every level after the above, I rest my case, only to add, 'There are none so blind as those who wish to be'!

I had one opportunity to be involved in high goal coaching, while working at Palm Beach. Shortly after arriving to begin another year of polo clinics, I was approached by a 7 goal player, Calle Garcia, to know if I was interested in assisting his 22 goal team, which was having a bad season, had lost their last 6 matches and only had one tournament left to compete in. The patron and No.1 was Billy Busch (2), an American; at No.2 was Fortunato Gomez(8) from Argentina; at No.3 Calle Garcia(7) from Cuba; and at No.4 the late Bobby Barry(5), an American.

Naturally I was interested and excited, but first had to ensure that everything was organised for my first clinic of that year, and to verify that I could be available at the required times. Then there was so little time, before their first round of this last tournament that it became clear to me that there was only one way to proceed. This was to have a simple team discussion, round a table, after which I would attend as sideline coach for their first match. The meeting round the table seemed to be very positive. I asked all of them to describe their 'thought processes' for all the set piece situations. In essence their answers demonstrated that their thoughts were not sufficiently connected to produce a structured team strategy. Yet we quickly achieved agreement between them for the future basic thinking in most situations, making each of them aware of what the other three were expecting from them.

At the first match they played well as a team, connecting with good anticipation, and won fairly easily. However I did pick up that Fortunato, who was incredibly quick to cover Calle in defence, was causing a muddle with Bobby, that left one opponent unmarked at crucial times, when goals were scored against them. This highlighted the classic problem of mixing different standards (handicaps), which only happens in polo. By first congratulating Fortunato on his speed and then indicating the problem, he gracefully accepted the point. The second match, against stronger opposition, was closer. But it was a good victory with the defence working much better, because Fortunato controlled his speed, not to interfere with Bobby, thereby reducing the occasions, when opponents were unmarked. Our team now had high morale and had two more comfortable wins, to qualify for the tournament semi-final. Here the opponents, who included top English player, Julian Hipwood, were the winners of the two previous 22 goal tournaments. Basically we had to accept that they were a better and faster team than our group of players, so that the only possibility of beating them was to obey the chapter in my book *Polo Vision*, called 'How to beat a better team'. The main concept of this is to reduce the speed of play, by avoiding the middle of the field, through regularly hitting the ball towards the boards along the sides, which can be achieved from widening the angle of most backhands.

Unfortunately Fortunato had his reasons for not agreeing with me to implement this tactic. The result was a disastrous first chukka which ended with the score at 0-3 against us. My dismay was diminished, while the players changed ponies, by Fortunato saying to me in front of the others 'Major, you were right and I was wrong, we must from now on take the ball round the sides of the ground'. From then on the opponents lost their superiority and by the end of the 4th chukka the scores were level. But for a miss by our team, of only inches from a goalpost, in the 5th we remained at an even score, when the last chukka commenced.

Out of the blue Murphy's Law struck, when the most unexpected reason prevented our tournament victory. Bobby Barry was hit by a sudden fever, yet continued playing, without telling anybody. Watching around the sidelines, there must have been at least a dozen 5 goal players, who could have come on as a substitute. Even so we only lost by 1 goal and we had given 3 away in the first chukka. Our victorious opponents went on to win the final easily, suggesting clearly that, free of any bad luck factor, my team should also have won. Hence I felt that I was cruelly robbed of the opportunity to enhance and accelerate the future of polo coaching, in high goal, at that time. Without doubt my team had improved enormously from my input, but people only remember winners. Nevertheless I had proved to myself the importance of my concept about coaching.

Billy Busch invited me the following year to coach his reconstructed team, but he changed the remit to cover other dimensions, including pony management. After much thought, reluctantly, I felt unable to commit to so many responsibilities in parallel with ten weeks of polo clinics. A similar opportunity never occurred for me at Palm Beach again. However more of the high goal teams, there, did start the practise of having coaches.

One afternoon I was standing with a large group of my clinic clients, watching the 3 p.m. high goal match. That morning while we were working on the wooden horses, I had emphasised the importance of the mallet head, for a brief moment, pointing exactly at the desired target. Furthermore I had invited them to critique each other, by specifically observing the mallet heads of others, during the swing, before contact was made, when hitting a ball. Suddenly there was a pause in the match, when the ball went over a backline, off a defender's mallet. The equivalent of a corner in soccer, known in polo as a safety 60, was awarded to the other team. This meant that 60 yards from and opposite, where the ball had crossed the backline, a shot at goal could be hit at goal, similar to a penalty shot.

Up stepped an 8 handicap American pro player, Dale Smicklas, who was renowned for his big hitting, to take the penalty. By coincidence there was a straight line between where we were standing, the ball and the centre of the goal. I noticed this and said to all my clients, 'We now have the perfect opportunity, from here, to see and then discuss where his mallet head points, during his swing.' We all watched intently as Dale hit a long high ball that missed the goal by a few inches, outside the left goalpost. Most of them agreed with me that his mallet head had pointed at the right-hand goalpost, instead of correctly at the centre of the goal. Therefore the ball was minutely mishit, because the mallet head had not turned a perfect circle.

The next day at another 3 p.m. match I saw Dale Smicklas amongst the spectators. At half time, while the crowd were walking on the field to repair the divots, made by the feet of the ponies, I approached Dale to talk to him about his missed penalty, how my clinic members and I had thought that his mallet head pointed right and why this caused the miss. To my surprise he openly admitted that he had never considered the importance of knowing where the mallet head pointed. He added that he had once been coached by an ex pre-Second World War and post-war 10 handicap player, who had never even touched on the subject. Our paths did not cross for another two weeks, during which I had not been present at any of Dale's games. When I happened to meet him inside the club I asked him about his success rate with recent penalty shots. 'Major havn't you heard, I have not missed one since you last spoke to me?' he replied. I hoped he might invite me for a drink to discuss the subject further, but he walked away making no other comment. The casual way in which he had applied my advice, without apparent gratitude, was probably typical of a pro, who was not regularly under the guidance of a coach.

I was always pleased, when invited to give extra lessons to residents and temporary visitors to Palm Beach. These included children, wives and even parents of the players, who were participating in the tournaments.

The children showed more enthusiasm than others, but I had to be careful to limit the amount that I taught them in one session. The wives could be prickly, when criticised, and the parents of players were apt to tell me what their problem was, while showing little interest in my opinion. Normally, I gave this coaching in the evenings. One advantage of this time of day was that there was no dusk in Florida, so that darkness arrived very quickly, clarifying the exact minute when my work had to stop. Also on many evenings we witnessed some extremely beautiful sunsets with glorious deep colouring.

There were several dimensions to social life at PBPCC. The most enjoyable was dining with or attending a drinks party with our personal friends. Less relaxed were the cocktail parties given for my clinic clients by the polo club. We also, about twice a year at a weekend, tucked in to a sumptuous brunch, at the polo clubhouse, before the Sunday match. At these a special concoction of Bucks Fizz was poured from large jugs, sending a number of cheerful spectators to enthuse over and support their chosen team, at the polo match.

Before the throw in took place, for this well attended Sunday game, the American national anthem was sung. Every week there seemed to be a different version, sung by a variety of singers, even choirs. This was followed by a grace and blessing from a jovial local priest, who cleverly included a topically amusing subject each week. After the prize-giving an enormous crowd would invade the bar at the polo clubhouse. When one eventually achieved a drink, in the hand, it was impossible to hear a word of what anybody was saying. Following a few experiences of the above, Maria Ines and I looked for excuses, to allow us to avoid that performance.

I arrived at Palm Beach one February to find that I had been allotted one of the white Cadillacs, which were provided to the club as a form of sponsorship, as my car. I felt as if I had earned my spurs or team colours, because it was clearly a privilege to enjoy the luxury of a car, with such prestige. To begin with I enjoyed the comfort and glamour of driving this smart car in place of the normal hired vehicle. However over time the negatives of being given a sponsored car started to dawn on me. Every Sunday I had to ensure that the Cadillac was spotlessly clean, outside and inside, before handing it over to take part in a VIP parade that happened before the big polo match of the weekend. Then I would have to wait until after the prize giving was over, before I could regain my only mode of transport. Also I became shocked, when frequently observing the fuel gauge being close to empty so quickly after I had filled the tank.

Naturally the consequences of driving such a conspicuous car attracted trouble. The first example happened, when I was invited to dinner to the enormous and famous Breakers Hotel by one of my clinic clients. I had left our condominium a little late and was hurrying too much to take notice of a 40 m.p.h. sign, just before joining a highway. Suddenly a police siren sounded and all the cars, in front of me, pulled over on to the hard shoulder and stopped. Luckily I copied their action, before seeing a search light resting its beam on one car after another, until finally coming to a halt on my roof. The other halted cars quickly disappeared, while I waited for the expected call of 'Get out of your car and put your hands above your head'. Instead a police officer opened the door of my car and requested some identification. I produced a credit card, which he examined before saying, 'What is a Major?' I explained trying to sound contrite and humble, to which he replied 'You were doing 80 in a 40 limit'. I stuttered that I was sorry but had not been aware of being in the 40 limit. After a brief further discussion to my relief he said, 'I still do not understand what Major means, but I love your accent and you seem to be a really nice gentleman; so on your way and watch your speed.'

The following year I went to Florida a few weeks ahead of Maria Ines. Then on a Sunday I had to drive, after the Sunday match, to meet her at Miami airport. The game went in to extra time, which delayed my intended departure. Hence once I had collected my Cadillac, I crossed the car park, driving at a decent speed, heading for the main road, that leads to the major highway to Miami. Unknown to me, the president of the company that owns Cadillac, was walking across that same car park, at that precise moment. Seeing my car he had waved in a friendly manner, expecting recognition, when he rapidly had to jump out of the way, to ensure of not being in any danger. The next day I was outdoors with a new group of clients, when the vice president of polo came up to me saying 'You nearly killed the president of Cadillac; we are going to pull the car.' I innocently replied that I did not have any rope in my car. The next day my Cadillac was replaced by a sports car, my petrol bill was halved and at weekends I no longer had to clean my car and present it to participate in the VIP parade.

A French baron came to Palm Beach one year as the patron of a high goal team, which was competing in several tournaments. For the most prestigious event three eminent French businessmen came to stay with the baron to give him support and enjoy the comforts of Palm Beach. Being very active men, on the days when their host was not playing, they mildly complained about being bored. This resulted in someone suggesting to them that they should register, the following week, for the Major's polo clinic. Hence these three total polo novices appeared as members of my polo clinic, on the next Monday. They were all competent horsemen and my memory of them, which is not very clear, tells me that they were relatively easy to teach and coach

Ten years later I went to the Guards Club, at Windsor, in England, to watch my son Sebastian, play in a high goal match for a French patron, Hubert Perodo. When Sebastian introduced me to Hubert, to my surprise, he told me that he had been one of those three Frenchmen, who together had attended my Palm Beach clinic. I was a little embarrassed that I did not immediately recognise him, although I did remember the clinic with three Frenchmen.

Hubert Perodo was an oil industrialist, who could afford to employ the very best players for his team. Yet to my amazement during the match that day, he failed to score any goals himself, although given many opportunities, from receiving many accurate passes, because he did not know how to hit a simple half shot and always missed with wild full shots. The half shot has always been the first shot that I teach, thus it was clear that his brilliant professionals accepted his money, but did not take the trouble, ever to revise with him, the technique of the 'half shot'. After that polo season, Hubert Perodo retired from polo and took up mountaineering. Sadly he was killed from a fall from a high steep slope.

History does not record whether he was using the simple protection of being attached to others by a rope. You have to suspect that he was not.

With my Palm Beach clinics, I regularly repeated my Irish polo school exercise, of a team, sharing the ball, from one end of the field to another, before attempting to score a goal. Hence when Billy Ylvisaker, the club supremo, was training with his high goal team, on an adjacent polo field to us, I challenged him to do the same drill. To our great amusement his team took four attempts before they succeeded in scoring a goal. There were mutterings that it was a good way to train, but as far as I know, it was never adopted by any other team. Teams for rugby, soccer, hockey and basket ball do endless training in this format, making it clear that the polo players are missing a trick.

My first year at Palm Beach I was 50 years old, however I was not invited to play in an annual over 50 tournament until a few years later. When I did I was grateful to Walt Kuhn for allowing me to pick my ponies from his string. Nevertheless my opponents were playing on a higher class of pony and, playing at No.3, I had to use all the tricks, including hitting wide angled backhands to the boards, at the side of the field. As expected my team was beaten in the two matches, played by us, yet I was delighted to be congratulated afterwards, on having played in exactly the same way as I coached and instructed my clinics. I was especially pleased that such notice had been clearly taken, by these older players, of how my system of teaching was carried out. Furthermore I was extra happy, if surprised, to know that I had, myself, successfully executed those tactics and concepts in front of a critical audience.

One afternoon I was with a group of clients, who were having a session with me on the wooden horses. Suddenly I felt a very strange sensation in both my feet. A little later the feeling increased, giving me considerable discomfort. After another 15 minutes I was in real pain and had to jump up and down, while I talked and critiqued the hitting technique of my clients. I wondered if they thought that I was mad, but managed to finish the lesson. Later that evening I saw a doctor, who quickly diagnosed gout, gave me a prescription and some pointers for my diet. I suppose it was just another part of the aging process, which seems to include the onset of unexpected ailments.

In hindsight, although I have no direct proof, I believe that my Polo Vision clinics at Palm Beach did become well known throughout most of the polo playing countries in the world. If so more publicity must have been generated, than what I was aware of. Yet knowing that representatives, of the not so small club PR department, were often present at other polo events, I became frustrated that none of them came to meet my clinic clients.

The American *Polo* magazine, of the day, had published advertisements, stating that I was the best polo coach in the world. At the Palm Beach weekly Sunday match, the commentator would occasionally echo the same message. Naturally my ego was delighted, but deep down I was not too impressed, because *Polo* magazine was not read much, outside of USA. Also I knew that, at that time, there were relatively few polo coaches in existence, making the title of 'best' rather meaningless.

My ambition has always been that polo coaching should become much more important, being deemed to be valuable for all players at every level. In the polo clubhouse there were many photographs of famous players and successful teams displayed. I proposed that photos of my clinic members should be added, but only after repeating this request many times was the required action taken. Then looking at the smiling faces portrayed in those photos, I was thrilled to know that all future visitors would know that coaching was a valuable part of Palm Beach polo.

A French brother and sister, in their mid-teens, took part in one of my clinics at PBPCC. They were very enthusiastic and kept up with the adults in every dimension, except the ball striking while playing chukkas, where the pressure affected their confidence. To help counter this difficulty I was frequently reminding both of them to aim at the ball with the palm of the right hand and not with the head of the polo mallet. I had much amusement and satisfaction, with both siblings, when pushing them to apply the right hand, during our clinic chukkas.

To make the hand concept work, I encouraged clients to verbalise the action with the word 'hand' when hitting, thereby helping their imagination to feel that the hand was passing through the bottom of the ball. With the French I often tried 'la main'. An example of the success of the above I remember that the brother escaped, against the play, with the ball, but had hit his first shot weakly. As he approached for his second hit, I reminded him verbally by calling loudly 'hand', but he remained silent and hit weakly again. So I accelerated my pony, to draw level and alongside him, as he approached the ball for a third attempt, yelling 'this time I kill you if you do not say "hand"'. He then screamed 'hand', lofting the ball directly at the goal, with a wonderful facial expression of joy and surprise.

The next day I endeavoured to convince the sister by suggesting that she tried to remember the name of a boy, whom she disliked and had wanted to slap his face. I had had previous success encouraging other ladies to do this trick. So as she approached for each shot, I called out the name of the boy, resulting in her striking the ball much better than ever before and being amazed that she was hitting so well. In later years I was delighted, on several occasions, to read about the sister playing well in France and being in several winning teams. Also I was saddened to hear that the brother had lost an eye in a polo accident, however in 2004, when I went to the Polo World Cup, in France, to promote my second book, *Playmaker Polo*, I was delighted to see that he was in the French team, which reached the semi-final. After the French team had won an earlier match, I went to talk to him and we much enjoyed friendly reminiscences together.

The famous fiction writer, Jilly Cooper, came to Palm Beach, to prepare and increase her knowledge about the polo world, before writing her next novel. To my delight she invited me to lunch, at one of the clubhouses, in order to learn from me the correct polo language and to understand all the technicalities, that can arise, during a polo match. Jilly was sufficiently pleased with our meeting, to insist on a repeat reunion, to confirm her new polo knowledge and ask further questions. I then invited Jilly Cooper to a small drinks party at our condo so that she could meet Maria Ines and a few of our local friends. Everyone was impressed by Jilly's charm and charisma, as she flattered all the ladies about their appearance, while complimenting the men on achievements, which she had artfully extracted from them.

When her book *Polo* came out, it included a number of raunchy episodes, attached to her polo story, but most important of all the continuity and the polo language were perfect, while the sales were extremely satisfactory for the author. I was included in the list of those, who were thanked for their assistance, and my name was also once in the text.

During an autumn, or American Fall, the status of my polo vision clinics was given a boost, by PBPCC organising an evening reception in New York for all those who had participated in my coaching programme, since the beginning in 1983. Laurie, the daughter of Billy Ylvisaker, was the principal organiser and through her efforts the attendance was better than I had expected, with everyone present excited at being part of a reunion. I felt honoured and thrilled that this was happening. To indicate my pleasure I tried to help Laurie to sell the message that a return visit to my clinics at Palm Beach would be well worthwhile. We also discussed some of the future plans of the world's top players at Palm Beach the following season.

Little did I, or anyone else present, know that the ownership of PBPCC would change a year later. The great Billy Ylvisaker, who had held all three key thrones of the mighty Gould Corporation, on whose behalf he had purchased the Florida land, where this unique club was then developed as a world leader, had been slowly losing control of the Gould Board. First of all he was replaced as President, then relieved of being CEO, so that as Chairman alone, he did not continue to have the power and influence over all the shareholders. Hence at the next AGM, in Chicago, a majority voted for this wonderful club to be put up for sale.

On a few occasions I was asked to sit with visitors at the Palm Beach Sunday match, in order to enlighten them about the finer points of the game, and to give explanations of events as they happened. The most memorable of these was a group of American Express customers, who had come for a day out that included a tour of the club, brunch in the polo clubhouse and grandstands seats at the polo. They were all highly appreciative of any of the information, which I gave them, besides being pleasant and interesting to talk to. Some of the questions they asked clearly demonstrated that spectators, who have not themselves played polo, would enjoy and benefit from extra information to what is provided by the normal commentator over the public address.

Added to the above, the attention to someone sitting close to you, is certain to be better and easier to concentrate on, than a voice over a microphone, in a stadium. On one Sunday by coincidence I sat behind two smartly dressed couples, with the ladies wearing large elegant hats. Normally games will vary from minutes of excitement and skill to less entertaining moments of boring action and stoppages. On this occasion, from beginning to end, the play was enthralling and exciting, with end to end play, brilliant skills at full gallop and an ever changing scoreboard, as both teams took turns to be in the lead. At half time these four people stood up, shook their clothes, adjusted hats and loudly said, 'This is so boring so why don't we go home?'

I have also given a similar service at polo games, in other American clubs, to be described later, and do not understand why it is not employed all the time, around the polo world. There must be experienced players, current and retired, who could be regularly employed to improve the enjoyment of spectator groups, while themselves appreciating the experience.

Near the end of one clinic a very eminent American doctor/surgeon, who had previously complimented me, by saying how much he was enjoying the introduction to polo, which I was giving him, spoke to me again. 'Major, I have just realised that you are employing the Socrates method of teaching,' he said. I hesitated with my reply, while trying to understand exactly what he meant, before I answered, rather weakly, 'Oh, did you?' Only after I had made several enquiries, did I establish that the British Army, by introducing me to the effective 'thinker questioning technique' that I applied whenever possible to my polo coaching, had influenced me strongly to extend this method in to a long line of connecting questions, which had caused this flattering comment. My main intention with each and every question is to make the whole class mentally search for the answer, before I named only one person to reply. Thereby the memory cells of all my clients were hopefully kept primed as were those privileged listeners to Socrates, who had walked the streets of Athens, the capital of Greece, before the time of Jesus Christ.

During my twelve annual visits to Palm Beach, Florida, the most dramatic day has to be when a Space Mission exploded high in the sky above us. It was a beautiful peaceful day, with a gloriously clear blue sky. I was outdoors working with a group of polo clients, when suddenly one of them pointed to a turbulent white cloud. This explosion smoke was visible for several minutes before beginning to evaporate. It was hard to believe that so many valuable lives had been lost at that moment of tragedy.

The most humbling few minutes that I experienced at this wonderful club happened on the golf course. After a difficult day at work, I was seeking a mode of relaxation by going by myself in a golf cart round a few holes of golf, expecting to be unobserved when hitting this little white ball. I was really enjoying myself, obeying the best golf advice that I had ever heard, which was not to record my score, never look for lost balls and award myself mulligans, whenever it suited me. Suddenly I hit a rare long and accurate shot to approach a green. When I reached the ball, I saw four golfers standing on the green around the hole. I tried to ignore them and avoid being seen and wait until they had finished and moved on. To my horror all four of them began waving their arms, in the motion that means, 'please pass through'. Then I recognised them as the four famous Heguy brothers, each one of them a 10 goal polo player. Fifteen minutes later, after at least ten terrible shots, I eventually sunk the put. I never looked at them, although I knew them all, but I could imagine how much they must have been laughing. In hindsight I do not understand why I did not relish that unusual good approach shot, pick up my ball and move to another golf hole or golf course, far from the Heguy brothers.

CHAPTER 16

Costa Careyes, Mexico and Cyprus

My Palm Beach days were over, but would be cherished by me for ever in the knowledge that ten years of visits to one place was probably sufficient in such a large world. Hence in February 1995, I found myself flying out for my first ever experience in Mexico.

My son Sebastian had been the intended beneficiary of an invitation to glorious Costa Careyes on the Pacific coast of Mexico. He had made great friends with an Italian boy, who had stayed twice at Whitfield Court, for polo training with me. The mother of the Italian youngster, owned a house in Costa Careyes, and had tried to entice Sebastian to stay with them there, for the past two Christmases, unaware of his phobia, at that time, for flying. The result of this was that she connected me to Giorgio Brignone, the owner of the polo club at Costa Careyes, in the hope that I would be invited to coach there, and bring Sebastian with me.

Giorgio Brignone, in a strange coincidence, which I was to discover later, had been literally derailed, when en route to Whitfield Court, to start his polo training with me. A leading Mexican polo player had met him in Mexico City, a short time before he was due to catch a booked flight to Europe, and had persuaded (kidnapped) Giorgio, into putting himself under Mexicans, in order to learn polo at a higher level, from the beginning. There is of course a false logic in that surmise. However in the meantime Giorgio had developed two beautiful scenic polo fields close to the Pacific Ocean. His father, Jean Franco Brignone had in the 1970s founded an elite residential settlement at Costa Careyes. To design it, he had attracted some brilliant international architects, who produced a range of houses, that all had the polapa roofs made from palm tree straw. This was the perfect construction for their climate, which was gloriously sunny in the winter months, because it provided open living rooms without windows.

The original development created a central hotel by a beach, and connected to a layout of the private houses, an Italian type collection of luxury apartments (casitas) and a few beach bungalows, by a network of cobbled roads, destined to maintain their condition for ever. A variety of beautiful beaches, together with an inviting warm sea, beckoned visitors to sunbathe, swim, canoe, and sail in a true paradise. I had set out from Ireland via Heathrow London, intending to spend a night there with Richard Briton Long. On arrival at Terminal 1, Heathrow, I had gone straight to a telephone box, to make a few calls before collecting my luggage, and proceed to Richard's flat. My travelling jacket had a large inside pocket, in which I had my passport and air tickets in what I regarded as a secure place, for the whole journey. I must have taken the Mexican air ticket for some reason, to tell a friend my flight timings. Richard was also flying very early the next morning to another distant destination, departing like me, from Terminal 4. Conveniently I accepted a lift in his car to the airport. As we arrived, my hand casually felt inside my coat pocket to discover that there was only a passport there, with no sign of an air ticket. That dreaded feeling of a disaster around the corner, filled my body from head to toe. However I said goodbye to Richard, and walked towards my check-in area, wondering what I would say. Pathetically I squeaked, 'I have lost my ticket' to be told to wait a minute, after which someone arrived to ask me, 'Is this your ticket?' Miraculously it had been found by an angel at the telephone in Terminal 1, and handed in to British Airways in Terminal 4.

I was met by a car and driver sent by Giorgio Brignone to Puerta Vallarta airport. The journey of a hundred miles to the south took nearly three hours, with parts of it being scenic and colourful. On arrival I was shown to my room in an enormous house, next to the sea, before being taken to a dinner party. I felt aware that I was amongst a very friendly, widely international group of relaxed people. Giorgio Brignone introduced himself, and there and then we started a polo friendship that was to last a long time, and change my life in many ways. During my first night in a house called 'Mi Ocho' I thought that a violent storm had engulfed the whole area. I wondered if I had brought bad luck with me and prayed that I would not wake up to find damaged structures and fallen trees all around Careyes. Happily I arose the following morning to find a really beautiful day, and no sign of any destruction. Gradually I realised that the noise had been nothing more than the sea breaking on the rocks, which were below the house. Furthermore I became fully aware that I was living in a magnificent home as the guest of Giorgio Brignone.

From the beginning I took full advantage of the glorious swimming that was available in swimming pools and the sea. In both the temperature was perfect, and the water refreshing to be in. The sun gave out a welcome heat and in only a few days, I had changed to a colour of golden brown all over. I was taken to see the two polo fields, much admiring the scenery, setting and the lushness of the grass surface. The Mexican ponies were of good calibre and were easy to play, the most important factor for teaching. Two days later I played my first Mexican chukka, made up of players, who included a Germany artist, an Italian entrepreneur, three brothers from Mexico City, a vet from Puerta Vallarta and Giorgio. There was a cheerful group of Mexican grooms, who gave us our ponies and some of them were eager substitutes for later.

Gradually the polo clinics, which I had come to give, started to take shape. The majority of my clients, at the beginning, came from the two big cities, Guadalajara and Puerta Vallarta. As told earlier the saying 'Necessity is the mother of invention' unrolled in front of me on these flat polo fields, in such perfect weather conditions. I found myself extending my playmaker philosophy, in new riding drills, plus exercises for striking and tactics that would serve me brilliantly until the end of my coaching career, besides providing the foundation of my second book. Giorgio and other local club players helped to complete chukka numbers when required. My clients appeared to be happy, making welcome comments such as 'This is the best instruction I ever had'.

After two weeks, I literally began pinching myself to check that life was this good, that I really was staying in such a paradise with pleasant people, while enjoying polo coaching and glorious swimming. Another incredible dimension to Costa Careyes was that there was never a crowd, yet always someone new, who was international and interesting to meet. Dinner parties were given fairly frequently and normally included a delicious fish dish. The Mexican brothers mentioned above at the polo were called Solorzano. Two of them were twins, named Salvador and Antonio who regularly came to Careyes in a bargaining arrangement with Giorgio, that gave them polo when they were needed, in turn for assisting with the pony exercising and work by the regular grooms as required. They were very helpful to me in my efforts to learn my way around the Careyes area, while we spent a few hours together.

Giorgio provided me with a car, which was an old Volkswagen Beetle that was not in the best condition. One day I took a wrong turn on the cobbled road, and instantly tried to make a 'U' turn. I failed to complete the movement in one swing of the steering wheel, forcing me to pull the handbrake, in preparation for reversing, to my horror the whole lever came away in my hand. Luckily I reacted quickly to flatten one foot on the brake pedal, while my other foot found the clutch, enabling me to put the little gear stick in to reverse. Then with further dismay I realised that the car was on the edge of an enormous drop, into a wooden area below me, meaning that a mistake would send the car plunging to the bottom. To move backwards required me to lift both feet, at the same time, off the brake and clutch, followed by pressing the accelerator a split second after. For one reason or another I was unable to carry this out, real fear gripped me, and I started sweating profusely. After about twenty minutes I was relieved to hear another car passing behind me, and was able to shout loud enough to attract the driver's attention. Luckily in that car, there were two strong men, who succeeded in putting their joint weight against the Volkswagen, while I was able to reverse it safely off the cliff edge.

The highlight of my first wonderful year at Costa Careyes, was the week that was reserved for the FIP Ambassadors Tournament. The Federation of International Polo had been set up to organise tournaments at different levels between countries all over the continent. To assist the implementation of these tournaments, an annual tournament was created for the appointed FIP ambassadors in all polo countries as a means of bringing them all together. It moved to a new country every year. Hence this was a first for Mexico, temporarily filling Careyes with interesting international people including the founding FIP President, Argentine Marcus Uranga, and his successor, the debonair Californian Glen Holden.

Four teams of equal handicap, made up of representatives from more than ten countries, all played each other, over the three days. I was able to have a lovely relaxed week, because I had no official duty at the polo. However, I could not resist giving some unsolicited advice, which seemed to be gratefully received. One wealthy American patron, who owned a chain of hotels, tried to justify to me why he had played badly on the first two days. He used the old excuse of blaming the Mexican ponies saying that he was unable to stop them when he needed to. I asked him if he was applying his legs before the reins on the pony's mouth. To my surprise he looked for a further explanation. Nevertheless after his third match, he was totally honest with me, by admitting that he had really enjoyed his ponies, stopping them easily, through always applying his legs first before his hands. The week was enhanced even more by a festival of social events, including an opportunity to dance on one evening. At this party I took courage and boldly invited all the wives of the principal hosts to dance with me. I joyfully encountered ladies who much appreciated a partner with some sense of timing, which normally signifies that their husbands do not have it.

One night I was invited to Casa Maya, a large international house, with an extra big polapa, that gave out contradictory messages of happiness and sorrow. It was owned by the Bittar family, from Winconsin USA, who frequently dispensed appreciated hospitality, including dinners of exotic delicious food. However at the dinner table sat their grown-up son, Ramsey, in a wheelchair being spoon fed. A brilliant student, when at university, he had been very badly injured in a laboratory accident, with the tragic result that he could not walk or talk, although he appeared to be able to understand a conversation around him, to read books and work a computer. Three full time nurses took care of him around the clock, adding character and beauty to the mixed atmosphere. The house is named after Ramsey's beautiful sister, who has an important job in the American financial industry. Their father is a well known heart specialist, and their mother had escaped from Lithuania in the Communist days. Over the next few years I was made exceptionally welcome by this kind family, who bore their wounds with great dignity, while showing courage and kindness to many, like me, who visited Costa Careyes.

Salvador Solorzano prevailed on me to invite him to Ireland for the summer of 1995. The Mexicans rated him as a 2 goal player, to which I did not agree, but optimistically hoped that I could improve him with good coaching. Sadly one evening he successfully persuaded me, against my will, to lend him a car to go to Waterford city. Tragically as he left the gated entrance to our driveway, to proceed down the main road to Waterford, he was driving on the wrong side of the road and crashed head on in to an unfortunate nurse, returning from a hard day's work, in a hospital. The poor nurse was badly hurt, our car was a write off and Salvador remained in pain for the whole summer, further degrading his performance in all polo matches. Already known for his forwardness to ladies, he added the wounded hero to his introduction, when meeting them at some of our local dinner parties. When strongly commiserated with, reports suggest that he looked for a little harmless physical sympathy, which raised some minor alarm bells, amongst more than one of the dinner hostesses.

Maria Ines joined me in glorious Costa Careyes for my second year there. She absolutely loved the never-ending sunshine, cleverly combining some swimming with her sunbathing. I coached a variety of nationalities, including Mexicans, in my polo clinics, besides meeting and conversing with some other very interesting visitors to Careyes. The big surprise was to discover that two incredible new exotic buildings had been erected at either end of Pelican Bay which has a magnificent beach. They looked like castles with a moat around them, an effect produced by the brilliant design of their large swimming pools. They were called Oriente and Occidente and each had, under a polapa, three main en suite double bedrooms, with a door opening on to the pool. Two more similar double bedrooms were in thatched cottages alongside a sixth, unbelievably fitted into to tower from the middle ages.

These magnificent constructions added much to the ambience of the whole area and were quickly put to use for the more lavish events of entertainment. Celebration of the Chinese New Year was lavishly carried out each year with Jean Franco Brignone, father of Georgio, revelling in the duties of Master of Ceremonies. Returning to my Mexican polo clinics, the old adage that 'Necessity is the mother of invention' allowed me then and there to develop full application of my playmaker philosophy, which now became established as a key part of my coaching. This enabled me to make the weakest participants take on every role for at least short periods of time.

One of the groom players, called Raul, blossomed as a player, from my coaching, together from assisting me, and he accepted my invitation to come to Ireland for summer 1996. However there was a nasty drama waiting to unfold when Raul finally landed at an Irish airport. An immigration officer initially refused his entry and said that he had to return to Mexico. Only after a telephone call to the Waterford Garda was the matter resolved. He settled in quickly at Whitfield and had good relations with my head groom, John O'Keeffe, with the training of all my younger ponies. He was also most helpful in the house and with the task of cutting the large garden lawns.

I continued with my coaching in this wonderful place every year until 2012, when I closed the Whitfield Court Polo School. Maria Ines accompanied me every year, and we invariably stayed in the same 'lodgings'. During the seven years we spent in Mexico we made many friends, several of whom came to Ireland during the 2010s to visit us. We decided that we would return to Mexico on holidays for as long as we could. We did not return in 2003, since we were in the process of selling Whitfield Court, and building a new house nearby. After the sale, which was highly satisfactory to us, I decided to go to Mexico for a month's holiday in 2004. Maria Ines did not accompany me, since she was very involved in the building of our new home. I made a big decision during that holiday. I decided that I would purchase a house there. I spoke to

Giorgio Brignone, and he was very enthusiastic about it. An apartment became available in their residential settlement, and I was offered first refusal. Jean Franco Brignone gave me a good deal, which I accepted, and hoped that Maria Ines would support me when I returned home. It was the first major deal that I had made since we married, everything else was jointly done by both of us.

Maria Ines was satisfied with the deal, and until 2011 we went to Costa Careyes for a month in February or March. We left the cold climate of Ireland for the beautiful climate and sunshine in Careyes. It was like coming home, since all our friends were there. I saw a lot of polo as a spectator which I enjoyed. It was doubly entertaining to watch the game from the sidelines, having spent so long coaching.

The story of everybody's life is that one thing leads to another. This happened to me with a sudden momentum in the 1980s, and it led to my coaching and playing polo for fourteen glorious years in Cyprus with the British Forces. Two coincidences led to this, one was I met an officer from the Irish Guards playing polo at Windsor, and he told me that he was about to be posted to Cyprus, and was aware of the coaching I was doing in the UK. I asked him to spread the word about it when he was over there. The other coincidence was General Langley, a friend of my father's who informed me that he was about to take charge as Commander in Cyprus. As a result I received an invitation to go to Cyprus in September 1982. When I arrived I found I was the guest of General and Mrs Langley in the comfort of Government House in Episkopi.

The British Forces were spread across the Greek sector of Cyprus in several locations. The sand polo field was located at Episkopi, which is halfway along the southern coast. Conveniently there was an RAF airfield nearby, maintained by a large attachment of the Royal Air Force. Close to the sea was an excellent sports complex that included golf, soccer, rugby and hockey fields. Nearby was a full size polo field that had an attractive view of Happy Valley.

The first year I had a large group of twenty people to coach, who were drawn from the Army, RAF, and civilians attached to base, including three Cypriots. My hours of work were 7.00 a.m. to 9.00 a.m. in the morning, and 4.00 p.m. to 7.00 p.m. in the evening. This allowed us to play polo, avoiding the midday heat. This meant generally that I was free to enjoy the scenic swimming pool at a local hotel everyday. I combined my swimming with reading, sunbathing, and listening to music.

The ponies were Arab and generally easy to ride. At first I put the group through my riding drills as detailed in my book *Polo Vision*. At 7.45 a.m. I started what could be called a stick and ball practice session – hitting the ball alone and then with another individual. At 8.30 a.m. I gave a tactic lesson using my toy horses in an army tent. Then at 4.00 p.m. we rode all the ponies to the polo ground, where we practised some of my team drills – before playing chukkas. There was always a rush to finish, and get back to the stables before darkness enveloped us. This left an hour to discuss the lessons learned from the chukkas, and to look at some new tactical opinions.

The second year group was larger, and included the General and his charming wife. They invited my wife Maria Ines for the second week, and we travelled to Jordan with the Langleys. This ended with a polo match in Amman – the capital. We also visited Gerassa and Petra. These two places stand out in my mind as the most amazing heritage sights I have ever seen. These were the two most memorable weeks of all the polo trips I ever took. Firstly the welcome from the Langleys, and the week as their guests was special. Secondly, having such a distinguished pupil as the General, added aura to the group. What I found was, that it made my work more worthwhile, better accepted and appreciated, besides creating a dimension of humour and enjoyment, never to be surpassed by any other group.

Looking back on my polo playing and polo coaching career, I was amazed that it took me into 32 countries, which I detail hereunder in alphabetical order:

America – Many States, Argentina, Australia, Austria, Barbados, Belgium, Brazil, Columbia, Cyprus, El Salvador, England, France, Germany, Greece, Holland, Hungary, India, Ireland, Italy, Jamica, Jordan, Kenya, Malta, Mexico, Northern Ireland, Pakistan, Scotland, Singapore, Spain, Switzerland, Thailand, Zimbabwe.

CHAPTER 17

Whitfield Court Polo Club

1976 HAS TO BE, FOR ME, IN RELATION to sport, the most memorable year of all. How can I forget that day, when I personally started a new sport within the area where I live, on my own land, using a field that had been specially prepared over three years. This had involved sowing and harvesting three crops of corn, under sowing with specially researched grass seed in 1975, and then cutting and rolling twice a week to achieve an appearance of a beautiful lawn. Those historical first chukkas have been previously described, during the build up to the opening of my residential polo school.

The big luck factor was that 1976 was the drought year of the century. This greatly helped the new polo ground to tolerate the rough treatment of ponies galloping over it, while incessantly stopping and turning on top of the new grass. The other fortunate happening was that we were starting the polo school and polo club together, because I soon discovered that the two were mutually supporting and even interdependent. Club members could join in to make up the numbers of the smaller polo school groups, while there were occasions, when the school clients were delighted to play in the club chukkas. The positive result, for the club, from the two operations, was that my initial members, Walter Halley, John Cranley, Edward Grant and Harry de Bromhead, were quicker to pick up the basics of the game than the normal beginners of polo do, in most other clubs. For this reason I was confident that they would acquit themselves well, when I invited a fairly novice Dublin team to play against them at Whitfield. The surprise of the Dubliners was clear and the report, which they took home, must have helped to encourage more of their club members to attend my polo school in future years.

During the second year of the Whitfield club, there was another helpful coincidence, when a village two miles away called Ballyduff came looking for a temporary soccer pitch, while they were developing their own. We investigated many areas of the farm, eventually selecting the field, which was next to, parallel and on the house side of our polo field. After a couple of soccer games had been successfully played, we realised that this field could be extended at the top to create a second polo field, if we accepted playing around a tree in the top left corner. Of course the tree could have been cut down, but it was a beautiful, and in the long term we began to appreciate that the roots of the tree, helped to drain the rain from that corner.

As time went by, after experiencing more heavy rain than usual, we were disappointed to find that much of the area above the soccer field on our second polo pitch was difficult to play on. However we continued to use it in wet weather, rather than negatively damage our excellent first polo ground, while still providing chukkas for people, who had travelled far to participate in the polo school or play with our club members.

A few years later an unlikely event provided an unexpected most welcome solution. A loyal farm worker, Martin Daniels, who had served my father, for many years, before me, requested an acre of land, on which our County Council were prepared to build his family a house. Another extensive search around the estate, to my surprise, found that there was only one place, at that time, suitable to cover all factors, including planning permission. Unbelievably it was on the bottom end, next to the main road, of the soccer/2nd polo pitch. Maria Ines and several of our friends were strongly against allowing this area to be built on, insisting that it would ruin the lovely scenery, in what we called the Upper Park, and cause a substantial loss of value, to our whole property.

Nevertheless, although I could not totally disagree with the above opinions, a strong instinct told me to proceed, despite knowing that my lovely wife was nearly always right about most matters and that the soccer club would not be happy either. Also I have previously mentioned that we had inherited, from my wonderful grandmother, this incredible local goodwill, which I wished to maintain, rather than see it deteriorate. Hence the soccer pitch was moved and marked out, on the top end of a slightly shortened second polo ground, where many football matches were successfully played, throughout the next winter. In a relatively short time, after the beginning of the following summer polo season, we were stunned to find, that the second polo ground was playing better than ever before, with that difficulty, after heavy rain, no more in existence. Clearly the effect of 44 feet, from 22 players, in two soccer teams, regularly running up and down on the surface, had beneficially compacted the soil. The result was of crucial importance, because from then on we were able to play, on our second polo field, in any summer weather conditions. Sometimes on extra wet days, I substituted the polo ball with a larger rubber or plastic one, with surprisingly good results.

From lack of funds the soccer club had to delay the completion of their new ground in Ballyduff, which meant that several extra years of the multi feet treatment was added to the positive process. I still find it hard to believe that, in the end, such a disputed good deed, was so handsomely repaid, leaving all parties very happy, especially polo players.

An early additional club member, who added much to the character of the club, was Noel Molloy. His family were amongst the leading butchers in Waterford and Noel was a senior representative of the National Butchers Association. He was also an enthusiastic golfer and sportsman, who had the gift of telling good stories. Often after chukkas, Noel entertained us with some wonderful and amusing tales. Another welcome new member was John O'Byrne. He came from a famous family of horsemen and, in the hunting field, he stood out with his outstanding riding style. Sadly John's back did not stand up too well to the rigours of polo and after a few years he reluctantly had to give up playing.

The most significant person to join our ranks, a few years after polo started in Waterford, was James Kennedy, who brought many valuable dimensions to our planning and club development. He was the managing director of the Waterford Branch of the American international company Bausch and Lomb. James went on to become the head of all their

European operations, besides being elected for a term as president of the Irish Chamber of Commerce. James participated in a full course with a polo school group, giving himself a depth of understanding about polo organisation. Later he imparted an enormous source of energy to future club planning, besides acquiring some valuable sponsorship, which allowed us to have established trophies, for our main annual tournament. He also introduced many constructive ideas, besides using his charisma, to give vital encouragement to me and other club members, when he became a very active president of the polo club. James's family has consistently contributed to our membership numbers and the creation of teams for Irish tournaments. His three sons George, James and Jerome are all gifted sportsmen, making them quick polo learners, when available from other commitments. Their mother Mary also bravely attempted to play, after structured lessons, but then generously made way for the three athletic siblings, whom she strongly supported vocally, besides doing much valuable club administrative work. Father and sons went on, as a conspicuously good family team, to win a tournament at the Moyne club, two years in succession. A description of this triumph follows later in the book.

As I was the only club member *in situ*, I had to keep on top of all dimensions of organisation. My previous experience with management, of army polo in two German locations and Tidworth, where I had been captain of polo, gave me a big advantage, for anticipating requirements and solving inevitable problems, as they arose. I always looked for opportunities to delegate club duties, although initially I would still supervise the tasks.

However there was one difficulty, which I never fully surmounted, and this did consistently test my patience. For the midweek chukka days, I would make out a written plan, of who was playing with whom and for the allotment of ponies. It should have been simple, with relatively small numbers involved, yet without fail, either a player, who had booked, failed to arrive, or one who had forgotten to call in any requirements, turned up expecting to play. I learnt to be very flexible, by asking members of my staff to fill in or drop out, but the fact that I never found a way to prevent such an inevitable annoyance, was not good for my blood pressure.

The use of grooms, playing in the chukkas, could yield a dual bonus. The morale of those involved was considerably raised, while the standard of play was frequently improved, through the increase of control that was handed to me. This happened because the grooms were trained, better than the club members, to fit in with my tactics, having practised and/or played with the smaller polo school groups, thereby learning to fit in with and apply much of my tactics. This automatically produced more spells of flowing play, because backhand and forehand passes were continually being given and received, through prior anticipation. Inevitably this participation of grooms in the club chukkas had to produce a negative factor from time to time, because of the unbelievable human trait of believing that enjoyable experiences, become your right, instead of your occasional luck. Although I was at pains to explain the situation, suddenly I would notice a discontented face of a groom, because he or she was not playing on that day. Then the morale bonus was temporarily reversed.

Over the years we had some very welcome lady members. For a mixture of reasons I always found that their inclusion was very beneficial. Obviously they brought an attractive dimension, which gave pleasure to male members and spectators, but also they were good at diffusing moments of antagonism, which arose between competitive males. Despite the fact that men have a strength advantage, especially when the pace of polo increases, females often show more enthusiasm and are apt to be more methodical. The former was clearly seen when we staged an annual ladies' match between Waterford and Dublin. The ladies behaved as if they were competing in a Gold Cup. Their excitement beforehand and celebrations afterwards, whether winning or losing, was healthy and a wonderful example to our male members.

The longest female member has been Denise Power, whose strong character and amusing personality has added much to the club both on and off the polo field. Denise has formed many teams for tournaments all over the Ireland, winning some good victories and always being welcomed wherever she goes.

We were surprised and thrilled when a few people from County Tipperary started to take an interest in the club. Peter Reilly, a solicitor from Clonmel, was the first to appear. He had an in depth fox-hunting background and quickly became hooked by the excitement of battle on the polo ground. Except for an unfortunate health interruption for a few years, Peter has probably been more consistent than any other, with his dedication to playing in Irish tournaments and forming teams for that purpose. He bought several ponies from my breed and has cleverly maintained an effective small string for many years.

Paul Ronan soon followed Peter, showing much courage in overcoming the handicap of being left-handed and therefore having to use his weaker (right) hand and arm. The hand and eye coordination factor, unknown to many, is a minimal disadvantage, if ongoing coaching, to keep the technique pure, is sensibly employed. Paul has done wonderful work both as club secretary and treasurer. Now his son, Paul, is also a regular playing member.

Fred Daly was also left-handed and rode with little technique and style, but possessed an enormous enthusiasm for sport and life, which helped our morale on his good days. Aiden Farrell came up from Tipperary to be coached by me in the Wicklow Arena. Finding that he lived much closer to Waterford, he quickly joined our club to contribute effectively by frequently putting together good teams, besides giving his valuable time to a long period as club secretary.

Over the years a considerable number of Waterford people have shown an interest in being involved with the polo club. Yet for reasons that are understandable, very few have committed to take up the sport seriously, for more than a few years. A surprisingly high percentage of them experienced an unpleasant relevant minor injury, which could not be cured in the short term. These included most of the original members, who gave the club such a good start. Others met factors outside polo that affected their freedom and ability to continue as regular members. Some because they changed their employment, or location of work and others had to move their place of residence. Hence polo did help us to enjoy meeting quite a cross-section of local people.

One character, who has lasted longer than most, is Chris Hennessy. He has also been a leading local flying instructor, to which he has given equal enthusiasm as the polo. He was very successful in the motor trade, which he terminated with a good sale at the right time. He was our chairman for a term, during which he made constructive changes and obtained welcome sponsorship. We always shared a laugh with him, when he frequently played in the wrong direction for one or more hits, before realising he was assisting the enemy. Eddie McDonald, a very successful builder from Tramore, enjoyed several seasons with us, playing in tournaments, before business demands curtailed his sporting interests. Also from Tramore the Flavin family, who had started their own polo cross club as well as a large horse trekking enterprise, added their steady participation to our club's activities. The father Pat has become a significant entrepreneur and his son John, who grew too tall to continue as a successful jockey, now promises to be a good player, if he is able to devote sufficient time to polo. Neil Breheny, whose home address is also Tramore, although he is a Waterford solicitor, has shown great enthusiasm in training all his own ponies from the start. He is himself a polo cross coach of distinction and therefore has always understood the value of instruction, which he has constructively sought.

The wire fence between our smart No. 1 field and useful second ground had served some constructive purposes, including preventing damaging incursions on to the fabulous surface of the best field. However we had been lucky that no ponies had collided with it and that injuries from wire cuts had been avoided. Hence when the members banded together to remove the whole fence, there was a feeling of relief and safety. Then later on we reaped other benefits when sideline boards were purchased and erected on No. 1, while the second field became a little wider. A good clover spray was obtained and applied to our best ground whenever the surface was becoming slippery from a fresh growth. This greatly improved the general safety and allowed the better standard of polo to be played a little faster.

Then my decision to allow the local greyhound coursing club to use our facilities for its annual competition, added several beneficial dimensions to the polo. They built at the top end a wire pen, which during the coursing events, provided a home for the hares and an excellent escape area for the majority, who were turned but avoided being caught. This provided a big improvement to our net, which was meant to prevent polo balls going in to the wood. Added to this an enormous builder's net was erected behind our goalposts at the bottom road end. Besides losing less balls, this decreased the risk of the passing traffic being struck and damaged.

An Italian/Irish polo player, called Gariaveli, was a member of the Dublin Polo Club. He had cleverly discovered an unbelievable way of producing, from Argentina, potential ponies for a very cheap price. Consigned to be killed for meat, in Europe, they had left South America for a long slow shipping voyage to Italy. There Gariaveli had purchased them, before sending them on to Ireland, where he was able to offer them at relatively low value to Irish polo players.

Led by the ingenuity of James Kennedy, our club decided to purchase six of, what we initially called, the Meat Ponies. James was well aware that fortuitously Eduardo Albaracine, a brilliant polo pony trainer, would be working for me at Whitfield during the next summer polo season. As explained elsewhere, as a favour for taking many of my clients to La Martina in Argentina, for their first year of operation, the famous Cambiaso family had offered to lend Eduardo, a 5 goal player, to me for this coming summer. Naturally I made a business deal with James, so that Eduardo, assisted by John O'Keeffe, who had also recently started to work for me in place of Jimmy Keane, could give some daily time to the training of these six Meat Ponies. Basically we ran an ongoing account between us giving a wide flexibility for whom would become the eventual owners of all of them. After a short time the allocation was clarified. James Kennedy, Peter Reilly, Paul Ronan and Chris Hennessy joined together as a syndicate to own Moro, Tronquito, Mariposa and Clavel, while I accepted the two worst, Lievre and Burro, for very small value, to join my ponies for the use of the grooms and as emergency reserve for club and school chukkas. My two, at first mainly umpired, but as years went by they filled some vital spots in chukkas and training sessions, when replacing some of my good ponies, who were injured or sick.

Meanwhile my own breed, now under the control of Eduardo and John, was growing and progressing very satisfactorily, except that numbers were in danger of becoming out of control, unless a few sales were made. Providentially after a few polo seasons, Chris left the syndicate while James, Peter and Paul, although complimentary about the genuineness of their four Meat Ponies, started asking for replacements that were a little faster, with an eye on my breed. Naturally I was hesitant to swop the elegant classy ponies, which I had bred, for these syndicate ones, who did not fit under this description, especially as I already had Burro and Lievre. But business is business and we entered in to negotiations, each claiming that we were being robbed by the other, whether we meant it or not. Finally a deal was struck, in which I received a few thousand and the remaining four meat beasts, in return for a group from my special breed.

Hence it is now hard to believe that, in the long term, everything worked out perfectly for the brave syndicate members and myself. They took my family ponies to play in many tournaments around the country with happy results, while my staff and I made great use of all six of the once scorned ponies, that had miraculously avoided their sentence to death. Moro and Tronquito adapted to being perfect school ponies, besides giving me some unbelievably incredible chukkas in practice and in matches. In fact when playing them I often came against one of the syndicate on my breed, and to their dismay, I normally outmanoeuvred them, by applying the advantage of my lengthy experience together with Moro and Tronquito's wonderful courage. Mariposa was played by many of my polo school clients and our local club members in matches and practice, giving satisfaction to most, while Clavel, after a winter of arena polo in Wicklow, was sold to the Herbsts, to become a stalwart for them and some of their clients. Lievre and Burro continued to exhibit moments of obstinacy, but were priceless for giving enjoyment to my staff, when filling numbers that completed long chukkas programmes.

To create and organise our own club tournaments I again had the advantage of my previous experience. In a short time our biggest annual event, the summer bank holiday three-day tournament at the beginning of August, appeared to gather a valuable reputation for efficiency and enjoyment. Naturally the dinner dance, in our beautiful stately home, added a significant dimension. However compliments from esteemed polo participants, like Craig McKinney, about the smoothness of each day's playing programme, was good proof of having satisfied customers.

I was always delighted by most of our members providing the willing team work, which was needed to cover all the basic details, to which James Kennedy and Paul Ronan added their special expertise. The weather naturally played a big part in influencing how many spectators were attracted to attend our August Tournament. We were delighted, on several occasions, when there was a thrilling final, watched by a large enthusiastic audience. Nevertheless there was a year, when the exciting finish went beyond an acceptable climax, because the teams were level, when the flight of the final shot, of the match, went high in the direction of goal, before curving sharply left, while passing over the posts. I was an umpire and, from my position on the field, I could not decide and rule, whether the ball had gone inside or over the left goal post. Hence when the young goal judge waved his flag, to signal a goal, I could not use my entitlement to overrule him. Ironically the young lad was the son of the member of a losing team, Paul Ronan, making me greatly admire his courage and honesty, when sticking to his decision, despite the commotion that followed.

As described earlier our possession of two impressive trophies, for the final and subsidiary final, named the Eduardo Albaracine and the Bausch and Lomb, respectively, added much to the atmosphere of the prize-giving ceremony.

In Ireland there is so much horse sport for children, that together with the Junior Gaelic Games, the competition for the involvement of children in other sports is intensely challenging. However through the inspiration and noble work of Greta Ormonde, in the Waterford area, we had two years of great activity, before other sports and events regained the dominant foothold.

In 1988 we were thrilled, when the Waterford pony club team went to Dublin, for a clear victory against a team from the rest of Ireland. Our team consisted of Sean Ormonde, Jenny Bulbulia, David Dawnay and Sebastian Dawnay, who combined excellently to dominate their opponents for much of the match. Following this Graham O'Sullivan from Dublin and

Victor Clarke from Carlow joined up with Sean Ormonde and Sebastian Dawnay, to cross the sea to England where they acquitted themselves well, although not winning the tournament. In 1989 Sean, Sebastian, Jenny and Victor lost in a great battle against an English team, but later when David replaced Jenny for a return match in Dublin, the result was reversed in our favour in an extremely high standard game.

The early days, which led up to the two successful years at Whitfield, were full of fun and excitement, with enthusiastic children all over our polo field. One of the Curran family arrived on a Thelwell type pony, which kept bucking him off when entering the field. Rose Tormey, Orna Ellickson and Danielle Ormonde came to practise and play with many of those mentioned above, all exhibiting substantial talent while raving about their enjoyment. A good finale to the whole adventure was the important involvement of both Sean and Danielle in Ireland's junior three-day event team, in which they achieved some very respectful results. They openly said that the polo had built in them a great enthusiasm for horses and competing in other equestrian events.

Our first and last international polo match at Whitfield Court Polo Club was between Germany and Ireland. We combine it with the one and only hurling exhibition match, on the polo ground, between Waterford and Kilkenny club teams. I was aware that there could be a problem with 30 hurlers and 20 polo ponies being prepared to play in the same area. Therefore I arranged for the polo players and ponies to do their pre-match exercise on the far side of the small wood, above the polo field, where they were out of sight from the spectators. This not only solved the difficulty, but also produced a fairly sensational surprise for visitors, when as the hurling finished the ponies emerged at speed from the wood.

My cousin, the Marquis of Waterford, and I were joined by two players from Dublin, to complete the Irish team. We were expected to be too strong for a fairly novice German team. However the four Germans had all been trained by me, either at Whitfield or in Germany, and their youngest played brilliantly to snatch a last minute win against us. We then had an enjoyable reception and trophy presentation, on the magnificent staircase, inside Whitfield Court, during which the

Baron Von Maltzahn, with the friendly nickname of Bad Baron, made a generous speech, about the success of my training in Germany.

Everyone departed the scene in an excellent atmosphere, but unfortunately the Germans forgot or possibly failed to agree, when and where, to invite us for a return contest in Germany. During many of the years, when our big tournament was in August, we were able to include a fund-raising dimension. We needed a little help from the Gods in at least three ways to achieve good results. These included non inclement weather, limited rival competition and good cooperation from polo players and spectators. We were seldom blessed with perfect weather, for all three days in August. Yet whenever the other restrictions were sufficiently circumvented, the sun also came out, to permit us to implement a charity event in order to raise funds.

We tried several different formats. The one I remember best was when I succeeded, after an intense and extreme effort, in procuring a fairly large show-jumping clock. This allowed all present, including competitors, to see the results in a totally transparent manner. I requested the members of each team, individually to submit to a short test against the clock, hitting the ball round an easy course. The best six went forward to a final on the third day, when they were all auctioned to the crowd. Then the purchaser of the winner received half the proceeds and the other half went to the selected charity. Another occasion we staged a competition, based on the recorded statistics about good and bad plays of all the members of every polo team. Then we created our own quick pick system and issued a different selection, to anyone who paid 5 euros or more. There could only be one winner, who collected half the pot, while the other half went to the nominated charity.

We were lucky to have very few accidents, on our polo fields, during all matches, games and practices related only to the polo club, not involving the polo school. The three most significant are described below.

Sadly the worst fall of all, happened to Ward O'Malley, the oldest and greatest character amongst our members. Ward had played polo in Iran, during the 1930s. There he had been a professional geologist in the oil business. He had retired to a place close to Tipperary Town, and therefore had a long drive, when coming to polo at Whitfield Court in Waterford. However he came regularly to play, and when he reached his 80th birthday, he commenced hiring a driver to bring him this lengthy distance to participate. Ward had a very high intellect, coupled to a wonderful sense of humour, which enabled him to tell many amusing stories. To get the opportunity to listen to many of his tales, I frequently invited him to stay a night with us, before a polo day. He used to put me to shame, by jumping on to a pony, quicker than I could and he rode all the ponies, which I gave him to play, extremely well. He was not the best at timing ride offs, yet could appear from nowhere to meet opponents perfectly legally.

What made his accident extra tragic was that it was so unnecessary, because it happened in a non competitive chukka. I was playing and to my sorrow, I saw the whole episode unfold. Another of our club members was riding a big good-looking thoroughbred, which he himself had procured and introduced to polo. Ward was playing my old pony, called Mariposa (Butterfly). The former started a solo run down the far side of the field, and hence rather than oppose him, I decided to allow him to get in front of me, expecting that he would soon miss the ball, leaving it behind for me to collect peacefully. Suddenly Ward went by me at Mariposa's top speed, before cutting the corner across the field towards the thoroughbred, reaching him just at the moment that he was turning towards the goal. This caused an ugly, ill timed, collision, from which Ward ended up underneath both ponies. Luckily an ambulance was quick to arrive from Waterford, to take the unfortunate Ward to our local hospital, where he remained in a coma for two days. Unbelievably and fortunately this great elderly man made a complete recovery, although he was never able to ride a horse again, but continued to recount his stories.

A most unusual breakage of tack, was the reason for our second memorable accident. In the middle of a practice chukka, another club member was thrown forcefully in to the air, before landing heavily on the ground, when his saddle girth broke. He was an esteemed member and never played polo again, which caused a big loss to our club. The third incident concerned a visit by a famous TV presenter, who wished to be filmed, for a very short period of time, to give the appearance of playing in a polo game. This was to be used amongst other happenings in Waterford, to provide clues in a TV game, in which names of locations had to be guessed. However this presenter refused to come for a rehearsal on a previous day, and on the day itself arrived so close to the time of filming, that our practice was ridiculously brief. I guided her through the short sequence of moves required, by riding next to her, keeping one hand on the reins of her pony. But then I was told 'leave me go, I will stop myself' while she continued moving towards the cameras, probably with a view to impressing her associates. Unfortunately her pony then refused to stop and a few extra paces the lady fell to the ground, breaking a finger. After a very long wait in the Casualty Department of Waterford Hospital, the finger was suitably repaired and a bashful TV presenter returned to England.

The whole club was delighted to learn, that we were going to be visited, on one day of our annual August Tournament, by the Chairman of the Hurlingham Polo Association, who was Mark Vestey. He had been a figurehead in British polo, both as a player and an executive in the world renowned association. As I had been in grateful receipt of generous hospitality from both Sam and Mark Vestey, when in England, I was extra pleased to host a lunch party, in our house, that day for Mark. He was most appreciative and in very good form with some amusing stories from English polo.

During the afternoon, at the polo field, Mark was full of friendly jokes about the application of the rules by our umpires. This is a type of English humour that is better ignored to avoid other traps. Then one of the tournament matches had a very exciting finish, causing much emotion from a group of English visitors, who were surrounding Mark. Naturally the gallant chairman and gentleman separated himself from their caustic comments, to give charming compliments to winner and losers for a thrilling spectacle. Mark duly departed giving the Whitfield Polo Club some welcome praise and encouragement, which added to our pleasure, that an HPA Chairman had taken the trouble to cross the sea to watch our main annual fixture. However I was a little sad that an opportunity to discuss the future of coaching in polo never arose.

Three isolated happenings bring back a combination of special memories, which remind me that I had had many wonderfully happy moments with my polo club at glorious Whitfield Court. First was at an August Tournament, in which my sons, David and Sebastian, playing together in the same team, reached the final. I had stupidly agreed to umpire, because for a variety of unexpected reasons, other suitable candidates, for the task, were not available. In the middle of the match David appealed for a foul by an opponent, which was for me, doubtful and in no way dangerous. When I did not blow I heard Sebastian, who was quite young in his mid-teens, say 'Oh typical Dad, he is biased against us, in order not to be thought to favour us.'

At the same time I was proud my sons were in the final and I regarded Sebastian's remark as a welcome compliment about my integrity. Then when the boys narrowly lost the game, I was relieved that no one would be shouting 'favouritism' and that David and Sebastian had been very sporting losers. It was a funny mix of emotions.

Secondly we much enjoyed, during one summer, having a charming good player from Argentina, as the club professional. Alejandro Traverso was a good pony schooler besides being a talented ball striker and very amusing company. Added to these skills, in the middle of a ferocious chukka of an August Tournament, he produced a brilliant improvisation to deal with a serious emergency. The gate from the polo field to the busy main road displayed a large sign saying that it had to be kept closed. In the middle of a match, in which Alejandro was playing, a late arrival had just driven through the gate and was obediently in the process of closing it, when another player fell from his pony, who took fright and flew at unreal velocity towards the road. Unbelievably the loose pony was through the gateway and on his way down the main road, towards Waterford City, before the gate had been shut. Without hesitation, Alejandro, who was on his pony, rapidly reached the gate, jumped off and handed the reins of his pony to the shocked and surprised car driver, before running into the middle of the main road. Coincidentally there was a weekend motor cycle rally nearby and at that moment motor cyclists were heading towards Waterford. Alejandro stopped one, climbed on as pillion passenger, and with minimum delay was giving chase to the frenzied polo pony. Half a mile down the road, history does not relay how, Alejandro stopped and caught the missing pony, jumped on to his back and returned undamaged to our polo field. Naturally he received a loud ovation from all the astonished players and spectators.

Thirdly at the August Tournament in 2001, I was treated to a presentation and celebration that meant more to me than I can possibly describe. Twenty-five years of polo had, by then, been played at Whitfield. When the ever active James Kennedy, realised the significance of the year, he quickly set about putting together all the arrangements for recognising the achievement. The great Micky Herbst, of Wicklow Polo Club, who was the first, in 1993, to instigate arena winter polo in Ireland, kindly came to make the presentation to me, and the principle evening party was jointly in honour of the club and me. Naturally I made a speech, in which I thanked all who had helped me in any way with the club, my family and the committee who had made this one weekend so special for me.

Not long after the above, fate and lucky timing, before the property crash arrived, caused my family and I to leave our beautiful home estate and wonderful house, purchased in 1916 by my brave widowed grandmother. That presentation and celebration made it much easier for me to accept that change and the memory is still sweet.

In 2002, when Whitfield Court was first put up for sale, the club moved to Tom Driver's farm, which was situated between Waterford City and Tramore Town. The new ground, other than having two wet patches requiring attention was the best unprepared polo field that I ever played on. After heavy rain the turf did not cut up badly, with only the top skin coming off. When there was a dry spell of weather, the ponies were not jarred or lamed by the conditions.

The location was some distance from any house, making it necessary to have a portacabin, which happened to have pink walls, for players and visitors to use. On the first day of one tournament, before playing, I went to ease springs in the cabin. To my horror my water appeared to be coloured red, suggesting the return of the cancer, for which I had been operated on ten years previously. I said nothing to my team, which included James Kennedy, before playing, with a heavy heart, but well enough for us to win and reach the final. The next day after the final, which my team lost, before rushing to Waterford Airport, for a flight to England, I returned to the cabin. I quickly noticed that my water was again red. This made a bell sound in my head, that reminded me that, ten years previously, this had only happened once, and not on two consecutive days. Therefore I invited James to ease springs in the cabin, in order to see what would happen to him. In what would have been an hilarious scene, for any watching spectators, to my delight, I saw another cascade of red fluid hit the bowl. At the same moment I observed that the sun was shining off the pink walls, giving the explanation for the red water. Relief surged through my brain and body in the knowledge that I had clearly experienced a false alarm. This wonderful news allowed me to enjoy my trip to England more than usual. James and I still laugh, when we meet and happen to recall that little comedy in the portacabin.

In 2004 I had both hips replaced within six months of each other. The operations were successful, but I was warned by the doctors not to attempt riding polo ponies again. Stupidly I ignored this advice, since I was feeling very well, and thought that nothing could happen. I got a nasty fall, and the hip joints were fractured, and from then onwards I had to use two crutches to get about. They restricted my movements greatly, particularly when driving, so I was completely sidelined as far as polo was concerned.

In 2006 the polo club moved from Driver's to a new location in Rockett's Castle by the River Suir near Portlaw. By then I was not actively involved in the management, but the club insisted that I would remain as chairman, being re-elected every year. I curtailed my visits and only attended matches and tournaments. In 2011 the majority of the club moved to Curraghmore, so the club became the Curraghmore Polo Club, my cousin Lord Waterford became president, and his sons were active members. I was then 78 years old, and had been involved with polo for over 40 years, my mobility was limited, so I quietly resigned from the club. My good friend James Kennedy succeeded me as chairman of the club.

I joined Waterford Rotary Club in 1981 and shortly afterwards became involved with an international committee with a view to supporting projects abroad. I was actively involved in the polo school, and I found it therapeutic. I also realised that I had spent all of my life adjacent to Waterford City, but had never got involved in anything other than the army and polo playing and coaching. I did not have a lot of spare time, but I attended as many meetings as I could, and got to know many interesting people. The ethos of Rotary interested me, and it soon became an active part of my life, and I promised myself that I would become more involved when I retired from the polo scene.

As mentioned already, we decided that we would sell our beautiful home when I closed the polo school. It was a decision that we made with great reluctance, but we felt that it would be too costly to maintain such a large house, which had 14 bedrooms, and we would have to employ domestic staff and gardeners to keep the place in pristine condition. The time to sell was then, the 'Celtic Tiger' had arrived for the Irish economy, new hotels and golf courses were being built, the banks were 'throwing money' at property developers, and we felt that the time had come to sell. The property, including the large farm was put on the market at the end of 2002. But it was late in 2003 before we found someone willing to take on such a property. We eventually sold Whitfield Court to a Northern Ireland based developer. The property suited his expectations of building an all inclusive leisure development. He planned a large hotel, Mark O'Meara was designing an 18 hole golf course, he would retain the existing stables, so there would be horse riding facilities, and fishing in the river within the estate. The cost of new development would be close on €100 million, and would be equal, if not better than Mount Juliet thirty miles away in Kilkenny. He applied for planning permission, and ran into all kinds of problems. The excellent goodwill which Granny Susan and my parents fostered with the local community vanished. The locals did not want this development to go ahead, and it took well over two years to 'get it over the line'. By then, the banks had tightened their regulations, they had overextended, and big money was no longer available by the time that planning permission came through. Whitfield Court was unoccupied and was vandalised, the 500-acre farm had been taken over by 'poachers' who hoped to get squatters rights.

We had decided that we would build new locally, so we retained a 20-acre field in Powersknock as an ideal site. The trauma of selling Whitfield was bad enough, but the thought of selling the beautiful antique furniture, which my parents and grandmother Lady Susan had acquired over the years, was too much to endure. Maria Ines decided that our next house would be so designed that it could incorporate the continued use of our lovely furniture. She spent months at the kitchen table sketching her vision of our next house. It would be a two-storey Georgian house, and she used a modular 6-metre square by 3-metre high in the 4 bedrooms and reception rooms. The entrance hall would be 6 metres wide, exactly like Whitfield Court, with a magnificent stairs. The normal floor to ceiling height in modern houses is normally about 8 feet, in her design it would be 3 metres, close on 10 feet. The new house would be 18 metres long by 12 metres wide, and 7 metres to roof eaves. It would contain 4 bedrooms 6 metre square by 3 metres high, all en suite. The kitchen, dining room, drawing room, and living rooms would be the same size. A library, with double doors would be built off the half landing on the stairs between 2 bedrooms on the side elevation. This was an ingenious use of space. My study was to be on the ground floor off the entrance hall. The scullery, wine cellar, hot press, boiler room, all of generous size, were behind the kitchen area.

There would be a single storey flat-roofed sun room 3 metres deep by 12 metres long off the south facing gable. Access to the kitchen and living room was through double doors off each. Instead of a glazed roof, there would be 4 fixed roof lights, each 4 foot square. The gable would have double doors and 4 windows. The attic would have a staircase off the bedroom landing and a space the length of the back elevation by 4 metres wide gave a working space of over 60 square metres. There were 6 Velux roof lights on the back elevation of the house.

Maria Ines went on the internet to find the best materials possible, the slates were imported from Spain, the timber double-glazed Georgian windows were sourced in Denmark, the central heating would be under floor using a German Siemens system so there were no radiators. When she had completed her research, we engaged an architect to prepare working drawings, and to apply for planning permission. Maria Ines gave emphatic instructions to the architect to follow her design only. He put the building out to tender, when planning permission was received, and a local Co.Waterford builder was engaged.

While we were waiting for our new house to be built, our good friends Louis and Kate Ronan lent us a house in Clonmel. We drove daily to the new house site. As well as architect supervision, Maria Ines acted as clerk of works, and continued to source materials. She wanted solid mahogany doors 8 feet high by 3 feet wide, they were proper proportions of the height of the rooms. She located a timber saw mill in Bunmahon, who had seasoned kiln dried mahogany logs which were cut into boards, and the doors were assembled in their joinery. Skirting boards, architraves, and window boards also came from the same source. The work was completed to the exacting standards set out by Maria Ines.

The site was chosen because it was a sloping field and the house was built at the highest point, which gave magnificent views. The entrance gate was electronically controlled, and a curved driveway was formed to a flat area in front of the house. There was a large double garage built close by at the same level to a similar design. We moved in to our new home in 2005. It was an anxious time for us, and we were wondering if our scheme was successful. It was, the pieces fitted perfectly into place. This rebirth of our home, could easily be described as a seventh lottery. The site was fenced, and a local farmer rented the remainder of the 20 acres for grazing. Our lifestyle was changed by the move, the new house was easier to manage and maintain, since it was a house of our own creation. After thirty years of living with Maria Ines, she once again showed her ingenuity through her skill in designing our home.

I now had plenty of leisure time and I was reasonably mobile, so I was able to devote more time to Rotary which interested me. Every year we went to Mexico for a month, usually in February while we still had cold Irish winters. The only cloud on the horizon was the continuing dilapidation of Whitfield Court. It was no longer our concern, we would never forget our time there, but it looks as if it was never occupied.

My eldest son David, born 1972, went to Headfort School in County Meath for primary education. He was very bright, his teachers spoke highly of him, so we decided he would go to Eton to follow family tradition. He was there from 1986 to 1991, returning to Whitfield Court during the holidays. In 1992 he went to the University of Bristol, and graduated in 1996 with a BA in Spanish. He was interested in sport, and played polo with great success in his youth. We thought that David might take it up as a career, but he was not prepared to follow that road. Initially he was interested in finance and he worked in private banking for a big firm in London, but subsequently became passionate about IT and saw good opportunities in that field. He began working as a web developer for a small firm in Barcelona and later moved to Buenos Aires with his family in 2005, where he works as a freelancer for clients there and abroad.

David met Aisha Lebron, a Brazilian national with Argentine parents, during an earlier trip to Buenos Aires in 1999 and the following year they married and went on to have two children, Lucia and Nicolás. Aisha was very supportive of my piano playing when she stayed with us and it was wonderful to have a daughter-in-law who shared my passion for music. David's family come to stay with us in Clashes Hall as often as they can, distance permitting, and I thoroughly enjoy the company of my grandchildren when they are over.

Our other son Sebastian was born in 1975 and was educated in Newtown School in Waterford. From an early age he played polo, and was determined to follow that career path. He is now a professional polo player, and to my delight, he has taken up coaching, and is registered with Hurlingham Polo Association (HPA). He reached a 5 goal handicap outside and an 8 goal handicap in the arena. He has played for and captained England and Ireland both indoor and outdoor and had played in all the major tournaments in the UK. He won the British Open Gold Cup at Cowdray Park with C.S. Brooksin in 1996 and reached the finals another three times. He won the Arena Gold Cup in the Royal County of Berkshire Polo Club six times. He has played for the England Arena

Polo Team on several occasions, as well as winning the Arena Gold Cup at the Royal County of Berkshire Polo Club. He is still playing as a professional in both field and arena polo.

In 2008 he purchased a small farm not far from Windsor, which already had stables, and he is running a livery business from there. He will use that as a venue for coaching, when it is up and running. Early in 2010 he told us that he had met and had fallen in love with a young lady, who was also involved with polo. He wanted us to meet her, so they came to Clashes Hall for a short visit. He brought Louisa Crofton to meet us, and you can imagine our surprise, when we learned that her mother, the Hon. Georgiana Crofton had come to Whitfield Court Polo School in 1976 (see details page 193). Louisa is a beautiful tall blonde lady, and she is employed as polo manager at the Royal County of Berkshire Club, where Sebastian is a professional player. Her full name is Louisa Crofton Hutchinson, her father Brent Hutchinson from Avonmore House Co. Wicklow, married Georgiana Crofton, only daughter of Sir Blaise Crofton, 4th Baron Crofton, and Ann Tighe, daughter of Group Captain Charles Tighe, from Rossana, Co. Wicklow. She was then known as Baroness Crofton.

As a child she fondly remembers holidays in The Red House, Woodstock, Inistioge, with her great grandfather Charles Tighe, and her grandmother Ann Tighe, who had moved from Rossana to Woodstock. Maria Ines and I were captivated by Louisa, she had a beautiful personality, and was very knowledgeable about polo management. On 1 January 2011, we got a phone call from Sebastian and Louisa, announcing their engagement. They decided to have a Civil Marriage in Windsor in March 2011. On the 17 December 2011 they had the marriage blessing at Kilmeaden, Co. Waterford, with a reception at Faithlegg Hotel nearby. This was mainly arranged by Maria Ines, and it was magnificently carried out. I was in good form, and I made a speech which went down well.

I have written at length about the six lotteries in my life, and I would like to add two more. My seventh lottery is the move to Clashes Hall in 2005. It was such a major decision for us, but it was worth it, and we derived so much contentment by doing it. My final lottery was my family, my sons David and Sebastian, their wives Aisha and Louisa, and my grandchildren Lucia and Nicolás. To have such a loving and caring family like ours must be considered a special lottery which Maria Ines and I cherish very much.

CHAPTER 18

Obituary of Hugh Dawnay and Tributes from Rotary

MAJOR HUGH DAWNAY PASSED away on Monday 28 May 2012. He died at Clashes Hall, in the arms of his loving wife Maria Ines, and his sons David and Sebastian. He was aged 79, born in December 1932. His funeral was on 31 May, to Sacred Heart Church, The Folly, Waterford. There was a Requiem Mass and the remains were taken to Cork for private cremation.

His funeral was attended by hundreds of locals, and people from all over Ireland. It was the end of an era, his grandmother, the widowed Lady Susan Dawnay, came to Whitfield Court with her four sons in 1916. His father Major General Sir David Dawnay, his mother Lady Katherine lived there all their lives, and the respect that the people of Waterford had for the family was shown by the turnout.

A Memorial Service was held on Friday 21 September, at the Royal Military Academy in Sandhurst, Camberley, Surrey. All the arrangements were done by Louisa Dawnay. The Service took place in the Royal Memorial Chapel at 2 p.m., followed by a reception in the Indian Army Memorial Room. The Service would have been pleasing to 'The Major'. It was carried out with great precision, the Duke of Edinburgh, Colonel in Chief of the Royal Hussars was represented by a General, all ranks of officers, including some who had served with him were there. Maria Ines invited several people from Rotary and polo to the ceremony. James Kennedy, and Des Purcell, paid glowing tributes to Hugh. His cousin the Marquis of Waterford was unable to attend, his sons Lord Henry Beresford Earl of Tyrone, and Lord

Charles Beresford, represented Curraghmore. Lord Patrick Beresford who played polo with Hugh and was a fellow pupil at Eton attended. Richard Dawnay, 12th Viscount Downe, was unable to attend, he was represented by his mother, Diana, Viscountess Downe.

Des Purcell representing Rotary wrote:

I am privileged to be invited by Maria Ines, Sebastian, and David to make a brief presentation on the enormous contribution Hugh made to his native Waterford, and in particular Waterford Rotary Club. Most of you are either former army colleagues of Hugh, or friends through polo here or abroad. We knew Hugh primarily through Waterford Rotary Club, not as Major Hugh, but as Hugh the extremely active Rotarian.

Following Eton and his military career, Hugh returned to Kilmeaden which had been the family home since 1916. He had spent most of his childhood and adult life abroad and enjoyed very little business or social contact in the local community. Hugh used Rotary as a means of addressing this, and over a period of thirty-two years was one of the most outstanding members of the club, and contributed greatly to it. As in the best traditions of most voluntary organisations, approximately 50% of the membership did 100% of the work, and Hugh was a very willing participant in whatever was afoot.

In 1986 Maria Ines and Hugh made their former magnificent home Whitfield Court available for the running of a Strauss Ball. As a function it was unique in our community, and never happened before. The proceeds were for a local voluntary hospital. It was a complete sell out, a monumental success and by the standards of the day generated a very substantial sum for the hospital. To nobody's surprise Hugh and Maria Ines invited Rotary to repeat the function the following year with an identical result.

Hugh joined Waterford Rotary Club in 1981, and that year coincided with an invitation for the club to set up an active international committee with a view to supporting projects abroad. He was a founder member providing unbroken service on that committee for thirty-one years. They raised money for a whole range of international causes. They ran film premiere nights to fund a dental clinic in an orphanage in Belarus primarily because one of members, dentist Dr Donal Tully, who is in attendance here today had a commitment in that direction. The project is still ongoing today. They supplied 200 wind-up radios to a school in Ethiopia that had no electricity. Fresh water wells were funded in India. Goodwill trips were taken to Northern Ireland during the terrible years of the 1980s, visiting clubs in the north and sharing fellowship with exchange visits was very important. I could go on, but really my brief was just to share a flavour of what was achieved.

On a lighter side, a notable feature of that committee was that meetings were not held in a local hotel but rather in members' homes. In the best traditions of things Irish, meetings shortly developed into gatherings marked by fine wine, strong camembert and cheddar, and the odd glass of vintage port. None of your Tesco special offer €5.99 aviation fuel for this distinguished gathering, or perhaps better described as 'Dad's Army'. Yes, they did Trojan work for voluntary causes abroad, but simultaneously developed an enviable expertise in the merits and demerits of Chateau Rothschild 1962, or similar modest fair. Is it any wonder Hugh was the linchpin of that committee for more than thirty years. That committee became the envy of the club, and membership extremely difficult. You'd have got ten men into a tank easier, than an invitation to join them.

It would be remiss of me not to mention a final project that was very close to his heart, and given his illness significant. For a number of years now we in Waterford Rotary Club have manned the local Christmas tree, erected by Waterford City Council in a project known locally as 'Remembrance Tree'. It was simplicity personified. The public of their own volition came up to the tree, filled in a card in memory of a loved one who had passed on, the card was tied with bow and ribbon to the tree, and simultaneously a voluntary contribution of whatever size was made. The entire proceeds without one euro deduction went to our local hospice. At the height of the economic boom at home in 2005, 2006, 2007, we were generating close to €50,000 a year out of a sustained four week effort. Your stint on the Christmas tree was three hours, and it was less than comfortable in the December cold, but remarkably even last December 2011, Hugh insisted on full attendance.

I have been asked specifically by Maria Ines, Sebastian and David to share briefly the following incident which has no connection whatever with Rotary.

A few years ago I was in Buenos Aires and my trip coincided with the Polo World Cup semi-finals. I had never attended a polo match, but was invited by Hugh to join him for the two semi-final games. Inevitably we were in the best seats in the stand, and I was enthralled by the speed and skill. After the first match we adjourned to the marquee for a little liquid refreshment. We were standing outside the tent with two glasses of champagne and this gentleman looked very hard at Hugh, walked past, then twirled around and states 'you're Major Dawnay'. Hugh replied in the affirmative. The gentleman introduced him self as being from Columbia and said and I quote, 'You wrote an outstanding book, and I have read it more times than any human on the planet. I can virtually repeat it line by line'. It sounded odd, but all this was happening at pace. Hugh thanked him for his kind words and asked, 'How do you know my book so well?' There followed the best one liner that either of us had heard in our lives. The Columbian gentleman said and I quote, 'I was reading it when I was kidnapped at gunpoint in Columbia, I was allowed keep it and it was the only thing that I had to read for four months in captivity until I escaped, stole a mule, rode through the night for three nights, hiding in woodlands during the day, found a friendly village, found the police station, and was rescued by helicopter shortly thereafter.'

The world is made up of two kinds of people: those who brighten a room when they go into it, and those who brighten a room when they leave it. Hugh Dawnay brightened many rooms, in many places, in many countries, for very many years.

I recently watched a very distinguished Nobel Laureate being interviewed, and when asked how he would like to be remembered, he replied and I quote 'as somebody who made a difference'. Hugh made a lot of difference to a lot of our lives across a range of areas – the army – polo – Rotary, our general community back home, and many other areas.

Yes, sadly he has gone, but the difference he made, the memories created, the fun shared, will live with us joyfully, happily for a very long time.

Des Purcell read this at the Memorial of Hugh Dawnay in Sandhurst.

Tom Sheridan from Waterford Rotary Club who served with Hugh on committees for many years wrote:

The Hospice Christmas Tree. For many years Waterford City Council erected a large Christmas tree in the heart of the pedestrianised retail area of the City at Barronstrand Street. A few years ago Waterford Rotary Club decided to raise money for the local hospice, by organising volunteers to attend the tree, and inviting the public to erect a card and a bow on the tree, in memory of loved ones who had passed on. Simultaneously they would be invited to make a voluntary subscription, the extent and nature of same entirely at their own discretion. The idea proved enormously successful and popular locally, and has been copied by various Rotary Clubs nationally. There were other collection points for the Hospice Christmas tree at major shopping centres, but the real focal point was the Christmas tree at Barronstrand Street.

The tree was manned for up to ten hours a day, depending on the opening hours enjoyed by local retailers. It was cold, at times wet, nevertheless very rewarding, and Hugh Dawnay played a major part in manning the Christmas tree. Even in December 2011, which was to be his last Christmas, he insisted on carrying out his stint for the duration, and the weather was particularly cold at that time, but he never complained or flinched.

At the height of its popularity, and during the Celtic Tiger era, this project raised up to €50,000 per annum, which was a truly enormous amount of money, which went without deduction to the local Waterford Hospice. It was a measure of his commitment to the project, and to Waterford Rotary Club, that even when ill, and suffering considerable discomfort, he insisted on participating to the fullest. It typified his views of voluntary service. If you put your hand up and volunteered, then there were no half measures, and he was impatient and intolerant with members who did not undertake this project with what he deemed to be an appropriate level of support.

Hugh brought this level on enthusiasm to his Rotary involvement for a period of thirty-one years. Reliability was his hallmark and joy to have on committee. Mind you it wasn't all work and no play. His affection for the odd glass (or two) of good Bordeaux were known and recognised, and the various Rotary projects through the years afforded him the opportunity for good fellowship, and the hearty exchange of views. His legacy in Rotary will be an example for younger members for many years to come. He will be sadly missed.

James Kennedy a great friend, had been to Whitfield Court Polo School, later joined Whitfield Polo Club, and still plays polo at Curraghmore Polo Club. He attended the Memorial Service in Sandhurst, and spoke there as follows:
Firstly I would like to thank the Dawnay family for inviting me to be part of this memorial service, thank you.

Hugh in his books and coaching always used mnemonics, I am going to use one today, using the word LEGACY. L for life, and polo was Hugh's life – both professionally and as a hobby. The quote that best describes this for me says, 'The dreams of great readers are not fulfilled but transcended, when you concentrate all your powers and energies on a pursuit that you love. Then abundance flows into your life – and all your desires are fulfilled.' Polo in Ireland was started in 1873 in the All Ireland Polo Club in the Phoenix Park in Dublin. History will recall that Hugh played a prominent role in this club, over the last 40 years, but also in the development of polo generally in Ireland.

It is difficult for us to imagine when we look back that when Hugh started to play in Ireland, there was only one club in the country. Today there are 8 HPA clubs – a number of private grounds – and a total of 140 HPA registered players. Hugh was involved personally in the start up of all these clubs, and the coaching of their members. But most importantly everyone is having a lot of fun playing polo!

E is for his extraordinary understanding of all aspects of the game, and his ongoing vision for the development of polo. His past contribution to Irish polo is immense, and because of what Hugh Dawnay has achieved, the sport will continue to grow for future generations. In the Waterford Polo Club, we have the Dawnay Cup which is much sought after each year. Last year the members in Waterford presented Hugh with the Playmaker Cup, a national trophy to be presented each year to the best playmaker.

To continue the LEGACY – G – is the Game. His vision was, that the game should be enjoyed whether we win or lose, realising that in no other sport can people ride brilliant horses for an hour in the game of kings. The game should always have a charitable element to it. His favourite charity was Bothar – the Gaelic for road – and the concept is to send a Noah's Ark of farm animals each year to African villages. This has been a huge success over the past 30 years.

A for adversity. Not only from his army training, but I believe it was in his DNA – his unique ability to deal with adversity – whether as a polo champion – or in his own life. He would look a problem straight in the eye – he often called the problem Murphy's Law, and was aware that Murphy was mostly bad – but he would deal with his problems with a great deal of humour and unwavering courage. He would look for learning from it, and believed that once in a while some good might be forthcoming in the future. In this way he boxed off his problems as he met them each day, and then got on with looking for any excitement that might be about! What a great lesson for us.

C is for Coaching. His tireless promotion of coaching everywhere he travelled. His vision was to see coaching at all levels in the game – club level – all tournaments whether large or small – we in Ireland were no exception to his rule.

'We must have coaching.'

Y is for YES. Tomorrow we say YES. We have a 2020 strategy for Irish polo with audacious goals, that may or may not be met – they may even be exceeded. Hugh has seen first hand the wonderful success you have had here in the UK, with so many young people into the game. Back in Ireland – as the founding President of SUPA – he worked with all the participants to help make it happen – polo clubs – schools and universities – and anybody else he could reach.

With the memory of Hugh Dawnay foremost in our minds, we will kick on the future to bring as many as can to play and enjoy polo 'The Sport of Kings'.

His Legacy will live on.

I will finish with a quote that Hugh had in his office.

A horse beneath me sure of foot and quick
My good right hand well serviced with a bamboo stick
The fine hit ball – the beat of flying hooves
Of life's delights – why here must be the pick.

Acknowledgements

Maria Ines Dawnay would like to thank James Kennedy for the invaluable encouragement he gave her husband Hugh, when he was writing his memoirs and also Tom Whyte for reading the memoirs and for his huge help in getting them published and Erica Ward for all the work she did for Hugh over many years.

She would also like to thank Colm Henry and Ricardo Motran AKA Snoopy for permission to use photos.